À la

IYETIE

NOT ONE JOT ...

par Catherine M·T.

14 déc 2023

À la famille de la Grille

par Catherine M.T.
Abbé Rolls

NOT ONE JOT ...

Personal Testimony

Fortunat Tshimanga-Mukadi

Library of Congress Control Number:		2013922068
ISBN:	Hardcover	978-1-4931-5025-0
	Softcover	978-1-4931-5024-3
	eBook	978-1-4931-5026-7

This book was printed in the United States of America.

Rev. date: 07/24/2014

To order additional copies of this book, contact:
Xlibris LLC
1-888-795-4274
www.Xlibris.com
Orders@Xlibris.com
543492

TABLE OF CONTENTS

PREFACE

A S A COMMON person, without any qualification in what people call 'theology' as science and history, it is a big challenge for me to discuss in public the very sensible religious matter of Ten Commandments. My second challenge, and not the least, was my weakness in English language. Indeed, having French as first language, I have hesitated to write in French or in English, both languages spoken in Canada.

I opted for English for two reasons. Torontonians would be my important readers and there are in large majority English-speaking people among the French-speaking Ontarians. Therefore, to reach the large audience, I chose English. Big challenge, is not? The other reason is that I attend an English-speaking congregation for worship and this would be my first audience, as my closest family.

Why do I write this book and why is it called 'Not One Jot'? I had a disorderly youth, as I grew up with a widowed mom unable to correct me when needed; thus, finding myself where my God has brought me now, I felt obligated to testify of His Love. The only way to be thankful to Him is to preach His Gospel around me to respond to His commission in Matthew 28 : 19, 20, "*Therefore go and make disciples of all nations, baptizing them in[1] the name of the Father and of the Son and of the Holy Spirit, and teaching them to obey everything I have commanded you. And surely I am with you always, to the very end of the age*".

Therefore, living in selfish North-American culture where we do not have time to listen quietly to your neighbor, everyone closed in his corner or always too busy, where even the married couples have not enough time for each other; and, as I do not have the means to have a TV or a radio station to preach and care for my neighbors, colleagues, friends, family

---

[1]   The biblical quotations are taken, except otherwise, from New King James Version.

members, relatives . . . I decided to write this Testimony about the holy Ten Commandment Law of the Creator of the Universe, specially the Fourth commandment of the Decalogue, which shows clearly that we are not product of the hazard nor are we here by accident!

Grown up in a Roman Catholic environment until my twenties, I myself discovered this Truth as taught in the Holy Bible, by reading a book, which changed forever my life. Here I have to be thankful to my elder brothers who had endured sacrifice to help me study and finish my high school degree which made me able to read, write and analyze. Without this, that book which transformed my life could not have any meaning to me!

I am not writing this book to offend or belittle any Christian denomination, especially those specifically cited in this Testimony. Many of those church members love their Creator and would like sincerely to believe the Truth and serve their mighty Creator and infallible Lawgiver, if they had opportunity to earnestly study His Word! Thus, time may come when some of them would open their heart to the eternal Light and follow the true Way to the eternal Life. Neither have I written it to boast myself or to extol those Churches whose members keep the Sabbath as being the unique ready for heaven, for, Judas was one of the twelve beside the Messiah more than three years, but we know he will not be found there!

Yes, there are many books written in this matter, however, someone can be interested reading a book only by its title, and also more importantly by its author.

The title 'Not One Jot' emphasizes the idea found throughout the Word of God asking people not to obliterate any of the smallest letter of His Ten Commandment Law, no matter how great they are, how powerful they pretend to be, how intelligent and wise they may be, how high their instruction could be, how big and rich their church seem to be. For these ten statements are the only ones through all the Scriptures, written by the mighty and holy Hand of the Creator.

Herein is discussed the origin, the importance and the perpetuity of God's Ten Commandment Law as the Moral Law of His eternal Government. And as Lawgiver and Supreme Legislator, He is the only One worthy to change His Law, nobody else is entitled to suppress, change or modify one point of this Law.

I was also inspired to write this book by many discussions I have with my relatives, my friends and colleagues to answer to some of their questions and concerns. I do not pretend having resolved all their questions and concerns; however, my aim is to give them much desire to continue to seek prayerfully and faithfully their Creator who is the One able to resolve, in the best way, their questionings and doubts. We have this promise, if *'we seek Him with all our heart, we will find Him, for He is at our heart's door knocking that we may let Him come in'*.

Moreover, there are some affirmations many times repeated in the book, only to insist and emphasize some important truths.

I would be missing a duty if I do not take the opportunity to thank in a special way sister Soneni Burombo who has gladly accepted to spend her precious time to read the manuscript and has helped me to fix some ideas by her important remarks. Only God she serves may pay her back for her benevolence. I express also my heartfelt gratitude to pastor Jacques Vaudré who, regardless of his multiple ministerial charges, had joyfully accepted to read the manuscript and had given me some remarks to make this Testimony come true. May God bless his ministry and his family.

I thank in special way the Toronto Bereans who supported me and encouraged me while I was still alone in this great City and they were my important supporters in my first steps to learn English language.

Finally, I would be incomplete if I do not have a word of thankfulness to my dear wife, my wonderful daughters, sons, grand children and daughters-in-law and sons-in-law for their matchless love for their Maker. Guys, you are doing so well! Wait for the coming of the King!

I—THE BOOK OF THE BOOKS

For whoever shall keep the whole law, and yet stumble in one point, he is guilty of all. For He who said, 'Do not commit adultery', also said, 'Do not murder'. Now if you do not commit adultery, but you do murder, you have become a transgressor of the law. So speak and so do as those who will be judged by the law of liberty. (James 2 : 10 - 12)

THE BIBLE, AS its Author, is spiritual and eternal, as it is written, "*Heaven and earth shall pass away, but my words shall not pass away*"; for His words are spirit and life. His Word is a lamp at the wanderers' feet who sincerely seek the true way to the Life, which is Christ, the living Word of God. It is sharper than two-edged sword, ready to wound the preacher and the hearer if they do not humble themselves before it and do not heed to its warnings and councils.

Reading the story of Jesus' life and death and how He was born in a cowshed; how He grew up by working hard as a carpenter for a daily living bread; how in His ministry, He fed the hungry and healed the sick ones; how He was betrayed, falsely accused, beaten and spat upon, though always forgiving and blessing; how the mob mocked Him and roman soldiers tore His hands and feet with nails to crucify Him on a rugged cross; His friends forsaking Him! O yes, only some women from Jerusalem were so saddened of His misfortune, that they mourned and followed the mob to see what next will come to Him!

I wonder and marvel at why and how He accepted to endure such great shame and torture, Him who reigned and ruled in heavens with ten thousand times ten thousands of angels serving Him! Him who created the Man perfectly made, and would recreate a new one to replace the one who got lost in sin! The explanation is found in these words, "*I have loved you with an everlasting love; therefore with loving kindness I have drawn you*" (Jeremy 31 : 3) Christ had given up all power which He shared with the Father, to save sinners such as every one of us. He inspired the prophets and apostles to give us a message to instruct us of His love and of our hope.

Through His Word, God speaks to us; He teaches and shows us His love and His concern about us and our seed: the life, the eternal life, through Jesus Christ, is the greatest gift we can possibly receive. Thus "Every chapter and every verse *and every line* of the Bible is a communication from God to them, *you and me* . . . if studied and obeyed, it would lead God's people, as the Israelites were led, by the pillar of cloud by day and the pillar of fire by night". (Ellen G. White— *Patriarchs and Prophets*, p.504, Margin added)

There is no other book like the Bible in the world; it is the voice of God Himself speaking to every creature and above all, to every man, every woman and every child. The true disciples of Christ should make of it their daily food, as were the Bereans who were searching to know the Truth that makes free! Truth is still truth, whether the majority believes it or not. Truth is still truth, whether it is popular or not. Truth is still truth, whether some people alter it or not. Truth is from and in God alone, as it is written, '*let everyone be a liar, but God is true*'. Truth is personalized in Jesus Christ, the living Word of God.

Because of its divine origin, let every human being put all his trust and love in the Word; it is our only shield and weapon of defense against the foes; it gives us faith and power, and at last the victory over the world and its vain pleasures. Let us make it our daily bread to energize our limited spirit and understanding.

The Church can best respond to Christ's call to be a lantern that shatters the darkness if only it leans faithfully on His Word; affording to understand it by the help of His Spirit, instead of trying to correct some of its parts, for only God is the One best Interpreter of His Word.

Let everyone who takes the Bible in his hands believe and be sure that each of its messages is addressed to him or her personally as an individual.

FORTUNAT TSHIMANGA-MUKADI

As it is put in a right way, "We are to open the Word of God with reverence and with a sincere desire to know the will of God concerning us", advises Ellen G. White. "Then the heavenly angels will direct our search. God speaks to us in His Word. We are in the audience chamber of the Most High, in the very presence of God. Christ enters the heart." (From the Periodical, *Signs of Times*, March 28, 1906)

Is this Holy Word read and applied according to God's Spirit which qualifies spiritual heirs of the Kingdom? By it, we are heirs of the covenant that God made with Abraham, Isaac, and Jacob. One day, the natural heirs, the Jewish people who now reject the Living Word of God in Christ, will have the veil removed from their eyes. And the Christian world that distort selfishly the Word will be found wanting. Until then, the whole Word of God, which brings salvation, must be preserved. So we have a fight on our hands to preserve the Word of God unpolluted with human sophistry and philosophy. Let us make no mistake. We are engaged in a solemn and a holy war for the Truth, also for the honor and glory of our Creator and Lawgiver. This war is between those who are for the Word and those against the Word, and it has been raging since the beginning of time, since the rebellion of Lucifer. But our weapons are not carnal, but spiritual.

The Word of God is unchanging in its divisive character. We see the divisive nature of the Word in the cross of Christ: on the one hand, there is the Word of salvation, and on the other hand, the Word of condemnation. Anywhere the Word is, there is division. Christ stressed it clearly, *"Do you suppose that I came to give peace on earth? I tell you, not at all, but rather division. For from now on five in one house will be divided: three against two, and two against three."* (Luke 12 : 51, 52)

God's Word is a separating word, and as a such, those who believe sincerely in it are duty bound to protect it and defend it against all attacks. We must also recognize the simple historical fact that the Church's greatest attacks have always arisen from within the Church itself. We are not the first, nor are we alone in the fight.

Paul in Hebrews 12 : 1 explains: *"Therefore we also, since we are surrounded by so great a cloud of witnesses, let us lay aside every weight, and the sin which so easily ensnares us, and let us run with endurance the race that is set before us."* From this passage, the dramatic imagery of an athletic contest used by apostle Paul, in which the competitors, Christ's true followers against Satan's army, in the arena, our world, are surrounded by the crowded tiers of an amphitheater, heavenly holy angels, shows how hard is the battle in which we are engaged. In a sense, the holy angels are not only watching us, but they are also involved in this competition against the foes among whom are the so-called Christians that revise selfishly God's Word, trying to make it suitable to them and feel themselves comfortable in their conduct, although wrong. It is why the Holy Spirit calls to our unceasing earnestness, that we may understand the oracles of God and have a systematic knowledge of the very battle upon the earth, which could prevent us from being carried about by every wind of doctrine. The wicked wind of doctrine is not always from out of the Church; but most of the time, it is among and around us, as Christians. For, being a Christian is not only being in a church, registered in some books, even occupying some position in the clergy or in the office; but we are so, by the fact that we believe in Christ, not as demons do, but by the faith manifested in our daily speech and deeds.

How do we know today Him who lived many centuries before we came to life? By the eternal Truth revealed in His Word. This Word is our leitmotiv (refer to Romans 8 : 28 - 30), our rule of life (see Galatians 6 : 16), our code of conduct (refer to1 Thessalonians 2 : 10, 2 Thessalonians 3 : 7), our GPS (Global Positioning **S**ystem) (see 2 Timothy 3 : 15). It shows the way to the eternal life through the Savior whose soon coming we are waiting for. We can keep our ways pure only by living according to the Word according to Psalms chapter 119, verse 9.

This Word is the Book of books, tried by many theories and philosophy but stands unshaken through ages, because nobody can teach the Eternal Creator or correct His sayings! He who *"has measured the waters in the hallow of His hand, measured the heaven with a span and calculated the dust of the earth in a measure? Weighed the mountains in scales and the hills in a balance? . . ."* (Isaiah 40 : 12), the Almighty Rock of ages, cannot mistake, forget or lie. His statements are not limited by the time, by the circumstances or by human science.

Therefore, no man as wise, learned and clever as he may pretend has any right, any power or any wisdom to add or suppress one jot to God's statement, unless it is an act of rebellion, which could call upon the transgressor the chastisement found in the book of Revelation, chapter 22 verses 18 and 19 : *". . . everyone who hears the words of the prophecy of this book: if anyone adds to these things, God will add to him the plagues that are written in this book; and if anyone takes away from the words of the book of*

FORTUNAT TSHIMANGA-MUKADI

this prophecy, God shall take away his part from the Book of Life, from the holy city, and from the things which are written in this book".

To the Lord Creator, there is no past or future, but the present, as He introduced Himself to Moses, "*I am who I am*". The past and the future in His Word are for our understanding, as finite creatures, subject to the time and seasons change.

In this life, one thing that is useful may be useful for some and not for others, maybe for a time and not forever; but what is true remains true for all people and for all time. Think of Pilate's pitiful complaint, "*What is truth?*", while the Truth was standing in front of him. The truth is in our hands and it is unlawful for anyone, though an apostle or a prophet, to teach otherwise than what we are taught in the Holy Scriptures. It is forbidden to add unto or take away anything from the Word of God. It does evidently appear that the doctrine thereof is perfect and complete in all respects. Neither may we consider the writings of any men of equal value with divine Scriptures, nor are we to consider custom or the great multitude or antiquity or succession of times and persons or councils, decrees and statutes as of equal value with the Truth of God, since this Truth is above all. Therefore, we have to reject, with all our hearts, whatsoever does not agree with the infallible Word of God; if not, the Scripture itself would be regarded as less reliable than reason and nature. Error or rebellion. The authority of the Holy Scriptures depends not upon the testimony of any human authority or prophet, but wholly upon God who is the Truth itself and the Author thereof; and thus it is to be received as such because it is the Word of God.

Many Bible teachers, to sustain their heresies, state, 'Paul says . . . Paul says . . . Paul says . . .', instead of saying 'The Holy Spirit, speaking in the holy Scripture, says . . . '. However, the Bible tells us that God is the author of every part of the Scripture. The unchanging character of Scripture as authoritative means that we have to allow Scripture itself to tell us how to regard it and how to interpret its statements. In quoting the Scriptures and specially Apostle Paul's writings, we have to be very careful and take into account the warnings of the apostle Peter, when he emphasizes, "*. . . Some things in Paul's letters are hard to understand, and people who are ignorant and weak in faith explain these things falsely. They also falsely explain the other Scriptures, but they are destroying themselves by doing this.*" (2 Peter 3 : 16, The everyday Study Bible, *New Century Version*). This distortion of Scriptures is so rampant today, as some so-called theologians reason, 'Didn't Jesus and His disciples go into the field and pluck the ears of corn to eat and this, on Sabbath day? Didn't He heal on the Sabbath . . . ? So why we cannot have the opportunity to do whatever we can to make the Sabbath day good for us?'

To distort the Scriptures is a sin against the Holy Ghost who inspired them. Jesus is very clear about this kind of sin, when He strongly warned, *"Therefore I say to you, every sin and blasphemy will be forgiven men, but the blasphemy against the Spirit will not be forgiven men. Anyone who speaks a word against the Son of Man, it will be forgiven him: but whoever speaks against the Holy Spirit, it will not be forgiven him, either in this age, or in the age to come."* (Matthew 12 : 31, 32)

Cain justified his sin instead of seeking God's forgiveness. Satan uses in the same manner distorted Scriptures to deceive those that are not taught in the Spirit of the Lord. For example, we read in Mark 2 : 21 - 28, *"One Sabbath Jesus was going through the grainfields, and as his disciples walked along, they began to pick some heads of grain. The Pharisees said to him, "Look, why are they doing what is unlawful on the Sabbath?" He answered, "Have you never read what David did when he and his companions were hungry and in need? In the days of Abiathar the high priest, he entered the house of God and ate the consecrated bread, which is lawful only for priests to eat. And he also gave some to his companions." Then he said to them, "The Sabbath was made for man, not man for the Sabbath. So the Son of Man is Lord even of the Sabbath"*. People use this Scripture to justify their wrongdoing on Sabbath, in seeking their pleasures on Sabbath.

However, what happened in that day in the corn field, is that the disciples and the Master were in an evangelistic mission and had to pass by that field. We do not know how long there were walking around. On that occasion, they started plucking ears of grain as they were going on. To the Pharisees, who were seeking an opportunity to accuse the Master on anything that was like unlawful to them, challenged Jesus on the question. They saw no real difference between the act of plucking one head of grain, and harvesting fifty or five thousand. Obviously, there is a difference between plucking a few heads of grain to eat at the moment, and taking time to harvest an entire crop for storing. What is the difference? The difference is in the intent. One man might have gone out to collect sticks on the Sabbath to build a fire to keep warm after a sudden cold snap: this man might have gone unpunished while another man who performed exactly the same act might have been stoned. One was reluctantly working to meet an unplanned human need, and the other was arrogantly flouting God's law. It was purely a matter of intent. Jesus' rebuke to His accusers showed the importance of saving a life, by recalling them of their own history, saying, ". . . have *you never read what David did when he was in need and was hungry, he and those with him: how he went into the house of God in the days of Abiathar the high priest, and did eat the show-bread, which is not lawful to eat, except for the priests, and also gave some to those who were with him?*" (Mark 2 : 25, 26).

What did this reply have to do with the Sabbath? Merely that a simple human need like hunger could, on an unintended occasion, unplanned circumstances in the life take precedence over the law; even the fourth commandment. Such an occasion in no way invalidates or sets aside the commandment: it is an exception to the rule to save one's life. Because the ultimate goal of the whole Law is to save life once lost (Mark 3 : 7).

In this circumstance, the apostles' plan and purpose was not to go and work in the field by plucking the corn ears! This text is not reported in the Scriptures to teach that we can work, kindle the fire, warm or cook the food blamelessly on Sabbath day! People and so-learned teachers read the Bible with the glasses that make them understand what pleases them and their followers. It is not strange that, for this end of times, some Christian teachers encourage their followers to remain in polygamy practiced by the pagans in their cultural societies, "because", they explain, "Abraham our father in faith had two wives and God blamed but Sarah because of her jealousy". So forget them the origin of marriage in Eden.

About Christ's healings on Sabbath, what we have to know is that, during the era before Christ, were developed some rules that were not known in Moses' time.

In SDA Encyclopedia, *Commentary References Series*, 10, p. 1109-1110, we read, ". . . at the same time, in some instances the Jewish attitudes reflected in the Gospel appear more severe than those found in classical Judaism. Thus as W.O.E. Oesterle has pointed out, the repeated criticism of Jesus for healing on the Sabbath . . . seems out of harmony with provisions in the Mishnah, allowing certain healing procedures, although this seeming difference may possibly be explained by the fact that Jesus' healings were performed on chronic cases." In addition, the Commentary gives possible explanation on Christ's attitude, "In each of Jesus' miracles of healing on the Sabbath the basic thought is the same, *'It is lawful on Sabbath to do good . . . , to save life . . . '* (Mark 3 : 4).

This, in the context of the fact that Jesus' recorded Sabbath healings were consistently performed on chronic cases who were not in immediate danger of death . . . , points to the conclusion that in these actions a dimension deeper than merely a physical healing is involved."

Everything will be well understood when He comes and it would be so late for many teachers that leaned more upon their philosophy and diplomas than upon the Spirit of God to correct their erroneous teachings.

On the other hand, who can blame or judge his God? Only Satan does.

Some believers refer to the writings of Ellen G. White as allowing them to kindle fire and cook on the Sabbath!

In fact, her statement, used proudly by many Sabbath's keepers to justify their way to organize parties and foolishness on Sabbath, is rendered as this, "While cooking upon the Sabbath should be avoided, it is not necessary to eat cold food. In cold weather, let the food prepared the day before be heated". (*Testimony for the Church*—6, p.357)

Without doubt, to heat and warm the food needs to kindle the fire, made with wood or coal, by stove or microwave.

Is there conflict here with the text of Exodus 35 : 1 1 - 3?

Not really, because, as it is said above, where is the great light, the Bible, the little one, Spirit of prophecy, is dimmed and becomes useless. For, Ellen G. White herself is so clear through all her writings by insisting and warning her readers, saying, "When questions arise upon which we are uncertain, we should ask, what says the Scripture?" So, when the Bible says clearly "*not cook, . . . not warm, . . . not kindle the fire, . . .*", we do not need more light or interpretation to understand what does this or that mean!

Always the true religion, studied in meekness of heart and prayer, helps to shed light on our path, if we avoid to take in account only what pleases us. If not, we bring trouble on ourselves as surely as sparks fly up from a fire, and Job has concluded, "*If I were you, I would turn to God and present my case to him. We cannot understand the great things He does . . .*" (Job 5 : 7 - 9, GNB Version)

"*For ever, O Lord, thy word is settled in heaven. Thy faithfulness is unto all generations.*" (Psalms 119 : 89, 90). The strain is more joyful, for experience has given the sweet singer a comfortable knowledge of the Word of the Lord, and this makes a glad theme. After tossing about on a sea of trouble, the Psalmist here leaps to shore and stands upon a rock. Jehovah's Word is not uncertain; it is settled, determined, fixed, sure, immovable. Man's teachings change so often that there is never time for them to be settled; but the Lord's Word is from of old the same, and will remain unchanged eternally. Some men are never happier than when they are unsettling everything and everybody; but God's mind is not with them. The power and glory of heaven have confirmed each sentence which the mouth of the Lord has spoken, and so confirmed it that to all eternity it must stand the same. It is settled in heaven, where nothing can reach it. In the former section David's soul fainted, but here the good man looks out of self and perceives that the Lord faints not, neither is weary, neither is there any failure in his Word.

These verses take the form of an ascription of praise: the faithfulness and immutability of God are fit themes for holy song, and when we are tired with gazing upon the shifting scene of this life, the thought of the immutable promise fills our mouth with singing. God's purposes, promises, and precepts are all settled in His own mind, and none of them shall be disturbed. Covenant settlements will not be removed, however unsettled the thoughts of men may become; let us therefore settle it in our minds that we abide in the faith of our Jehovah as long as we have any being.

God is not affected by the lapse of ages; He is not only faithful to one man throughout his lifetime, but to his children's children after him, yes, and to all generations so long as they keep His covenant and remember His commandments to do them. The promises are ancient things, yet they are not worn out by centuries of use, for the divine faithfulness endures for ever. He who succoured His servants thousands of years ago still shows Himself strong on the behalf of all them that trust in Him. "*Thou hast established the earth, and it abides*". Nature is governed by fixed laws; the globe keeps its course by the divine command, and displays no erratic movements: the seasons observe their predestined order, the sea obeys the rule of ebb and flow, and all things else are marshalled in their appointed order. There is an analogy between the Word of God and the works of God, and specially in this, that they are both of them constant, fixed, and unchangeable. God's Word which established the world is the same as that Which he has embodied in the Scriptures; by the Word of the Lord were the heavens made, and specially by Him who is emphatically '*The Word*'. When we see the world keeping its place and all its laws abiding the same, we have herein assurance that the Lord will be faithful to His covenant, and will not allow the faith of His chosen ones to be put to shame. If the earth abides, the spiritual creation will abide; if God's Word suffices to establish the world surely, it is enough for the establishment of the individual believer.

FORTUNAT TSHIMANGA-MUKADI

II—THE UNFAILLING WORD

I have more understanding than all my teachers, for your testimonies are my meditations. I understand more than the ancients, because I keep your precepts. I have restrained my feet from every evil way, that I may keep your word. I have not departed from your judgments, for You, Yourself have taught me. As you therefore have received Christ Jesus the Lord, so walk in Him, rooted and build up in Him and established in the faith, as you have been taught . . . (Colossians 2 : 6, 7).

THE CLAIM THAT God's Word is bound to time and shackled to the culture of its time does not do justice to God's revelation. According to Jesus, the content and the message of the Word of God does not change along with changes in the world. Jesus says of the permanence of His Word: *"Heaven and earth shall pass away: but my words shall not pass away"* (Luke 21 : 33).

In this restless and uncertain time two things remain unchanging, God and His Word. This permanence brings comfort and security to those who trust in Him and in His Word, which promises salvation in His Son. The covenant God has made with His people is unshakeable, for God, who cannot lie, has both made a promise and confirmed it by an oath (refer to Hebrews 6 : 13 - 18). The unchanging promise of God and His Word is the source of our hope for eternal life. A living hope such as this, provides a sure and steadfast anchor for the soul in this turbulent world. Since the beginning of time, God has not changed His will, nor the Word by which He communicates His will, toward mankind. He revealed to the prophet Malachi: *"I am the Lord, I change not"* (Malachi

3 : 6), and the apostle James described Him as *"the Father of lights, with whom is no variableness, neither shadow of turning"* (James 1 : 17).

God and His Word Are Inseparable as they cannot be separated from one another. Scripture bears witness that they are one: *"In the beginning was the Word, and the Word was with God, and the Word was God"* (John 1 : 1). The written Word of God reveals His will and its eternal truth. Even though written by sin-corrupted man, it was authored by the Holy Spirit (see 2 Peter 1 : 20, 21). Thus attempts to find differences between God's will and His written Word are foolish.

The Word of God is not an intellectual statement but the revelation of God to man through servants He has chosen. It is God who chooses the times and means by which He reveals His will toward mankind: *"God, who at sundry times and in divers manners spake in time past unto the fathers by the prophets, Hath in these last days spoken unto us by his Son, whom he hath appointed heir of all things, by whom also he made the worlds"* (Hebrews 1 : 1, 2, KJV).

Let us put in our mind that Old Testament reveals 'Promise' and The New reveals 'Fulfillment'. It is impossible to understand the mysteries of God or His Word with the powers of reason, for as the apostle Paul wrote to the Corinthian congregation: *"The natural man receiveth not the things of the Spirit of God: for they are foolishness unto him: neither can he know them because they are spiritually discerned"* (1 Corinthians 2 : 14, KJV). Yet the Holy Bible has come under increasing scrutiny and skepticism since the beginning of the Age of Enlightenment. Some parts of it are rejected, even though eyewitnesses have reported them, because the type of proof required by modern scientific methods cannot be found. As a result, 'enlightened man' has experienced a falling away from God and the teachings of Holy Scripture (see 1 Thessalonians 2 : 3).

The Bible is now examined mostly from the literary and historical points of view instead of its spiritual content and wisdom. Modern man no longer believes that the teachings of the Bible are applicable for this present time of complexity, neither is he ashamed to belittle Scripture and even God.

The God of eternity has not changed however. The God of the Old Testament is the same God as Him of the New Testament. The Old Testament reveals God's promise of a Savior to sin-fallen man and the New Testament is the fulfillment of that promise. The Old Testament is more than a historical account of ancient Israel or just an ancient literary work of the kind found in other nations of that time. Rather, the Old

Testament is the revelation of God's salvation plan through the history of His chosen people. The everlasting covenant that God established with Abraham and his seed remains and belongs to those who are His children, not after the flesh, but by faith, that is to those who believe as Abraham their spiritual father believed (Genesis 17 : 7; Romans 9 : 7,8; Galatians 3 : 7)).

The Word is not bound to time but is timeless and always suitable for instruction and teaching in life. Grace and the Word of God have always taught the children of promise to avoid sin and to live a godly life in their generation (read Titus 2 : 11,12). On the other hand, it is he who does not have the light of God's Word who becomes a slave of his generation and is easily swayed by the norms and opinions found in a changing society. Without an unchanging and eternal frame of reference, the life of man is without a spiritual and moral direction. Without God's Word, there are no absolutes and one can only live relative to the rest of society. Jesus prayed for His own that they would be sanctified by the truth of God's Word (refer to John 17 : 17).

God and His Word remain unchanged and eternal and will continue after the world ceases to exist, for "*heaven and earth shall pass away: but my words shall not pass away*" (Luke 21 : 33).

When quoting the Holy Scriptures, we must speak of the sacred things with reverence; not allowing a most light trifling expression to escape our lips. Handling the Bible in our hands, we have to know that we have the Light from above to lead us to salvation through faith. We should not run through its pages, but let us compare verses with other verses in prayer; not having many teachers, for the time has now come, where many of teachers today do not endure the right doctrine but speak after their lusts for their own perdition and of their disciples. For us, let us be wise to listen to the Bible speaking to us, by its steady study, not despising the prophecy.

The psalmist magnifies the Creator and urges us to obey Him fully in all things, that we may be lifted up on high, "*The earth is the Lord's, and all its fullness, the world and those who dwell therein. For He has founded it upon the seas, and established it upon the waters. Who may ascend into the hill of the Lord? Or who may stand in His holy place? He who has clean hands and a pure heart, who has not lifted up his soul to an idol, nor sworn deceitfully . . .*" "*Lord, who may abide in Your tabernacle? Who may dwell in*

Your holy hill? He who walks uprightly, and works righteousness, and speaks the truth in his heart; He who does not backbite with his tongue, nor does evil to his neighbor, nor does he take up a reproach against his friend . . ." (Psalms 24 : 1 - 4; 15 : 2, 3)

There are always and there will be more and more people, as the end draws near, who will do their own will contrary to God's Word. Obviously it is not man's prerogative to change God's law for any reason; but "Faith works by love to produce a life of obedience and fruits unto holiness. Faith results not only in a right relationship to God, but also in cooperation with Him that makes possible a likeness to Christ in both spirit and conduct." (SDA Encyclopedia—*Commentary References Series*—10, p. 392). For, '. . . *if anyone is in Christ, he is a new creation; old things have passed away; behold, all things have become new. Now all things are of God, who has reconciled us to Him through Jesus Christ, and had given us the ministry of reconciliation . . .'* (2 Corinthians 5 : 17, 18). And the psalmist enforces, "*O how I love your law! It is my meditation all the day. You through your commandments, make me wiser than my enemies; for they are ever with me.*" (Psalms 119 : 97 - 102)

God Himself has taught and continues to teach us through His holy Word, making us drink of the pure water of His Holy Source. As born again Christians, we are the new creations in Christ; Christ is in us and we are in Him and in His heavenly Father. (Read John 1 : 12, 13, 1 Corinthians 6 : 16, 17 and Ephesians 1 : 17 - 21). And Paul once more emphasizes in 1 Corinthians chapter1, verse 23 saying, '*You are Christ's, and Christ is God's*'.

So why people of God, gathering for the praise of their holy Redeemer, after being prepared on the sixth day for such a holy Assembly, find themselves being all 'sinners'! At many pulpits, we hear always these proclamations of being sinners! You may say it is by modesty and humility, and also fear of self-sufficiency and arrogance! Maybe. However, the term 'sinner' is explained as 'a person who sins, a transgressor'; meaning, one who commits sin continually. Sin is defined as 'transgression of divine law; any act regarded as such a transgression, especially a wilful violation of some religious or moral principle; any reprehensible action, serious fault or offense. (Webster's Universal College Dictionary, 1997)

What is 'sin' according to the Bible?—'Sin' is the transgression of the law, "*Whoever commits sin also commits lawlessness, and sin is lawlessness*"

(1 John 3 : 4).—'Sin' is of the devil, "*He who sins is of the devil, for the devil had sinned from the beginning. For this purpose the Son of God was manifested, that He might destroy the works of the devil.*" (1 John 3 : 8).—'Sin' is all unrighteousness, "*All unrighteousness is sin: and there is a sin not leading to death*" (1 John 5 : 17).—'Sin' is the omission of what we know to be good, "*Therefore to him knows to do good, and does not do it, to him it is sin*" (James 4 : 17).—'Sin' is the thought of foolishness, "*The devising of foolishness is sin, and the scoffer is an abomination to men*" (Proverbs 24 : 9).—'Sin' is all the imaginations of the unrenewed heart, "*Then the Lord saw that the wickedness of man was great in the earth, and that every intent of the thoughts of his heart was only evil* (Genesis 6 : 5).—'Sin' is whatever is not of faith, "*But he who doubts is condemned if he eats, because he does not eat from faith; for whatever is not from faith is sin* (Ro. 14 : 23). What can we retain from all these biblical definitions and explanations of the word 'sin'! God our Creator gave to men the laws and commandments that they may do and keep them for their happiness here below and for eternity. Therefore, when we realize sin's stranglehold on the world, people are either ignorant of their responsibilities to God and fellow man, or no longer care what God thinks. God's ministers, priests and prophets are responsible to make their God's teaching and ways as sharp and clear as they can, so that those they teach can understand, not just the basics, but as broadly and deeply as possible so that it can be lived, instead of wasting the precious time in vague sermons and legends and useless stories of human philosophy and boastfulness.

Sadly, people have a vague knowledge of what sin is, as well as a weak appreciation for the dangerous filthiness of sin, which can prevent us from entering God's Kingdom. We live in an exceedingly sinful time in which we are confronted by sin from every side, even from within ourselves, if we are carnal, instead of being spiritual. Sin is so exhibited that most people seem to treat it with indifference until things like rape, murder, thievery, lying, gossip, teenage pregnancy, abortion, drunkenness . . . hit each of us, if at all. So many are unaware of what sin is, that they ignorantly or willingly participate in it. Medical statistics show that in America, over one million unborn children are aborted each year, and Christian people euphemistically call this a 'privacy right', hiding from the reality that they are murderers, which the laws of the land should prosecute! What else can one honestly call heinous as the taking the life of an unborn human being created in God's image?

Wrong ideas about holiness usually lie in wrong ideas about human corruption. The responsibility of the Christian to seek the holiness of God provides the very reason God requires works, because it is written, *'Be holy, for I am holy.'*

The awful thing of this common ignorance of sin is that, without a firm understanding of human corruption, we have little appreciation of the radiant glory of God's holiness toward which we are to strive! Sin lies exposed as the root cause of humanity's corrupt condition, but many, even in the Christian Church, do not appreciate the depth of persistent corruption in them. Vague, dim and indistinct understanding of sin will never serve a Christian well, which must always apply his mind to growing in understanding how to throw off spiritual vagueness and simultaneously glorify the Father and His Son. If one does not grasp the depth of his carnal heart's disease, it will constantly deceive him into thinking he has little to do to overcome, thus dragging him into pride. The human heart is so sick that God tells us in Jeremiah chapter 17 verse 9 that it is incurable!

It is vitally important to know whether we can live above sin or not; because, if sin is unavoidable, it must be excusable; and if sin is avoidable, it is inexcusable. Certainly, God would not condemn anybody for not doing that which is impossible to him or her to do. In order to know whether we can live above sin or not, it would be helpful to find a Biblical understanding of what sin is, especially in the sense of the guilt that condemns an individual.

To know what sin is, it is best to eliminate what sin is not. Sin is not temptation, for Jesus was tempted, yet without sin (Hebrews 4 : 15).

There are two qualities that must exist in order for something to be a 'sin' that condemns a person: knowledge of what is transgressed, which is God's Law (1 John 3 : 4; Romans 4 : 15), and wilfulness in the choice, (James 4 : 17; Genesis 2 : 17).

Most definitions of sin involve 'missing the mark'. This infers two things; one knows the target, and one has the ability to aim. Sin, rightfully defined, is a wilful transgression of a known law of God. Sins of ignorance per se, are not sins in the sense of bringing condemnation upon an individual. We do not punish a child for murder if he thinks a gun is a toy, and he kills someone. If one knows that killing is wrong, and he chooses to kill, it is a sin that brings guilt and condemnation. This should be sufficient information to define 'sin' so we can know what the Bible is talking about when it refers to an act of sin. It is why Christ came to this world to make known His Father's Will (John 18 : 37; 9 : 41); it is why He is tarrying His return, that the Gospel of salvation may be brought to everyone, then the end will come (Mathew 24 : 14). For this reason also, God sent many prophets to make His will known. Not only that, He commanded them to write His sayings in the Book, which is now read by all succeeding generations. And as it was not enough, He sent also His only begotten Son in the flesh to this world to teach and prove the true way to love, obey and worship His holy Father and inspired His disciples to write a Testament which should be taken to its real value, the Word of God. He concluded His mission on earth by stating that if He did not come, people would not have sin (John 15 : 22 - 24).

God hates sin, He wants us likewise to hate it, because it gets us into trouble, causes sorrow of heart, and in the end brings death. But when involved in it, as soon as we sincerely repent and confess our sin to one we have wronged, that very moment we are forgiven. Let us confess our sins to God, who only can forgive them, and our faults to one another. If we have given offense to our friend or neighbor, we are to acknowledge our wrong, and it is his duty to freely forgive us. Then we have to seek the forgiveness of God, not of a priest or pope, or of a prophet or theologian, because the brother we have wounded is the property of God, and in injuring him, we have sinned against his Creator and Redeemer (see 1 John 1 : 9; 2 : 1, 2; 2 Samuel 12 : 13; Leviticus 19 : 17; Matthew 18 : 15).

The Bible distinguishes two kinds of people in the world: The sons of men, indissolubly connected with the sinful nature in the flesh inherited from the birth and by nature: *'Behold, I was brought forth in iniquity, and in sin my mother conceived me'* (Psalms 51 : 5), as by nature he does not know nor serve his Creator: this is our first birth, on one hand; and on the other, the sons of God whose heart is renewed, they know Him, love Him, serve Him and obey Him: '. . . *Fear God and keep his commandments, for this is the whole duty of man'* (Ecclesiasts 12 : 13, King James Version) and by baptism, they are born again; this is the new birth in the spirit or the second birth. Did you get the word used in this verse here? It is the *'whole duty'* of man to keep God's commandments. God always traces a line between the two camps.

The converted Christian is not primarily 'a sinner', that is, not to be characterized by sin. He is called to walk in the light as Christ is in the light (1 John 1 : 7), to live victoriously by the power of the Holy Spirit, to be a saint and a child of his heavenly Father. He is called to be partaker of the divine nature, in other words, to become Christ-like. Yet, the old nature stays with him until God calls him home to heaven or until Jesus returns, whichever comes first for such a person. Therefore, the converted Christian must know how to win the battle against sin and his lingering propensity to sin. Indeed, being baptized and becoming Christian does not mean that we will be carried through life on flowery beds of ease. As members of a fallen race, we are subjected to sickness, accidents, and tragedy like everyone else. Furthermore, we encounter the added struggle of spiritual conflict with the Evil one and the lifelong battle against our own sinful tendencies. Yet the Lord always sustains us through each trial and works to bring good out of the most trying circumstances. We have but to ask for His help!

Some have maintained that there is no conflict within the Christian heart because of the supposition that the old nature governed by the flesh has been eradicated. Nevertheless, this is not true according to the Scriptures taken as a whole. Naturally, the flesh is to become increasingly subdued to God as the Christian learns by grace to walk in the Spirit; although, the tendency to sin is never eliminated in the flesh. So the Christian is never released from the necessity of consciously choosing to go in God's way. There is no escape from the need to depend on God's forgiveness. And here is the key found in God's Word, '*Sin not, but if you sin, we have an advocate . . .*' Then what to do? Confess, repent and abandon your sin, you will live!

Thus, to understand Romans 7 : 14 - 23, the believer who holds the law of God in high regard will, like Paul, find himself in something of a battle. One part of him will give assent to the goodness of the law, but another part of him will rebel against it. In response to the principles of God outlined in the law, one part of the believer will aspire to great deeds, but another part will pull him back from achieving them. Challenged by the law to be done with lesser things, the believer may resolve to change his ways only to find that, like the dog which returns to its vomit, he goes back to do again the things he loathes.

In Romans 1, verses 18 to 22, Paul saw the carnal man's behavior as an object of God's wrath, and spoke of children of wrath (Ephesians 2 : 3), led by the spirit that works in the sons of disobedience (verse 2), dead through sin and trespasses (verse 5), full of the works of the flesh (Galatians 5 : 19). Of the mind of the flesh, Paul says that it is death and enmity against God, for ". . . *to be carnally minded is death, but to be spiritually minded is life and peace. Because the carnal mind is enmity against God; for it is not subject to the law of God, nor indeed can be*" (Romans 8 : 5 - 7).

As converted Christians, the Bible identifies us with the righteousness of Christ rather than the wretchedness of sin. It states clearly that we were [*past tense*] all sinners. The key thing to remember is that 'we were all sinners', sinners who cannot be redeemed by our own merits; yet, ". . . *while we were sinners, Christ died for us.*" (Romans 5 : 8) to demonstrate the great love of His Father toward us; therefore, ". . . *if anyone is in Christ, he is a new creation; old things have passed away; behold, all things have become new*" (2 Corinthians 5 : 17).

Praise the Lord.

Hast thou not known? hast thou not heard, that the everlasting God, the LORD, the Creator of the ends of the earth, fainteth not, neither is weary? there is no searching of his understanding. (Isa 40 : 28)

GLORY AND HONOR to the Mighty and Most High Creator GOD!

Are we the unplanned and accidental result of evolution through natural selection? Or are we the handiwork of a Supreme Being, the Allah of the Koran and the Yahweh of the Torah? Do we owe our existence to the Aztec or Babylonian gods, or to some alien creatures from outer space, or to one of many gods worshiped in African and Indian cultures? What is the truth about our origin?

Today the theory of evolution is taught with pump and emphasis to students and promoted in the media as if it were proven fact. Not at all! The truth of the matter is, however, the theory of evolution is just a theory. Its scientific foundations are actually somewhat shaky. Thus molecular biologist and author Michael Denton gives this insight into Charles Darwin and his theory, stating, "The popular conception of a triumphant Darwin increasingly confident after 1859 in his views of evolution is a travesty. On the contrary, by the time the last edition of the Origin was published in 1872, he had become plagued with self-doubt and frustrated by his inability to meet the many objections which had been leveled at his theory." (Michael Denton in Evolution: A Theory in Crisis. ["Darwin, Charles Robert," *Microsoft® Encarta® 97 Encyclopedia,* ©1993-1996, Microsoft Corporation]).

Thing unseen for years, since this evolutionary theory exists, more and more scientists holding doctoral degrees have gone on the record expressing skepticism about Darwin's theory of evolution and calling for critical examination of the evidence cited in its support. One of them said "I signed the scientific dissent from Darwinism statement because I am absolutely convinced of the lack of true scientific evidence in favor of Darwinian dogma . . . Nobody in the biological sciences, medicine included, needs Darwinism at all" (Raul Leguizamon, M.D. pathologist and professor of medicine at the Autonomous University of Guadalajara, Mexico).

Darwin's theory of natural selection could not be thoroughly tested in his day due to the limitations of the scientific equipment available at that time. Today's scientists are able to study the complicated systems within even the simplest single-cell organisms. By the help of such equipments, many people had come to think of single cells as being less complex than multi-cellular organisms, as Darwin thought that the first organism was a cell. Darwin can be excused for thinking so because the equipment to look inside the cell and see what was going on just did not exist then. Today, the story should be different! Now that scientists have the sophisticated equipment to look inside the cell and find enormous complexity. Amoebas move as humans move although they do not have muscles; but microfilaments. Humans digest their food; they do respiration, so does the amoebae. They are much smaller than humans are; they do not have but one cell but they do all of the things multicellulars do and they are just as complex.

The complexity of even the simplest life form is one of the reasons why many scientists are becoming increasingly dissatisfied with the evolutionary explanation, with its reliance upon pure, unguided chance. There is good reason for scientists to question the power of chance. The evolution through a long series of random, unguided mutations, seems to be a practical impossibility. This fact casts a cloud of doubt over the entire evolutionary scenario.

The philosopher Daniel Dennett wonders, "When we turn to Darwin's bubble-up theory of creation, we can conceive of all of the creative design work metaphorically as lifting in Design Space. It has to start with the simplest replicators, and gradually ratchet up, by wave after wave of natural selection, to multicellular life in all its forms. Is such a process really capable of having produced all of the wonders we observe in the biosphere? Skeptics ever since Darwin have tried to demonstrate that one marvel or another is simply unapproachable by this laborious and unintelligent route. They have been searching for a 'skyhook,' something that floats high in Design Space, unsupported by ancestors, the direct result of a special act of intelligent creation." (Daniel Dennett: *Colloquium Papers:* Darwin's "strange inversion of reasoning", *June 15, 2009*)

"There is no evidence in the fossil record of one kind of creature becoming another kind. No transitional links or intermediate forms between various kinds of creatures have ever been found. For example, the evolutionist claims that it took perhaps fifty million years for a fish to evolve into an amphibian. But, again, there are no transitional forms. For example, not a single fossil with part fins . . . part feet has been found. And this is true between every major plant and animal kind . . . There is simply no evidence of partially evolved animals or plants in the fossil record to indicate that evolution has occurred in the past, and certainly no evidence of partially evolved animals and plants existing today to indicate that evolution is occurring at the present . . . Even if a creature shared characteristics belonging to two separate groups, however, this would not necessarily make it a transitional link as long as each of the characteristics themselves is complete and not in the process of transition from one type of structure or function into another type of structure or function." (Ranganathan, B.G. *Origins?*, p. 19-20, 25—Carlisle, PA: The Banner of Truth Trust, 1988.)

"Darwin stated, 'Why, if species have descended from other species by insensibly fine gradations, do we not everywhere see innumerable transitional forms? Why is not all nature in confusion instead of the species being, as we see them, well defined?' . . . the outstanding characteristics of the fossil record is the absence of evidence for evolution . . . The point to remember . . . is that the fossil problem for Darwinism is getting worse all the time" (Johnson, Phillip. *Darwin on Trial*, p. 46, 50, 57—Washington, D.C.: Regnery Gateway, 1991)

More and more Scientists are now looking for shortcuts, miraculous jumps out of the realm of chance. Many are frankly awed by their discoveries, finding more and more clear evidence of intelligent design in nature. Intelligent design, of course, requires a Designer. When one says that matter or energy is infinitely old, one assumes that the material out of which the billions of stars were built, existed simultaneously. When we are aware that each star contains billions of tons of materials, and that the balance of the raw material is much more than the material which is contained in the stars and planets, we realize the improbability of such an idea. We cannot conceive that all these quantities of materials existed at once and that nothing of it was preceded by non-existence.

To say that only a portion of the material is infinitely old, and that the other portions came to existence at a later stage, is to admit the need of a creator, because the inanimate material does not increase by self-reproduction. Only living beings are capable of multiplying by self-reproduction. Surely, to allow any gradual increase in the material quantity is to admit the need of a creator. There is something that we all know, that was born after the existence of the earth, namely the 'life'. Some scientists state that earth was too hot, while some of them say it was too cold for any kind of life to exist on it. It took the earth millions of years to become a suitable place for life. Life, therefore, is, undoubtedly, a newborn.

Science, however, tells us that life does not originate from non-living being. Through Pasteur's experience, which took place in the 19th century, using his sterilized soup, he proved beyond any doubt that life does not originate from inanimate material. The scientists of today are still unable to disprove his conclusion.

The earth, along with its atmosphere, at the time of its formation was sterile and unproductive. Transforming the inanimate materials, such as carbon, hydrogen, nitrogen, calcium, and iron into a living being could not be done through a natural process. It must have been done miraculously. Therefore, the existence of life on this planet is a shining evidence on the existence of an Intelligent, Supernatural Designer, Who testifies of Himself that He's '*The Life*' (John 11 : 25, 14 : 6; 1 John 1 : 2 . . .).

Surely, as a matter of fact, the scientists for several decades have tried ceaselessly to unseal the secret of life and to explain its commencement on this planet; but their intensified efforts so far did not produce any substantial knowledge in this field. The presence of life on this planet is, no doubt, a great wonder that could not happen without a supernatural cause. Man has unsealed many secrets in the universe, advanced in his scientific and technical knowledge, landed on the moon and even reached the most high skies; but in spite of all this, he is still unable to produce a leaf of a plant or a seed of an apple.

What about life out of earth? Does life exist anywhere in the Universe apart from on Earth? Scientists have been searching for life elsewhere in the Universe for more than 100 years. What are the chances of success?

As the likelihood of intelligent life existing elsewhere in the solar system disappeared, people began to think about the possibility of life existing farther away in the universe. There was no point in looking for life on the remaining solar system planets, because, apart from Earth and possibly Mars, all the others were simply too hostile to support life as we know it. Historically unsuccessful, life on Mars has often been hypothesized, although there is currently no solid evidence of life there at present, some scientists have theorized that there is evidence of fossilized microbes in the meteorite. The existence of Life out of our Earth is only a mere theory, once again!

In the same way, the Qur'an, holy book of Islam, does cite the transformation of the inanimate earth elements into living being as a sign of God's existence: ". . . and a sign to them is the dead earth: We made it alive and brought forth from it grain so they eat of it and We made therein gardens of date-palms and grapes, and We made springs to flow forth therein." (36 : 33 - 34).

O yes, Christ emphasizes clearly, "*I am the Life . . .*"

The clearest portrayal of a designer and his work is found here in the Torah. The Creation account itself records a systematic progression of creative acts culminating in the creation of Man. The prophet Jeremiah emphasizes this intelligent design when he writes about the Special Designer: "*He has made the earth by His power, He has established the world by His wisdom, and has stretched out the heavens at His discretion.*" (Jeremiah 10 : 12). Yes, by His discretion, no need of witness or helper!

Creation theory, as found in the Bible and other sacred books, does not attempt to provide a scientific description of God's creative acts. Instead, it suggests the meaning, the purpose and the goal of Creation. "*By faith we understand that the worlds were framed by the Word of God, so that things which are seen were not made of things which are visible.*" (Hebrews 11 : 3) "*By the word of the Lord were the heavens made, and all the host of them by the breath of His mouth. For he spoke, and it was done; He commanded, and it stood fast.*" (Psalms 33 : 6, 9). The Qur'an shares the basic biblical view of Creation this way: "Lo! your Lord is Allah Who created the heavens and the earth in six days, then mounted He the throne. He covered the night with the day, which is in haste to follow it, and hath made the sun and the moon and the stars subservient by His command. His verily is all creation and commandment. Blessed be Allah, the Lord of the Worlds!" (Qur'an, chapter 7, verse 54, Pickthal translation.)

Notice that the Qur'an recognize like the Bible that the night precedes the day, even though people afford to ignore this eternal truth. We will discuss about it later.

The most important thing about these verses, as far as our human understanding of creation is concerned, is that accepting the universe as creation is a matter of faith rather than of scientific proofs. Therefore, we can understand the universe in detail by scientific investigation, but we see it as the creation of God because of our personal trust and confidence in the Creator. All other ways to consider it being uncertain. Maybe we tend to discard this old Book as an irrelevant collection of useless fables, legends, and traditions, specific to certain people or cultures; however, its value lies far beyond the realm of science, dealing with concepts that cannot be analyzed in a laboratory.

This Book of books addresses many questions that science cannot answer. Science can talk about how the universe behaves and how things take place within the universe. It cannot explain why such thing exists rather than another. It cannot really explain the fundamental question of existence.

O Yes, only the neglected pages of Scripture actually offer accurate insights into our origins. That is, we are not here by accident neither by chance. We are a part of a Creator's design. Such Creator, as any designer, should have a plan, some real purpose, for our existence in this universe. As He said, "*Let Us make man in Our image, according to Our likeness; let them have dominion over the fish of the sea, and over the birds of the air, and over the cattle, over all the earth and over every tree whose fruit yields seed; to you it shall be for food*" (Genesis 1 : 26) Wow! Amazing enough! "*. . . in Our image, after Our likeness . . . to have dominion . . .*"! So created were we to be like God!

We see here the story of Creation depicting Jehovah as having great ambitions, high hopes, for the human race by creating them in His own Image. In the innocence they had been in the beginning, they had the privilege of a direct communication with God, a kind of an intimate, personal, face-to-face relationship with Him. As the work of creation finished with Man, God marked the end of creation with a day of rest, thus establishing the weekly cycle for human life. "*Thus the heavens and the earth and all the host of them were finished. And on the seventh day God ended His work which He had done, and He rested on the seventh day from all His work which He had made. Then God blessed the seventh day, and sanctified it, because in it He rested from all his work which God had created and made."* (Genesis 2 : 1 - 3)

God created the entire world in six days, not because He could not finish it in one day, but because He wanted it that way; and then He rested on the seventh day, not because He got tired (refer to Isaiah 40 : 28 - 29) but to mark the importance of His act of creation. The Sabbath too is, though, a creation in and of itself, because, what it does is to put the rest from the six days of labor in perspective for human beings. Therefore, God created nothing on the seventh day. Instead, God created a context in which everything that has been created in the natural world, the material world, and life itself, can really be appreciated, enjoyed, and celebrated on the seventh day. By creating the Sabbath, God gave to human beings an opportunity to emulate Him, to enter into *'His Rest'* and thereby to signify their special relationship with Him as their Lord and Creator.

Pope John Paul II said, "The 'Sabbath' has . . . been interpreted evocatively as a determining element in the kind of 'sacred architecture' of time . . . It recalls that the universe and history belong to God . . ." (Pope John Paul II, Apostolic Letter, *Dies Domini*, 1998). John Paul's reference to the sacred architecture of time supports the biblical assertion that our Creator designed the seven-day weekly cycle for us, and to make it holy, He blesses only one of the seven days of the week.

Thus, the week differs from all other units of time. For we know that the story defines a day as a period of darkness and light, evening and morning. It is caused by the rotation of the earth upon its axis. More precise units of time, hours, minutes, and seconds, are simply fractions of the day, set up by the will of Man. And the year is the period required for the earth to orbit the sun. The month, as we know it today, is loosely based on a full cycle of lunar phases, but it has been adjusted to make 12 months equal one year. ". . . However, the week is a different story altogether. It is an arbitrary period related to no natural phenomenon. The earliest record of the week is found in the literature and archaeology of the ancient Semitic peoples who inhabited south-western Asia prior to 2000 BC" (E. J. Bickerman, *Chronology of the Ancient World*, Ithaca: Cornell University Press, 1968, p. 58.). Where did they get the week? Was it imbedded in their past as a result of the Creator's design? Those are the questions!

Is the week really an arbitrary, artificial unit of time? Astronomer and anthropologist Anthony F. Aveni suggests that some chronobiologists are convinced that the seven-day cycle is designed into our very nature. "The seven-day biorhythm in the human body is one of the recent discoveries of modern chronobiology. It manifests itself in the form of small variations in blood pressure and heartbeat as well as response to infection and even organ transplant: for example, the probability of rejection of certain organs is now known to peak at weekly intervals following an implant." (Anthony F. Aveni, *Empires of Time: Calendars, Clocks, and Cultures*, New York: Basic Books, Inc., 1989), p. 100).

The widespread acceptance of the seven-day week over thousands of years of history is additional evidence supporting the divine origin of the weekly cycle. Nevertheless, if the week of Genesis has survived the thousands of years since the original creation week, why has recognition of the Creator not been preserved just as successfully?

We have the book of Genesis that provides the answer as to the downfall of the human family. In fact, if you read Genesis chapter 6, verse 5, you will see the Bible says that the thoughts of humanity were evil continually. So, God decided to clean up the world and sent the Flood. "*Now the flood was on the earth forty days. The waters increased and lifted up the ark, and it rose high above the earth. The waters prevailed and greatly increased on the earth, and the ark moved about on the surface of the waters. And the waters prevailed exceedingly on the earth, and all the high hills under the whole heaven, were covered.*" (Genesis 7 : 17 - 19).

God's punishments always occur after persistent refusal to listen by humans to many calls and warnings for repentance and confession of sins.

IV—THEN, WHAT?

For God so loved the world, that he gave his only begotten Son, that whoever believes in him should not perish, but have everlasting life. For God sent not his Son into the world to condemn the world; but that the world through him might be saved. He that believes on him is not condemned: but he that believes not is condemned already, because he has not believed in the name of the only begotten Son of God (John 3 : 16 - 18)

THE BIBLE MAKES three fundamental claims.

First, the Bible claims that the God of the Bible exists and is the one true God: *"In the beginning God created the heavens and the earth"* (Genesis 1 : 1); *"We must believe that God exists"* (Hebrews 11 : 6) and *"To you it was showed, that you might know that the LORD he is God; there is none else beside him. Out of heaven he made you to hear his voice, that he might instruct you: and on earth he showed you his great fire; and you heard his words out of the middle of the fire. And because he loved your fathers, therefore he chose their seed after them, and brought you out in his sight with his mighty power out of Egypt; To drive out nations from before you greater and mightier than you are, to bring you in, to give you their land for an inheritance, as it is this day. Know therefore this day, and consider it in your heart, that the LORD he is God in heaven above, and on the earth beneath: there is none else.* (Deuteronomy 4 : 35 - 39)

The complexity of our planet points to a deliberate Designer who not only created our universe, but also sustains it today. The Earth's size and corresponding gravity holds a thin layer of mostly nitrogen and oxygen gases, only extending about 50 miles above the Earth's surface. If Earth were smaller, an atmosphere would be impossible, like the planet Mercury. If Earth were larger, its atmosphere would contain free hydrogen, like Jupiter. Earth is the only known planet equipped with an atmosphere of the right mixture of gases to sustain plant, animal and human life.

The Earth is located at a right distance from the sun. If the Earth were any further away from the sun, we would all be frozen, if it be closer and we would burn up. The Earth remains this perfect distance from the sun while it rotates around the sun. Its rotating on its axis allows the entire surface of the Earth to be properly warmed and cooled every day. In the same manner, the moon with a perfect size and is at a distance from the Earth for its gravitational pull, thus creating important ocean tides and movement so ocean waters do not stagnate. Then how our massive oceans are restrained from spilling over across the continents and destroy their inhabitants!

Oh, consider the water, colorless, odorless and without taste, and yet no living thing can survive without it. Plants, animals and human beings survive mostly of water, about two-thirds of the human body is water. It allows us to live in an environment of fluctuating temperature changes, while keeping our bodies a steady 98.6 degrees. As a best solvent, water makes the various chemicals, minerals and nutrients be carried throughout our bodies and into the smallest blood vessels and enables food, medicines and minerals to be absorbed and used by the body. Evaporation takes the ocean waters, leaving the salt, and forms clouds which are easily moved by the wind to disperse water over the land, for vegetation, animals and people. It is a system of purification and supply that sustains life on this planet, a system of recycled and reused water. Glory to the Creator!

Yes, we are wonderfully made! The human brain takes in all the colors and objects you see, the temperature around you, the pressure of your feet against the floor, the sounds around you, the dryness of your mouth, even the texture of our keyboard. Our brain holds and processes all our emotions, thoughts and memories; at the same time it keeps track of the ongoing functions of our body like our breathing pattern, eyelid movement, hunger and movement of the muscles in our hands. The science discovers that the human brain processes more than a million messages a second. This screening function is what allows you to focus and operate effectively in your world. The brain functions differently than other organs. There is intelligence in it, the ability to reason, to produce feelings, to dream and plan, to take action, and relate to other people.

What about the eye which can distinguish among seven million colors and handles more than 1 million messages, simultaneously. Evolution focuses on mutations and changes from and within existing organisms. Yet evolution alone does not fully explain the initial source of the eye or the brain, the start of living organisms from nonliving matter.

Scientists are convinced that our universe began with one enormous explosion of energy and light, which they now call the '*Big Bang*'; but they have no explanation for the sudden explosion of light and matter.

The universe has not always existed. It had a start and who or what caused that? Scientific explanations are incomplete and even weak. Much of life may seem uncertain, but look at what we can count on day after day: gravity remains consistent, a hot cup of coffee left on a counter will get cold, the earth rotates in the same 24 hours, and the speed of light doesn't change, on earth or in galaxies far from us.

How is it that we can identify laws of nature that *never* change? Why is the universe so orderly, so reliable? The greatest scientists have been struck by how strange this is. There is no logical necessity for a universe that obeys rules.

The DNA code informs, programs a cell's behavior. All instruction, all teaching, all training comes with intent. Someone who writes an instruction manual does so with purpose. In every cell of our bodies, there exists a very detailed instruction code, much like a miniature computer program? The DNA code in our cells is made up of four chemicals that scientists abbreviate as A, T, G, and C. Well, just like one can program his phone to beep for specific reasons, DNA instructs the cell. DNA is a three-billion-lettered program telling the cell to act in a certain way. It is a full instruction manual. There are chemicals that instruct the DNA code in a very detailed way exactly how the person's body should develop.

We know God exists because he pursues us. He is constantly initiating and seeking for us to come to Him. Unlike any other revelation of God, Jesus Christ is the clearest, most specific picture of God revealing Himself to us.

FORTUNAT TSHIMANGA-MUKADI

Indeed, throughout the major world religions, Buddha, Muhammad, Confucius and Moses all identified themselves as teachers or prophets, but none of them ever claimed to be equal to God. Surprisingly, Jesus did. That is what sets Jesus apart from all the others. He said God exists and you have to look at Him to see God. Though He talked about His Father in heaven, it was not from the position of separation, but of very close union, unique to all humankind. Jesus said that anyone who had seen Him had seen the Father, anyone who believed in Him, believed in the Father.

He said, "*I am the light of the world, he who follows me will not walk in darkness, but will have the light of life.*" (John 8 : 12). He claimed attributes belonging only to God: to be able to forgive people of their sin, free them from habits of sin, give people a more abundant life and give them eternal life in heaven. Unlike other teachers who focused people on their words, Jesus pointed people to himself. He did not say, follow my words and you will find truth. He said, "*I am the way, the truth, and the life, no one comes to the Father but through me.*" (John 14 : 6)

To prove His divinity, Jesus did what people cannot do and performed miracles. He healed the blind, the crippled, the deaf, even raised a couple of people from the dead. He created food out of thin air, enough to feed crowds of several thousand people. He walked on top of a lake, commanding a raging storm to stop for some friends. He told people, if you do not want to believe what I am telling you, you should at least believe in me based on the miracles you are seeing. Jesus Christ showed God to be gentle, loving, aware of our self-centeredness and shortcomings, yet deeply wanting a relationship with us. Jesus revealed that although God views us as sinners, worthy of His punishment, His love for us ruled and God came up with a different plan by taking the form of Man and accepted the punishment for our sin on our behalf. Jesus died in our place that we may live. Of all the religions known to humanity, only through Jesus will you see God reaching toward humanity, providing a way for us to have a relationship with Him.

So, does God exist? Looking at all these facts, one can conclude that a loving God does exist and can be known in an intimate, personal way.

Second point, the Bible claims to be an inspired revelation of God's will. This topic is more documented in chapters 2 and 3 of this Testimony. However, let us for instance ask ourselves the question, what is unique about the Bible that sets it apart from all other religious books ever written?

Throughout time, skeptics have regarded the Bible as mythological, but archeology has confirmed it as historical. Opponents have attacked its teaching as primitive and outdated, but its moral and legal concepts and teachings have had a positive influence on societies and cultures throughout the world. It continues to be attacked by pseudo-science, psychology, and political movements, yet it remains just as true and relevant today as it was when it was first written. It is a book that has transformed countless lives and cultures throughout the last 2000 years. No matter how its opponents try to attack, destroy, or discredit it, the Bible remains; its veracity and impact on lives is unmistakable.

The accuracy which has been preserved despite every attempt to corrupt, attack, or destroy, from within or without the Christendom, is a clear testimony to the fact that the Bible is truly God's Word and is supernaturally protected by Him. It should not surprise anyone that, no matter how the Bible is attacked, it always comes out unchanged and unscathed. After all, Jesus said, *"Heaven and earth will pass away, but my words will never pass away"* (Mark 13 : 31). After looking at the evidence, one can say without a doubt that, yes, the Bible is truly God's Word.

Finally the third point, The Bible claims that Jesus is God's Son. In John chapter 20 verses 26 to 31, Jesus allowed Thomas to call him *"my Lord and my God"*. To have eternal life, we must believe that He is the Christ, the Son of God. The Samaritans claimed Jesus was indeed the Christ, the Savior of the world (John 4 : 42). Each person is responsible to consider whether or not these claims are true. This requires giving careful consideration to the evidence, such as is presented through this book. Our eternal destiny hangs in the balance. If we conclude the claims are true, we are then responsible to learn to present the evidence to others (see 1 Peter 3 : 15; Philippians 1 : 7, 17). All people, believers and unbelievers, need to carefully study the evidence for the claims of the Bible.

Islam considers Jesus as a respected prophet, but not the Son of God. In Islam, Jesus has no earthly father and is born through the breathing of the 'Spirit of God' on Mary. However, Jesus is not considered the Son of God. (*Jesus: A Brief History* by W. Barnes Tatum 2009, page 217, *The new encyclopedia of Islam* by Cyril Glassé, Huston Smith 2003, page 86). Rather, the Quran compares the nature of his birth to the birth of Adam, who had neither mother nor father, (The Noble Quran V.3 : 59 - 60)

In the writings of the Bahá'í Faith, the term "Son of God" is applied to Jesus (Lepard, Brian D, 2008, *In The Glory of the Father:*

The Baha'i Faith and Christianity. Bahá'í Publishing Trust. pp. 74-75), but does not indicate a literal physical relationship between Jesus and God (Taherzadeh, Adib, 1977, *The Revelation of Bahá'u'lláh, Volume 2: Adrianople 1863-68*. Oxford, UK: George Ronald. p. 182). It is symbolic and is used to indicate the very strong spiritual relationship between Jesus and God (Lepard, Brian D, *Idem*), and the source of his authority (Taherzadeh, Adib, *Idem*). Shoghi Effendi, the Guardian of the Bahá'í Faith, also noted that the term does not indicate that the status of Jesus is superior to other prophets and messengers, that Bahá'ís' name 'Manifestations of God' includes Jesus, Buddha, Muhammad and Baha'u'llah among others (Hornby, Helen, ed., 1983, *Lights of Guidance: A Bahá'í Reference File*. New Delhi, India: Bahá'í Publishing Trust. p. 491). Shoghi Effendi notes that since all Manifestations of God share the same intimate relationship with God and reflect the same light, the term Sonship can in a sense be attributable to all the Manifestations (Lepard, Brian, *Idem*).

Muslims frequently ask that if Jesus were really God's Son or God in the flesh, why did not Jesus know the date or the hour of the Judgment? *"But of that day and hour no one knows, not even the angels of heaven, nor the Son, but the Father only."* (Matthew 24 : 36). Or, if Jesus were God in the flesh, why did He say, *"The Son can do nothing of his own accord but only what he sees the Father doing . . . The Father is greater than I . . . I can do nothing on my own authority."* (John 5 : 19, 14 : 28, 5 : 30). Muslims will ask rhetorical questions such as, 'Wouldn't God know the last hour of Judgment?' or, 'If Jesus were God, why did He say, *"the Father is greater than I"*?'

The answer lies in what Christ's Sonship on earth entails. The passage that best addresses it is Philippians chapter 2 verses 5 to 8: *"Let this mind be in you which was also in Christ Jesus, who being in the form of God thought it not robbery to be equal with God, but made Himself of no reputation and took upon Him the form of a servant and was made in the likeness of men: and being found in fashion as a man He humbled Himself and became obedient unto death, even the death on the cross."*

Here Christ emptied Himself. The Sonship of Christ is revealed in this: He was revealed as God in the flesh, and yet submitted to God the Father as Man. He was limited as a Man, and He glorified God the Father. The analogical term 'Son' best describes Christ's relationship with God the Father.

Christ's exalted relationship is even seen in the very verse Muslims choose to attack His Sonship. In Mark 13 : 32, Christ says, *"But of that day and hour knows no man, no, not the angels which are in heaven, neither the Son, but the Father."* Here, Jesus places Himself above men, and above the angels. Jesus describes Himself alone in a category in relation to God.

Likewise, Christ, when saying that He does nothing of His own accord, states that *"whatever the Father does, the Son does likewise"*. Christ establishes His Sonship and puts Himself in perfect harmony with God. Even Muhammad is declared in the Qur'an as a sinner in Sura 48 : 2, but Christ walked in perfect harmony with the Father. As Muhammad failed to understand what "Son of God" signified, so today, many Muslims continue to misunderstand Christ Jesus' nature, even though the prophet Muhammad advised them to believe in Jesus.

Jesus is not God's Son in the sense of a human father and a son. God did not get married and have a son. God did not mate with Mary and, together with her, produce a son. Jesus is God's Son in the sense that He is God made manifest in human form (John 1 : 1, 14). Jesus is God's Son in that He was conceived in Mary through the Holy Spirit. Luke 1 : 35 declares, *"The angel answered, 'The Holy Spirit will come upon you, and the power of the Most High will overshadow you. So the holy one to be born will be called the Son of God.'"*

During His trial before the Jewish leaders, the High Priest demanded of Jesus, *"I charge you under oath by the living God: Tell us if you are the Christ, the Son of God"* (Matthew 26 : 63). *"Yes, it is as you say"*, Jesus replied. *"But I say to all of you: In the future you will see the Son of Man sitting at the right hand of the Mighty One and coming on the clouds of heaven"* (Matthew 26 : 64). The Jewish leaders responded by accusing Jesus of blasphemy (Matthew 26 : 65 - 66). Later, before Pontius Pilate, The Jews insisted, *"We have a law, and according to that law He must die, because He claimed to be the Son of God"* (John 19 : 7).

Why would His claiming to be the Son of God be considered blasphemy and be worthy of a death sentence? The Jewish leaders understood exactly what Jesus meant by the words 'Son of God'. To be the Son of God is to be of the same nature as God. The claim to be of the same nature as God, in fact be God, was blasphemy to the Jewish leaders; therefore, they demanded Jesus' death, in keeping with Leviticus 24 : 15. The book of Hebrews chapter 1 in verse 3 expresses that very clearly, "*The Son is the radiance of God's glory and the exact representation of His being.*"

Another example can be found in John 17 : 12 where Judas is described as the "*son of perdition.*" John 6 : 71 tells us that Judas was the son of Simon. What does John 17 : 12 mean by describing Judas as the "*son of perdition*"? The word *perdition* means 'destruction, ruin, waste'. Judas was not the literal son of 'ruin, destruction, and waste', but those things were the identity of Judas' life. Judas was a manifestation of perdition. In this same way, Jesus is the Son of God. The Son of God is God. Jesus is God made manifest (John 1 : 1, 14).

V—THERE WAS THE NIGHT FIRST . . .

"Therefore do not cast away your confidence, which has great reward. For you have need of endurance, so that after you have done the will of God, you may receive the promise: 'For yet a little while, and He who is coming will come and will not tarry. Now the just shall live by faith; but if anyone draws back, My soul has no pleasure in him.'" (Hebrews 10 : 35 - 38).

THAT THIS ADMONITION is addressed to the Church in the last days is evident from the words pointing to the nearness of the Lord's coming: *"For yet a little while, and He that shall come will come and will not tarry."* In addition, this plainly implies also that there would be a seeming delay and that the Lord would appear to tarry. The instruction here given is especially adapted to the experience of Christians at this time in which we are living.

When a person becomes a member of the Body of Christ, such a person is expected to possess a passionate connection with Christ by a practical knowledge of Scriptures, a regular daily time in studying them, as did the Berean Christians, and above all, a prayerful life. On the other hand, the ministers of the Gospel have to know how to help members grow in spiritual maturity and discipleship; they should not '. . . think that they must proclaim the solemn, sacred message in a theatrical style. Not one jot or title of anything theatrical is to be brought into our work. God's cause is to have a sacred, heavenly mold. Let everything connected with the giving of the message for this time bear the divine impress. Let nothing of a theatrical nature permitted, for this would spoil the sacredness of the work . . . The enemy will watch closely and will take every advantage of circumstances to degrade the truth by the introduction of undignified demonstrations'. (Ellen G. White, *Evangelism*, p. 137, 138).

The true followers of Christ have to seek with prayerful and earnest effort for a passionate connection with Christ. One cannot connect sincerely and trustfully with someone whom he does not know well enough: thus, the practical knowledge of the Master is needed through the Bible study! I do not say by a weary reading of this holy Book; but by its steady study combined with the help of its Author, one may know Him as He must be known according to His providence, for He promised, *"Ask, and it will be given to you; seek, and you will find . . ."* (Matthew 7 : 7). *"And whatever you ask in My name, that I will do, that the Father may be glorified in the Son. If you ask anything* [Thank Lord!] *in My name, I will do it."* And *". . . I will pray the Father, and He will give you another Helper . . . the Holy Spirit, whom the Father will send in My name, He will teach you all things and bring to your remembrance all things that I said to you"* (John 14 : 13, 14, 16, 26, emphasis added)

Wonderful promises!

By God's grace and through the right encouragement of the fellow members of the community of faith, an individual may live in harmony with the principles of God's Word. This is not an easy task, as the cosmic conflict between Christ and Satan, between evil and good, between truth and lie, is raging throughout the Universe. Satan, consumed by hatred toward Christ and His salvation on behalf of His Saints, is confusing the vast majority of people by distorting the Truth concerning God and His holy Law!

In this conflict, there are but two camps, one for Christ and another for the Enemy. There is no middle ground, for *"He who is not with Me is against Me,"* says the Lord, *"and he who does not gather with Me scatters abroad"* (Matthew 12 : 30). Many Christians, blinded by ignorance, lifestyle, human philosophy, lust of the flesh and self-confidence, have difficulty to discern the border between the two camps, because Satan transforms himself into an angel of light, and when he intervenes in men's affairs, he is so subtle that he transforms himself into a loving and faithful Bible teacher.

The fact that people that are in any so-called 'Christian' church, not relying on the Word, feel confident and sure to be saved and not being in Satan's camp, forgetting there is only One Way to Life. Because of His humanity as we still are, the Son of Man was tempted and fiercely buffeted by Satan in a way higher than in which we are; so loved He the solitude of the mountains, of the desert and of the night in which He had communion with His heavenly Father in earnest prayers. This is what those that have taken a leadership in the Church should be doing unceasingly on behalf of their followers. Not everyone who hails unceasingly 'Lord, Lord' is necessarily following this unique Way to the eternal Life. Therefore, one believer could be in the Way or not! There is no middle ground. Because of multiple denominations claiming the name of Christ, everyone should earnestly study the Word of God to make sure he or she is in the Way!

The division, let us say the confusion among Christians is the fulfillment of the Lord's warnings when He prophesied, *"Do you suppose that I came to give peace on earth? I tell you, not at all, but rather division. For from now on five in one house will be divided, three against two, and two against three . . ."* (Luke 12 : 51ss). So prayed He that His true followers might be kept from doing evil, for, though they are in the world, they were not of it.

Christ foresaw His Church history throughout generations, full of betrayals among leaders, of false teachings invading His Truth, of church leaders becoming so powerful and proud that they would behave as heathens. Some proclaiming themselves 'God' for the name by which their followers call them, such as "Holy Father, Master . . .", to make themselves important and above all civil, military and religious authorities.

Therefore, they got lost in the Church.

How can someone in the Church get lost? Because many put the Church above Him who gave up Himself to save the Church, when the rules established by the Church overshadow, contradict and even suppress the unchangeable Sayings of the Creator. When some leaders have acquired so great power that makes no place for Christ in the Church members' heart! When many of them strive to accumulate diploma upon diploma that have, the most of them, nothing to do with the Master's teachings but only for the sake of being seen and praised of men! Some who stand in the pulpit make the heavenly messengers in the audience ashamed of them.

FORTUNAT TSHIMANGA-MUKADI

The precious and eternal Gospel that has cost so much to be brought to the world is abused and even despised. There is common and cheap talk, grotesque attitudes and working of the deceitfulness; there is with some teachers rapid talking; with others a thick and indistinct utterance. However, everyone who ministers before the people should feel it a solemn duty to take himself in hand. He should first give himself to the Lord in complete self-renunciation, determined that he will have none of self, but all of Jesus (read Ellen G. White, *Testimonies to Ministers*, 1896, p. 339). When put in some position in the Church hierarchy, some think having reached the holiness or all power to give to their words the worthiness that equals and even surpasses the Bible sayings, forgetting that they are but dust, born in sins and grown in sins.

By their disobedience, our first parents lost their likeness to their Maker: His well-nigh likeness became obliterated, His mental capacity in them lessened and His spiritual power dimmed. By God's decision and then, the hereditary laws, Adam's descendants inherited these new acquired weaknesses. Thus, as long as they will not lean on the power from above, they will be subject to errors and wrong behaviour and decisions. The holy Bible teaches us in 1 Corinthians 10 : 12, "... *let him who thinks he stands take heed lest he fall*". Therefore, those who accept Christ, and in their first confidence proclaim, 'I am saved', are in danger of trusting to themselves. Instead, our only safety is in constant distrust of self, and dependence on Christ; we are never to rest in a satisfied condition, and cease to make advancement, saying, 'I am saved'. When this idea is entertained, the motives for watchfulness, for prayer, for earnest endeavor to press onward to higher attainments, cease to exist; and we would not reach the standard which Peter calls, A CHOSEN GENERATION, A ROYAL PRIESTHOOD, A HOLY NATION, A PECULAR PEOPLE (1Peter 2 : 9, 10). By these Scriptures, the other extreme to avoid is what we said above, to debase himself to a sinful state, proclaiming unceasingly that 'I am sinner', by mere hypocrisy, somehow!

Nevertheless, the history of the Church is thus revealing; with all these coldness and false teachings increasing so far. Christ's commission to the Church is to deliver the "Good News" of salvation to all nations and the establishment of a community in which individuals can strengthen one another and continue to canvas the world with the eternal saving message of the Gospel.

The Holy Spirit has done His part of inspiring the holy people the writings of the Book, which must be taken as an unchangeable Word of God. Let us be less preoccupied to deliver our beliefs and catechisms for which we strongly stand, instead of standing with boldness for the pure "Good News" that came out of the mouth of the Savior and making them the centre of our theology! The mission of the Church is not to compromise with the world, not to conform to it, not to imitate the world in its perversions; but the purpose of the Church, as an arena of God's grace, is to change the world, to transform it and to be an instrumental agency of its conversion. Under Satan's instigations, some Christian teachers insist in their sermons that the important thing for salvation of the souls is but to believe, in stressing Romans chapter 3 verse 28, taken wrongly out of its context, although the verse 31 clarifies the idea, saying, ". . . *we establish the law.*"

We know by the Church History that between the close of the apostolic age and the beginning of the reformation in 1517, many basic biblical truths yielded already to falsehoods grounded in Roman and Greek philosophy and culture. In addition to this, the leaders acquired the desire for power and self-exaltation. Christ and His teachings gave place to the human teachings and wrongdoings: the people chose sin rather than righteousness, rebellion rather than obedience, self-centeredness rather than Christ-centeredness. Even those that condemned in the past these practices, espoused at their turn the same behavior. Others have set up their own rules of living to appear being better Christians than others are, and this, out of the Word. So stressed it clearly the Lord, ". . . *all their works they do to be seen by men. They make their phylacteries broad, and enlarge the borders of their garments. They love the best places at feasts, the seats in the synagogues, greetings in the marketplaces, and to be called by men, Rabbi* [minister] . . . *Rabbi* [father] . . . *Rabbi* [doctor] . . . *Rabbi* [bishop] . . . *Rabbi* [master] . . ." (Matthew 23 : 5 - 7, *emphasis added*). He concluded this with an important admonition, "*But you, do not be called 'Rabbi'; for One is your Teacher, the Christ, and you are all brethren. Do not call anyone on earth your father; for One is your father, He who is in heaven. And do not be called teachers; for One is your Teacher, the Christ* (verses 8 to 10).

I have heard other deceptions among Christians, with their leaders encouraging them to accept work positions where they have to work on Saturday, saying, ". . . Go to work to obey your boss and to keep your job, only bring Saturday day salaries to the Church treasure as free offering; do not use it for your benefit". What does God need the most, is it our money or our soul for which He has paid a high price! Nevertheless, the truth is, when applying for any job, consider first the work schedule. If this can lead you to work on Saturday, drop it and continue prayerfully your search for another job. If the conditions of work change while you are in any work position, discuss the matter with your boss and get an agreement to be released from working in holy hours of the Sabbath day. If an agreement is impossible, drop the position or change the department within the company. I know that some folks living in the countries where the workweek is from Monday to Saturday have much difficulty to accommodate themselves with the work schedule. It is a big challenge for such ones! Anyway, God knows and will provide: only obey, trust and pray and wait for deliverance!

In case of a position where you are the only one to help and save life in your specialty, therefore perform the task and do not get paid for those hour or task, considering yourself as benevolent helper to save life. If the check pay is automatically issued to you, then give it to the Church treasure or other no-profit agency involved in helping the needy ones.

If one pushes people to break God's holy Law, the same becomes a contender with his Creator and places himself and his followers in Satan army (Matthew 5 : 19, 20)! The attack against Christ's Church is not always from outside, but the Enemy uses the very members of it to introduce the falsity with the goal to deceive even the elect if he could (Matthew 24 : 24, 25)!

Though the Church is under attack, God is providing the way for a "Remnant" to escape in leaning upon Him by love and trust. Damage is done and will be done again to it, but the Remnant ones, in the end, will not be destroyed, because Christ will not allow that to happen. For this, Christ is so clear "*My sheep hear My voice, and they follow Me. And I give them eternal life, and they shall never perish; neither shall anyone snatch them out of My hand . . . I and My Father are one.*" (John 10 : 27 - 30). Those Remnant saints, now invisible, are the sole depository of "Good news" and a salvation bearer agency! For, there is but one Christ, which is not divided on one hand, and there are false 'Christs' on the other; one God who pays everyone according to his or her deed. Therefore, "Christ's Church will survive. The winds of lawlessness and fanaticism will blow; the dust storms of doubt will stir up clouds of confusion; the gentle zephyrs of Laodiceanism will put thousands of God's people to sleep; but His Church will survive" (Mark Finley, *Solid Ground*, Review and Herald Publishing Association, 2003)

Our battle is more subtle and more dangerous than it had never been before. After the physical persecutions suffered by the true worshipers under the roman empire and afterward under other false 'Christians' in the past, today we face the spiritual persecution from all these numerous 'Christian' churches teaching the falsehoods along the days in the name of the Crucified One, helped in this by the modern sophisticated technology of communication; in such a way that the 'little children' are deceived and led to "WORSHIP THE BEAST AND ITS IMAGE" in a subtle way; as it is written, *"For then there will be great tribulation, such as has not been since the beginning of the world until this time, no, nor ever shall be. And unless those days were shortened, no flesh would be saved; but for the elect's sake those days will be shortened."* (Matthew 24 : 21, 22). O yes Lord, please shorten those evil days to help us survive!

Be yourself holy as Him who called you is holy. Last-day true worshipers of God must live daily in full commitment to Him and to holiness, in obedience to the entire Law of the TEN COMMANDMENTS according to the powerful and eternal messages found in Revelation 12 and 14. In these prophecies, obedience to the law of God is a sign of submission and loyalty to the Master of the Universe. In this, the fourth commandment occupies a highest position among the other nine; for it emphasizes God's creative power; therefore, removing the creative power from the attributes of our God, He ceases to be the God who made us as we are and places us where we are! Without this special quality of Creator made manifest in the fourth commandment, our worship becomes idolatry; then, we do not know what and Whom we worship! Our worship becomes but a mere fanaticism or a vain routine, a blind formalism!

It is not in vain that Satan in Eden reached his goal toward our first parents in alluring them with the idea that, in eating the forbidden fruit, they will be 'as gods'. What they did not discern was in the second part of the message; for Lucifer concluded subtly, *". . . knowing good and evil"*. Created perfect in God's image, they knew already the 'good' for they were created perfect. Then they longed for more that would make them 'like God', only to find themselves naked, and hid themselves!

'Remember the Sabbath to keep it holy . . .' is controversial to most professing Christians, for God instructs to observe it, but many simply choose to ignore it. Yet, the fourth commandment is the all-important test commandment. How we keep it demonstrates our willingness to

honor our Creator and walk in His ways. God's Word describes it as a *sign* identifying the people who seek to obey God; it is the only command upon which a *covenant* was made (Exodus 31 : 13 - 16). The two commandments that are the most lengthy, detailed and well explained, the second and the fourth, are the ones that most Christian churches have chosen to alter for their own convenience.

Genesis, which means "Beginnings", speaks almost immediately about the subject of the Sabbath as the seventh day of the week; it is as though God wanted this issue clearly established in the minds of the Bible's readers from the outset of their study of His inspired Word: the "Creation chapter" of this first Book of the Bible concludes, "*Thus the heavens, and the earth and all the host of them were finished. And on the seventh day God ended His work which He had made, and He rested on the seventh day from all His work which He had made. Then God blessed the seventh day and sanctified it, because in it He rested from all His work which God had created and made*" (Genesis 2 : 1 - 3). God made the Sabbath as a time for man to rest from the previous six days of work, knowing that man would need this rest physically, mentally, emotionally and spiritually. It is a time to break away from the daily routine, commune with God, and reflect on our purpose for being here. God blessed and sanctified this time, making it holy. When God confers such honor upon anything, we should take special notice! Many scriptures make clear why He set the Sabbath apart from the rest of the week, commanding Man to work six days. He wants Man to provide a time of rest for himself and his family and manage his life and finances in accordance with His laws.

The faithful teachers of the Gospel of Christ must proclaim today that salvation is by faith in Christ, the true and living faith leading believers to obey all the requirements of the Law of our loving and eternal Legislator. This is the theme song of the Scriptures from Eden to Eternity:

- Genesis 2 : 16, 17, what is known today as the Man's original sin is from disobedience to the command of God;
- Exodus 19 : 5 - 6, obeying God places Man in special elevated position to Him;
- Deuteronomy 11 : 26 - 28, disobedience leads to the curse and obedience to the blessing, see also James 1 : 25
- 1 Samuel 15 : 22, 23, obedience surpasses offerings and tithes;

- Jeremy 31 : 33: God promises to write His Law no longer on the stones, but in Man's heart and mind that it may lead him continually in his life;
- Matthew 5 : 16 - 19, Christ did not come to destroy His Father's Law which will last as long as the earth and heaven will last, thus everyone should keep it thoroughly;
- James 2 : 10 - 12, we are called to obey to every point of the Law according to our profession of faith;
- 1 John 5 : 3, our love toward our Maker is expressed by obedience to His commands;
- Revelation 12 : 17, Satan is enraged against the faithful obedient Christians;
- Revelation 14 : 12 - 14 show clearly that obedience to the divine Law leads to holiness, without which nobody can see God.

When confronted by the greatness of God, His justice and His salvation, men and women must surrender to Him in faith and obedience. To fear God is, in fact, to keep His commandments (Deuteronomy 8 : 6). There are no substitutes for faithfulness, trust and obedience to our Maker when it comes to being fortified in whatever battles and challenges we face on any level of our Christian life.

Heaven and earth shall pass away, but never His Word! Yes indeed, *"the grass withers, the flower fades. But the word of our God stands forever."* For His words *". . . were now written! Oh that they were inscribed in a book! That they were engraved on a rock with an iron pen and lead forever."* (Matthew 24 : 35; Isaiah 40 : 8; Job 19 : 23, 24).

To him is much given, to the same is much asked. We know by the holy Bible that a 24-hour day goes from sunset to sunset. In addition, the Koran, holy book of Islam, shares the same basic biblical view of Creation that ". . . Allah . . . covereth the night with the day, which is in haste to follow it, and hath made the sun and the moon and the stars subservient by His command . . . !" (*The Koran*, chapter 7, verse 54, Pickthal translation). This is logical and correct, for it is from the Creator who made that the night comes first, and then the day! *"And God called the light Day, and the darkness he called Night. And there was evening, and there was morning—the first day"*. (Genesis 5 : 1, *Darby*), say the Scriptures.

However, the Prince of darkness had suggested to the world to consider the day from midnight to midnight. This confusion makes people to consider the natural first hour of the day as seventh hour in the morning, and the natural beginning of the night, as seventh hour of the night, mainly in the western culture: this is to say, when the night starts, we have already started to count its hours; the same for the day. Confusion of the high-learned confusionists! We all have fallen in the error, that even the educated persons cannot discern the error to count the beginning of a time from its middle! "*How can a young man cleanse his way? By taking heed according to Your word. Your word I have hidden in my heart, that I might not sin against You. Forever, O Lord, Your word is settled in heaven. Your word is a lamp to my feet and a light to my path. I have sworn and confirmed that I will keep your righteous judgments.*" (Psalms 119 : 9, 11, 89, 105, 106)

Despite the multiple variables that can affect when the physical solar light actually appears on the horizon according to where we live on our planet Earth, the concept of having post-meridian hours should represent the time between sunset and sunrise. A full 24 hours day is considered made of one daylight and one night, but it is still called a day. So we have everywhere on this planet a conceptual agreement of twelve hours (sometimes more, sometimes less according to which earth latitude one lives) of daylight starting at a conceptual daytime versus our current practice of saying midnight is the beginning of the 24 hour day.

Do you get what I am saying? Let me make it clearer. The terms 'AM and PM' are derived from 'Ante Meridian and Post Meridian'. '*Ante*' is a Latin word for the English word '*Before*' and '*Post*' is a Latin word for '*After*'. Meridian is the accusative form of Meridis, meaning midday. That makes no sense to a logical person, since midnight is meaning 'middle of the night'. Therefore, how could it then be the beginning of the daylight? And in the same way, that wouldn't make sense for PM, because afternoon is now at 12:00 PM, and then 11:59 PM is at night time, so PM can't mean morning and night time, neither AM night and daytime altogether! In this, even those that hold the multitude of great diploma are unable to refute it! Science without conscience is but death of the soul!

Let us reset the reference of time so that the first hour of daylight is 1AM, versus it being in the middle of the night. There may have been some plausible, obscure reason for the way time is currently referenced to, but we live in a modern society founded on reason and scientific integrity. Therefore, it makes sense that 'night' time and PM should be during the night, and 'morning' time and AM should be during daylight hours.

VI—NATURE-WORSHIP ORIGINS

But there were false prophets also among the people, even as there shall be false teachers among you, who privately shall bring in damnable heresies, even denying the Lord that bought them, and bring upon themselves swift destruction. (2 Peter 2 : 1)

THOUGH GOD HAD dramatically demonstrated His power and His displeasure with people not following His way, Mankind soon forgot again. They started to build again idols to themselves instead of worshipping their God; and the whole idea of the weekly cycle, which showed six days of work and the Sabbath was forgotten. What mankind did was to merely incorporate the weekly cycle into astrological tables instead of remembering the God of Creation.

How did the whole earth have moved to worship idols and believe in human philosophy instead of keeping God's cycle of the week along the History? The human history teaches us the downfall and revitalization of the seventh-day Sabbath:

God establishes Sabbath at end of Creation Week
2450	The Flood (Genesis 7 : 4 - 8 : 6)
2000	Seven-day week in Sumerian civilization prior to this date Abraham keeps God's commandments
1011-971	King David rules Israel (2 Samuel 5 : 10 - 25)
500	Birth of Buddhism
445	Nehemiah to Jerusalem to rebuild city and to reform Sabbath keeping (Nehemiah 13 : 6 - 22)

331	Alexander the Great overthrows Persian Empire
170	Antiochus IV tries to eradicate Jewish practices—including Sabbath observance
30	Roman Emperor Octavian dedicates captured Egyptian obelisk to the sun god
4	Birth of Jesus (Matthew 1 : 23 - 2 : 5; Luke 2 : 1 - 20)
31	Crucifixion of Jesus (Matthew 27 : 33 - 40 - 56; Mark 15 : 22 - 41; Luke 23 : 33 - 49; John 19 : 17 - 30)
64	Nero burns Rome (?), persecutes Christians
70	Jerusalem destroyed by Roman army under Titus (Daniel 9 : 23, 27; 11 : 31; 12 : 11; Matthew 23 : 36 - 24 : 2, 15 - 20; Luke 13 : 34; Mark 13 : 14 - 18)
90-99	Synagogue prayer devised to help identify Sabbath-keeping Christians who worshipped in synagogues with Jews
115-140	Epistle of Barnabas written in Alexandria; first anti-Sabbath literature. Christians in Alexandria replace Sabbath with Sunday
135	Jerusalem destroyed again; Jewish religion banned
144	Marcion, first great 'Christian' heretic, promotes Sabbath fast
150	Justin Martyr reports Sunday observance by Roman Christians
218-222	Emperor Elagabalus brings Syrian sun worship to Rome
270-275	Emperor Aurelian establishes sun worship as state religion of Rome
284-305	Emperor Diocletian worships the sun and persecutes Christians
306-337	Constantine—first Roman emperor to adopt Christian religion
313	Constantine legalizes Christian religion
314-335	Pope Sylvester I promotes anti-Jewish Sabbath fast
321	Edict of Constantine: first law concerning Sunday observance
570-632	Life of Muhammed, founder of Islam
590-604	Pope Gregory I identifies Sabbath keepers with anti-Christ
1054	The "Great Schism" splits Roman Catholic—Greek Orthodox churches
1070	Margaret, Queen of Scotland, initiates reform of Sunday observance
1720	Conrad Beisel, Sabbath-keeping founder of Ephrata Cloister, arrives in Pennsylvania

1742	Count Zinzendorf proposes Sabbath observance to Moravian community in Bethlehem, Pennsylvania
1273-1352	Life of Ewostatewos (Eustathius), Ethiopian reform who called for revival of traditional Sabbath observance in Ethiopia
1350	Strigolniks in Novgorod, Russia, observe the seventh-day Sabbath
1324-1384	Life of John Wycliffe, popular English 'reformer', who with colleagues produce first English translation of Bible in 1382.
1401-1410	English Parliament passed "Act for the Burning of Heretics" by which people were tried in English court for, among other things, observing seventh-day Sabbath
1431-1435	Roman Catholic Council of Basel condemns Sabbath observance by Jewish converts and in Bergen condemns Sabbath observance in Norway.
1475-1504	Russian reform movement includes observance of seventh-day Sabbath, but Russian Orthodox Council of Moscow condemns pro-Sabbath reformers; then in 1504, Ivan Kuritsin and other Sabbath-keeping reformers are burned to death in Moscow
1517-1518	Martin Luther posts his 95 Thesis, starts Protestant Reformation and appeals to pope for a general church council
1534	Henry VIII separates English church from Rome
1540	Andreas Fischer, Sabbath-keeping Anabaptist preacher, is murdered in Slovakia
1544	Christian III, king of Denmark and Norway, imposes fines for keeping the seventh-day Sabbath in his realm
1545-1563	Roman Catholic Council of Trent affirms authority of tradition, church's right to 'change' the Sabbath
1546	Oswald Glaidt, former Sabbatarian Anabaptist partner of Andreas Fischer, is executed by drowning at Vienna
1551	Russian Orthodox 'Council of 100 Chapters' approves seventh-day Sabbath worship in Russian churches
1553-1558	Reign of Queen Mary I (England); she tries to reestablish Roman Catholic Church in her realm
1560	Constantino Ponce de la Fuenta, Spanish priest who taught observance of seventh-day Sabbath, dies in Inquisition prison
1598	King Henry IV (France) issues Edict of Nantes, protecting rights of French Protestants (Huguenots)

1626	Jesuit priest Afonso Mendes arrives in Ethiopia as patriarch of the Roman Catholic church in that country; advises Emperor Susenyos regarding anti-Sabbath reforms; civil war ensues
1628	Theophilus Brabourne publishes first English-language book promoting seventh-day Sabbath
1650	English Parliament orders burning of James Ockford's book advocating observance of seventh-day Sabbath
1663	King Charles II issues the Rhode Island Charter which includes the grant of religious liberty within the Rhode Island colony
1665	Stephen and Anne Mumpford arrive in Rhode Island; first known seventh-day Sabbath observers to arrive in the colonies
1671	First Seventh Day Baptist church established in America by Mumford and friends (Newport, Rhode Island)
1682	Peter Chamberlen, prominent English physician and "Seventh-day Man," blames pope for changing the Sabbath from Saturday to Sunday
1684	Francis Bamfield, one of the "Seventh-day Men," dies in London prison after his arrest for preaching to Sabbath-keeping congregation
1701	Eustace of Flay takes 'Letter from Heaven' (sic!) to England to encourage reform of Sunday observance in the kingdom.
1708	Pope Innocent III proclaims a Crusade against the Albigensian heretics of southern France
1731	Pope Gregory IX establishes the medieval Inquisition
1773-1852	Life of Ewostatewos (Eustathius), Ethiopian reform who called for revival of traditional Sabbath observance in Ethiopia
1830-1895	Life of Maniilaq, the Eskimo prophet who learned about the seventh-day Sabbath from one he called "the Grandfather"
1844	Millerite Adventists disappointed when Christ did not return during this year. A handful of Millerite Adventist preachers and lay people begin to observe the seventh-day Sabbath; this leads to the eventual establishment of the Seventh-day Adventist denomination
1851-1864	Taiping Revolution in China; the Ten Commandments and observance of seventh-day Sabbath were at the heart of the movement
1859	Charles Darwin's book 'On the Origin of the Species' is published

1888	Senator Henry Blair calls for a national Sunday law; his proposal never makes it out of committee for consideration by the US Congress
1896	William Saunders Crowdy founds Church of God and Saints of Christ, a Sabbath-keeping denomination
1900	Owkwa, Amerindian village chief, learns about Sabbath, monogamy, etc., from supernatural messenger (!).
1926-1986	Herbert W. Armstrong accepts the seventh-day Sabbath as authentic biblical doctrine; goes on to found the Worldwide Church of God. Herbert W. Armstrong dies in 1986; new leaders of the Worldwide Church of God eventually renounce the seventh-day Sabbath
1998	Pope John Paul II issues apostolic letter, Dies Domini, upholding essential nature of the Sabbath but claiming the Roman Catholic Church's authority for the Saturday-Sunday change

The content of this Timeline is for general information only to help people to follow the long way taken by the seventh-day rest covered with the blood of innocent people. Its primary value is to show the chronological relationship between various individuals and events, but not for an academic or scientific proof. The dating of many historical persons and events, particularly those earlier than 1000 BC, is subject to ongoing debate and research. Most items on this Timeline are adapted from the content of The Seventh Day television series.

This is a long way for the Sabbath-keeping people. For those that love and fear the Lord,

Oh come, Let us sing to the Lord!
Let us shout joyfully to the Rock of our salvation.
Let us come before His presence with thanksgiving
Let us shout joyfully to Him with psalms.
For the Lord is the great God,
And the King above all gods.
In His hand are the deep places of earth;
The heights of the hills are His also.
The sea is His, for He made it,
And His hands formed the dry land. (Psalms 95 : 1 - 5)

Though the world has forsaken God that made them,
And lightly esteemed the Rock of their salvation,
By provoking His jealousy and anger with strange gods,
Whom they knew not and which did not create them.

Oh Come, Let us worship and bow down;
Let us kneel before the Lord our Maker,
For He is our God,
And we are the people of His pasture,
And the sheep of His hands.
Today, if you hear His voice: (Psalms 95 : 6 - 7)

But men worshiped the host of heavens upon the housetops;
They turned back from their Creator.
For that, the Master of the universe complained against them as people
that draw near to Him with their mouth, to honor Him with their lips,
While their hearts were far from Him.
He said of them as worshiping Him in vain,
For they teach the commandments of men for doctrines.

"Do not harden your hearts, as in the rebellion, your ancestors were at Meribah,
As in the day of trial in the wilderness,
When your fathers tested Me;
They tried Me, though they saw My work.
For forty years I was grieved with that generation,
And said, 'It is a people who go astray in their hearts,
And they do not know My ways.'
So I swore in My wrath,
'They shall not enter My rest.'" (Psalms 95 : 8 - 11)

For they are altogether brutish and foolish and their customs are vain:
They glorified in their vain wisdom and did not learn from the Almighty
How to walk before Him in meekness and fear!
They trample the Truth underfoot to cherish what they
Like to hear, according their evil ways!

Oh, sing to the Lord a new song!
Sing to the Lord, all the earth.
Sing to the Lord, bless His Name;

Every day tell how He saves us.
Proclaim the good news of His salvation
From day to day.
Declare His glory among the nation
His wonders among all peoples.
For the Lord is great,
And greatly t be praised at all times. (Psalms 96 : 1 - 4a)

He sent His Son to demonstrate His righteousness and to be the light for us, so that we cannot anymore walk in darkness.
As His servants, let us demonstrate His righteousness and let our light shine upon the earth to teach the heathen the good things that He has done for Adam's sons and daughters!

He is to be feared above all gods,
For all the gods of the peoples are idols,
But the Lord made the heavens.
Honor and majesty are before Him;
Strength and beauty are in His sanctuary. (Psalms 96 : 4b - 6)

Nevertheless, you put your trust and confidence
In the man who today is
And whose breath lasts but a time.
You honored the creature and displeased your Creator!
Also you changed His eternal Word of life
In the vain old stories good for the illiterates.
You did not refrain your evil from putting human philosophy
Above the Word of God.

Give to the Lord, O families of the peoples,
Give to the Lord glory and strength.
Give to the Lord the glory due His name;
Bring an offering, and come into His courts.
Oh, worship the Lord in the beauty of holiness!
Tremble before Him, all the earth. (Psalms 96 : 7 - 9)

Instead, we have changed His Temple into a hideout for robbers or kitchens for gourmands where to organize our parties for enjoyment, forgetting the high purpose of our coming before the Lord! However, He stands at the door and knocks that we may hear His voice and open to let Him come in our heart for our healing and our transformation . . .

For the true disciples of the Resurrected Saviour, praise to God is an expression of worship, lifting-up and glorifying the Lord. It is an expression of humbling ourselves and centering our attention upon the Lord with heart-felt expressions of love, adoration and thanksgiving. High praises bring our spirit into a pinnacle of fellowship and intimacy between us and God; it magnifies our awareness of our spiritual union with the Most High God. Praise transports us into the realm of the supernatural and into the power of God. *"Blessed is the people that know the joyful sound: they shall walk, O LORD, in the light of thy countenance"* (Psalms 89 : 15).

True worship or praise is not 'merely' going through some fleshly feelings and motions as the Pharisees, whose worship was for many of them an outward show and not a devotion from the heart, such one condemned by Christ (see Matthew 15 : 8); it should be a genuine praise to God made in humility and sincere devotion to the Lord from within.

Unpretentious praise and worship pleases the Lord: He delights in the love and devotion of His children made in spirit and truth (see John 4 : 23). Praising God is an expression of faith, and a declaration of victory, that we believe God is with us and is in control of the outcome of all our circumstances (see Romans 8 : 28). Praise is a *"sacrifice,"* something that is offered to God sacrificially, not just because we feel like it, but because we believe in Him and wish to express our thankfulness. (see Hebrews 13 : 15).

Sadly, all too often, praise to God is something that many people leave at church, an event that happens only when they come together with other Christians. However, praise should be a part of the believers' lifestyle, inter-mingled as a part of their daily prayer-life. At work, in the car, at home, in bed and anywhere, praise to the Lord brings the refreshing of the Lord's presence, along with His power and anointing. *". . . I will bless the LORD at all times: his praise shall continually be in my mouth"* (Psalms 34 : 1).

Since praise manifests God's presence, we should realize that praise repels the presence of the enemy, Satan. An atmosphere which is filled with sincere worship and praise to God by humble and contrite hearts is disgusting to the Devil. He fears the power gained in the name of Jesus, and flees from the Lord's habitation in praise. *"Whoso offereth praise glorifieth me: and to him that ordereth his conversation aright will I show the salvation of God"* (Psalms 50 : 23, King James Version).

When the children of Judah found themselves outnumbered by the hostile armies of Ammon, Moab, at Mount Seir, King Jehoshophat and all the people sought the Lord for His help. The Lord assured the people that this would be His battle. He told them to go out against them, and He would do the fighting for them. So what did the children of Judah do? Being the people of 'praise', Judah actually means Praise, and knowing that God manifests His power through praise, they sent their army against their enemies, led by the praisers! So, they went on, ahead of the army declaring, *"Praise the Lord, for His mercy endureth forever!"* And the scripture says, *". . . when they began to sing and to praise, the LORD set ambushments against the children of Ammon, Moab, and mount Seir, which were come against Judah; and they were smitten"* (2 Chronicles 20 : 22).

When God's people begin to praise His Name, it sends the enemy running! Therefore, let us become a people of praise, and we will experience the release of the power of God on our behalf.

VII—WORSHIP HIM IN HUMBLENESS

"Let the words of my mouth and the meditation of my heart be acceptable in your sight, o Lord, my strength and my Redeemer" (Psalms 19 : 14)

AS THE END of time is at hand, the warnings of the Spirit of Christ are to be regarded as more important and more earnest than at any other time before. This is the command of the Master, ". . . *If any man will come after me, let him deny himself, and take up his cross, and follow me. For whosoever will save his life shall lose it; and whosoever will lose his life for my sake shall find it.*" (Matthew 16 : 24, 25)

The Christian life in this wicked world is not of ease and pleasure or of vain rejoicing, clapping of hands and loudly laughing; for a Christian is not only a stranger herein, but also most importantly he is in a battlefield against the forces of darkness. He is walking in a narrow way, made of temptations, and spiritual thorns, and the cross, and the tears. As Christ consoled women from Jerusalem saying to them, "*Daughters of Jerusalem, weep not for me, but weep for yourselves and for your children . . .*" (Luke 23 : 28) Why, Lord? Christ explained, ". . . *if they act like this now when life is good, what will happen when bad times come? . . . You will hear about wars and stories of wars that are coming . . . Nations will fight against other nations; kingdoms will fight against other kingdoms. There will be times when there is no food for people to eat, and there will be earthquakes in different places . . . At that time, many will lose their faith, and they will turn against each other and hate each other. Many false prophets will come and cause many people to believe lies. there will be more and more evil in the world, so most people will stop showing their love for each other . . . There will be more trouble than there has ever been since the beginning of the world until now, and nothing as bad will ever happen again . . . False christs and false prophets will come and perform great wonders and miracles. They will try to fool even the people God has chosen, . . ."* (Luke 23 : 31; Matthew 24 : 6, 7, 10 - 12, 21, 24, The Everyday Bible Study, New Century Version)

Then the Master insisted, *"But pray ye that your flight be not in the winter, neither on the Sabbath day . . . he that shall endure unto the end, the same shall be saved."* (Matthew 24 : 20, 13)

So let no one imagine that, ". . . it is an easy thing to overcome the enemy, and that he can be borne aloft to an incorruptible inheritance without effort on his part . . . Few appreciate the importance of striving constantly to overcome; they relax their diligence, and as a result, become selfish and self-indulgent; spiritual vigilance is not thought to be essential; earnestness in human effort is not brought into Christian life". (Ellen G. White—*Testimonies for the Church*—5, p. 540)

Apostle Paul is so clear when he invites everyone of us to buffet his body and to make it his slave, lest possibly, after preaching to others, one should be disqualified; *"for"*, he insists, *"if ye live after the flesh, ye shall die: but if ye through the Spirit do mortify the deeds of the body, ye shall live"* (Romans 8 : 13)

The Christian life is thus one of duty, responsibility, of integrity of character and of commitment on the right way, of right doing and holiness. To build a character worthy of the Christlike life, we must form a disciplined and trained personality, that we acquire the habits and language of higher life.

The God we serve, because of His spotless love for His people, stands at the door of each of His son's heart and pleads, *". . . if any man will come after me, let him deny himself, and take up his cross daily, and follow me. For whosoever will save his life shall lose it: but whosoever will lose his life for my sake, the same shall save it . . ."* (Luke 9 : 23, 24)

For, when our lives ". . . are filled with striving for advance, security, and pleasure, we do not experience the fullness of life that Jesus offers . . . the only way we can truly follow Christ is to disown ourselves; this has to be a full, complete death to self . . ." (*The Gospel of John*, Adult Sabbath School Bible study, 1ˢᵗ term, 2004, p. 77)

To save the rebellious sons and daughters of Adam from eternal death, God would choose any other mean instead of the shameful cross. The death on the cross was a hideous, painful and detestable death, worthy for the great and very dangerous criminals. Our Creator found that only that kind of hideous death to penalty of Adam's sin was worthy, because of the greatness, the holiness and the nature of Whom that sin had offended.

The cross emphasizes for us how much sin must be hated and avoided, though small it may be! The way that leads to our salvation is but one of sacrifice and self-denial and the Lord asks each of His disciples to take his part of the cross and follow Him, step by step. Not by imitating year by year, as a theater, the 'Way of the cross' as some Christian churches do; but by a daily holy living, made of earnest prayers, sacrifice and self-denial; fighting against the devils with the spiritual weapons, as described in Ephesians, chapter 6, verses 13 through 18.

And then, constantly ridding ourselves of everything that gets in the way, such as search of all kind of greatness and honor, self-glorification, wrath, gluttony, inconstancy in God's business, heresies, hatred, superficialness, laziness and jokes in worship, lasciviousness, seditions, . . . keeping instead our eyes fixed on Jesus, on whom our faith and strength depend.

It is important to note that the perfection, without which no one can see Christ, is "a life-long work, unattainable by those who are not willing to strive for it in God's appointed way, by slow and toilsome steps. We cannot afford to make any mistake in this matter, but we want day by day to be growing up into Christ, our living Head". (Ellen G. White— *Testimonies for the Church*—5, p.500)

Most of the time, during our work days of the week, we do not have enough time to consecrate ourselves completely to our Lord in a full communion worthy to His greatness and holiness, as His beloved Son, our pattern, was doing while on this world.

Thus the Sabbath day, the prayer meetings, individual or corporate prayers and fasting and all other chosen worship times are the best opportunity to consecrate ourselves fully, spiritually and earnestly to prayer, instead of organizing parties and entertainment, to occupy the mind and the thoughts with stoves, fire, plates, guffaws, dances and making unnecessary noise! In our business and work, each minute counts and is spent totally to accomplish what is appointed to us. But when comes the time dedicated to worship the Creator, not only we make ourselves so tired and hurried, but also we do not care coming late and leave before the end of the service, for our heart is where our main interest and riches are.

We should instead jealously guard the edges of the Sabbath. Remember that every moment of the day is consecrated to the Creator God.

For a best preparation for that holy day, the coming Sabbath must be kept in mind since the sunrise on preceding Sunday. Then, on following Friday, ". . . let the preparation for the Sabbath be completed. See that all the clothing is in readiness and that all cooking is done. Let the boots be blacked and the baths be taken . . . If you make it a rule you can do it. Let not the precious hours of the Sabbath be wasted in bed. On Sabbath morning the family should be astir early . . . We should not provide for the Sabbath a more liberal supply or a greater variety of food than for other days. Instead of this the food should be simpler, and less should be eaten, in order that the mind may be clear and vigorous to comprehend spiritual things". (Ellen G. White—*Testimonies for the Church*—6, p.356, 357).

Let everyone, pastors, elders and all department leaders set a good example for the members by coming at the place of worship on time and behave as the Spirit of Prophecy and the Word of God teach! If not, we are accountable to God for our neglect and boasting, by doing our own will in His holy Day. He is the Author of our life and the universe. Placed under His care by our faith, let us stop to be too careful of ourselves as if the Great Physician ignored the needs of our souls: what the soul can lack, He supplies in His own way and time. "Be sure that the Sabbath is a test question, and how you treat this question places you either on God's side or Satan's" (*Selected Messages*—3, p. 396), and in this, there is no middle ground. For the Law of the Lord ". . . *is perfect, restoring the soul; the testimony of the Lord is sure, making wise the simple. The precepts of the Lord are right, rejoicing the heart; the commandment of the Lord is pure, enlightening the eyes. The fear the Lord is clean, enduring forever. The judgments of the Lord are true, they are righteous altogether.*" (Psalms 19; 7 - 9; The New American Standard Bible)

Sometimes we are troubled or ashamed or afraid to obey and teach God's requirements as it should be in the presence of the pagans and other Christians to comply sometimes with them, as did apostle Peter

FORTUNAT TSHIMANGA-MUKADI

when found gathering and eating with the gentiles! The Master warns us against such an attitude, saying that the one who will be ashamed of Him before men, He will be ashamed of a such before His Father and the angels in that day. To do God's will is not to be considered as a legalism, as some professed Christians cry to the legalism when it comes to keep holy the Sabbath day which God blessed and made holy. For ". . . the Sabbath in Christian perspective is diverted of all legalism: its observance, like that of the other nine commandments, cannot be for the purpose of salvation; rather, the Sabbath is a joyful act of thanksgiving for the gift of faith and life; it can only be kept truly by the Christian as a result of salvation . . ." (SDA Encyclopedia—*Commentary References Series—10*, p. 1106)

Some pretend that keeping the Sabbath in accordance of all requirements of our Maker is putting on people a somewhat burden!

If obeying God's requirements can be seen as a burden, thus we ignore the price paid for our salvation, we do not love our Creator, we do not know Him all right and we are not worthy of His love. If we cannot tread the path that He had shown us to walk therein, saying *"Take your cross and follow me"*, thus our worship is a vain marketing show and a mere formalism: a pleasant pastime or maybe a natural work to earn the means of a living!

The price set before us is so great and glorious that we can, we must accept some sacrifice where the duty requires it, knowing that the victory is sure, by God's grace. For, our divine Pattern had trod this stony way to save us, and He asks us to take daily our cross and follow Him. We know where He has gone to prepare for us a place, that where He is we may be also. On our behalf, He spent forty days and forty nights praying and fasting in the wilderness because of the importance of the work that He had to do, and because He came on Satan's own ground where we are still.

Before going to the cross, He prayed earnestly with cry and tears all night, *"Holy Father, keep through thine own name those whom thou hast given me, that they may be one, as we are . . . Sanctify them through thy truth: thy word is truth."* (John 17; 11, 17)

For this, "God's followers are to keep Christ ever in view, inquiring at every step, 'Is this the way of the Lord?' A holy desire to live the life of Christ is to fill their hearts. In Him dwells all the fullness of the

Godhead. In Him are hid all the treasures of wisdom and knowledge". (Australian SDA Union Conference Record, Feb. 1, 1904)

Apostle Paul urges us, ". . . *so run, that ye may obtain* [the prize]. *And every man that striveth for the mastery is temperate in all things. Now they do it to obtain a corruptible crown; but we an incorruptible. I therefore so run, not as uncertainly; so fight I, not as one that beateth the air: but I keep under my body, and bring it into subjection; lest that by any means, when I have preached to others, I myself should be a castaway*" (1 Corinthians 9 : 24 - 27). "Man must heartily co-operate with God, willingly obeying His Laws, showing that he appreciates the great gift of grace. Feeling his dependence upon God, having faith in Christ as a personal Savior, expecting efficiency and success only as he keeps the Lord ever before him—it is thus that man complies with the injunction, '*Work out your salvation with fear and trembling*" (Signs of the Times, Sept. 25, 1901)

The Christians as a people consider themselves possessing the true and everlasting religion for the salvation of the souls and for the coming life in heaven, when they compare themselves to other religion believers. The sad thing is that, when it comes to show a life and a character in harmony with what is taught in their eternal reference, the 'Holy Bible', the diploma and graduation, the worldly philosophy and the human so-called theology are more praised than the Bible destined to sharpen a higher and holier character. Consequently, every morning a new 'Christian' denomination is established, pretending to possess all the saving Truth.

Today, the Christian churches are the most popular on Earth, even though the Christians do not constitute the majority of world population. However, it is difficult for the observer to recognize the Christ's doctrine in His believers' behavior! Though using the same Bible, they are so different, even opposed to one another that no one can discover Christ's character in any of His so-called followers! It is not exaggeration to say that there is not one 'Christianity', but there are 'christianities'. Setting their philosophy above the Word of God, many Bible teachers dissect verses and give them the diverse meanings, which would fit to their thoughts, in such manner that the confusion and divisions are so important that the Bible is most of the time forgotten, and even, denied!

Some "sit in judgment on the Scriptures, declaring this or that passage is not inspired, because it does not strike their minds favorably. They cannot harmonize it with their ideas of philosophy and science, 'falsely so called' (1 Timothy 6 : 20). Others for different reasons, question on portions of the Word of God. Thus many walk blindly where the enemy prepares the way". (Ellen G. White—*Selected Messages—1*, p. 42)

Acquiring worldly grades, diploma, knowledge, honors. malice . . . is useful for our human growth and perhaps for the material advantage and interest. Where it becomes dangerous is when this human ability is used to oppose, to correct or to replace the eternal divine Will of the Creator. From Eden to this time, Satan leads people to interpret and put the clear requirements of our God in the way that suits to him. From Cain to Judas until now, men place themselves under the power of the Enemy by following his suggestions. Instead, placed toward God's Word, we should be considered ignorant, poor and illiterate, needing to be taught and be filled with heavenly wisdom and science, found in the Bible. Now, ". . . it is not the province of any man to pronounce sentences upon the Scriptures, to judge or condemn any portion of God's Word. When one presumes to do this, Satan will create an atmosphere for him to breathe which will dwarf spiritual growth. When a man feels so very wise that he dares to dissect God's Word, his wisdom is, with God, counted foolishness. When he knows more, he will feel that he has everything to learn. And his very first lesson is to become teachable". (Idem)

VIII—THEY CLAIMED A CARNAL KING

For there is no partiality with God. For as many as have sinned without law will also perish without law, and as many as have sinned in the law will be judged by the law; (for not the hearers of the law are just in the sight of God, but the doers of the law will be justified). (Romans 2 : 11 - 13)

A PECULIAR PEOPLE, A holy nation, Israel was chosen by God as His special Treasure. He was their God and King. He intended to reign over them and minister to them through the prophets, the priests and the judges.

However, they asked Samuel, to establish a king over them to judge them *"like all the nations"*. Samuel was saddened about the attitude and prayed to Jehovah, the loving and kind King who encouraged Samuel and said, *"Heed the voice of the people in all that they say to you: for they have not rejected you, but they have rejected Me, that I should not reign over them."* (1 Samuel 8 : 7)

Samuel explained and depicted to the people all the kingly rights and their obligations toward the royalty, not to discourage nor make them afraid, but to help them make the right choice, and then concluded: ". . . *'He* [the king] *will take a tenth of your sheep. And you will be his servants. And you will cry out in that day because of your king whom you have chosen for yourselves, and the Lord will not hear you in that day'."* (verses 17 and 18)

But the people shouted and affirmed their trust in the earthly kingdom and a carnal king and they said: ". . . *'No, but we will have a king over us; that we also may be **like all the nations**'* [emphasis added]; . . . *and that our king may judge us, and go out before us, and fight our battles'.*" (verses 19 and 20)

The same claim is still heard in the Church of Christ where members and leaders always want to be like the world, to rule over God's people as do the earthly monarchs, to be like other nations! They bring into the Church the human traditions of pomp and display while calling upon the Most High, and then suppress or lessen the Law of the Lord on the pretext of calling the nations to the faith.

So they reject to follow the God Creator of the Universe, and choose to be ministered and instructed by human laws; betraying each other.

With time, the gap between God and those that claim to be His people deepened more and more; for the love of God was not in their heart. However, "Love to God is the very foundation of religion. To engage in His service merely from hope of reward or fear of punishment would avail nothing. Open apostasy would not be more offensive to God than hypocrisy and mere formal worship." (*Ellen G. White—Patriarchs and Prophets, p. 523*)

The falling of the chosen people, encouraged by the self-confidence, went on bitter and bitter! If they had prayed, '. . . empty us of all our glory, all our boasting, and all our pride; let our righteousness, our wisdom, on Thy cross be crucified; fill us, then, with all Thy fullness, all Thy will work Thou in us; in Thyself is nothing lacking; make us, Lord, complete in Thee . . . ', they might remain in the favor of the Lord and grow unceasingly faithful and pure.

Christ, our Pattern, relied always on earnest prayer and the Holy Scriptures references during His earthly life. To be like Him, as a Christian goal, anyone must ". . . *walk just as He walked*", according to His example which the Christian should follow His steps. Apostle John testified," *He who says he abides in Him ought himself also to walk just as He walked* (1 John 2 : 6; (Read also 1 Peter 2 : 21)

The path followed by God's Church is far from what the Savior wanted her to follow, in the same manner, as did the ancient Israel! Yes, as in the time of old, the Lord yet continues to plead and testify against His people of every age, and this in many ways, saying, "*Turn from your evil ways, and keep My commandments and My statutes, according to all the law which I commanded your fathers, and which I sent to you by My servants the prophets. Nevertheless they would not hear, but stiffened their necks, like the necks of their fathers, who did not believe in the Lord their God. And they rejected His statutes, and His covenant that He had made with their fathers, and His testimonies which He had testified against them; they followed idols, became idolaters, and went after the nations were all around about them, concerning whom the Lord had charged them that they should not do like them."* (2 Kings 17 : 13 - 15)

In the beginning of the Israelite royalty, in the case of Saul, David and Solomon, the people were asking God to give them a king, but later kings succeeded to kings by conspiracy and 'coup d'état'!

Moreover, the nation was divided in two kingdoms, Israel and Judah, fighting sometimes one against the other, according to the kind of the rulers or the commanders chosen by the people, not by the prophet. The Spirit of God was no longer among them, though they continued to claim to be God's chosen nation, using together the same Temple to worship and the same Torah to study and teach!

Diverse nations invaded and conquered the divine nation, and thus took kings and people in captivity. Even the Temple, which made them proud, was not spared. As the prophet Jeremiah predicted, *". . . 'Then you shall break the flask in the sight of the men who go with you, and say to them, Thus says the Lord of hosts: Even so I will break this people and this city, as one breaks a potter's vessel, which cannot be made whole again . . ."* (Jeremy 19 : 10, 11). O that clay jar! I remember my poor mother's beautiful clay jar, which she was proud of! It was for storing the drinking water, it occupied the center of her unique room thus attracting the visitor's curiosity. So mom explained to the curious visitors and friends that the jar always occupied second place in her heart after her son, which I was! For, as widow, she had neither parents nor siblings nearby! One day, from school in a hurry, glad to be at home and hug my beloved mom who, unfortunately, was not there! Thus, no chance to stop on time, I accidentally hit the jar, which broke in pieces! As I loved mommy so much, I felt all the sky falling on me; so, forgetting my own injury, I fled and hid myself far away from home! Let every one imagine the saddened widow losing the two things she loved the most in that time of her poor life! She left everything and went out crying to find me first and bring me home!

FORTUNAT TSHIMANGA-MUKADI

Moreover, how many crying and lamenting prophets did God send out to His rebellious people, only to find them hardening their heart! As result, the Israelites were thus subdued to successive foreign powers: Babylonian, Media-Persian, Greek, and Roman, according to the prophecies, such as the wonderful prophecies found in the Book of Daniel, chapters 2, 7 and 8.

At the first coming of the Lord Jesus Christ, the Roman Empire was the conqueror and master over the rebellious Israelite people; and of this time the prophecy was accomplished regarding the birth, the death and the ascension of Christ, and the birth of the Christian church.

History shows that Roman Empire provided to the early church both stability and mobility that assisted the early Christian missionaries in spreading the gospel and the church.

The roman military outposts created a network of roads and secure travel by land and sea: the missionaries were thus able to span the whole Roman Empire before its end in the fifth century.

Pagan Roman power was followed by the Roman church power, each one with different points of view and purpose, persecuted the Christians: the papal authority believed to be the "*little horn*" of Daniel 7 : 25 persecuted the saints of the Most High by a hideous system called *Inquisition,* that the Christ's prophecy would be fulfilled, "*They will put you out of the synagogues: yes, the time is coming, that whosoever kills you will think that he offers God service. And these things they will do to you, because they have not known the Father nor Me.*" (John 16 : 2, 3)

Rabbi Marc Gellman and Monsignor Thomas Hartman in their book '*Religion for Dummies, p.63*' explain the growth of the Catholic Church in this way, "From its humble beginnings as a relatively small sect that attracted people from lower classes, the Catholic Church grew in influence both spiritually and politically. When the Western Empire fell in the fifth century, the Church and its pope were the only effective force for order in the West. From there, the Church grew to an empire in its own right, holding dominion over all secular, political, and spiritual realms in Western Europe. The Church even had its own army, which it used to maintain its holdings."

This Catholic army, organized in Crusades, first waged war to the Muslim to conquer the 'Holy Land' during the time between the eleventh and thirteenth century, and then organized the fierce inquisition against the Protestants from the fifteenth through eighteenth centuries!

The inquisition shed a hideous darkness on Christianity. In the name of Christ, Christians killed other Christians with inexplicable atrocity, not because those latter did not believe in the Master or in His Word; but because of their faithfulness and steadfastness to the pure Truth taught by the Bible, Truth which questioned the Church leaders of their errors and evil behavior. These faithful ones preferred to reject the human laws, which were replacing God's will and paid this by their own lives!

The Church for which Christ prayed for unity, broke down and dissentions rose among the Christians and they parted the Bible as the roman soldiers parted the garments of Jesus at His crucifixion.

This partition of the Bible truth led to the great disorder, which is found among the Protestant beliefs, with the magma continuing to break down until today, in such a manner that sects claiming to be Christian and possessing the sole and pure Truth, rise every morning.

Some of the leaders proclaiming themselves prophets, messiahs, gods . . . all this, in the Name of Jesus!

Among those that were persecuted yesterday for their faith, rose up the new fierce dissentions, even though they claim each other to be Christ's faithful followers!

All this because ". . . Those who have no time to give attention to their own souls, to examine themselves daily whether they be in the love of God, and place themselves in the channel of light, will have time to give to the transgressions of Satan and the working out of his plans" (Ellen G. White—II Selected Messages, p. 20-21)

Many of these dissentions are created by trying to change the 'Law and the Prophets', to neglect the eternal Truth and to put human traditions, their reasoning and philosophy, above the eternal Word of life, by shutting their ears to the warnings of the Spirit, "*you will not add, you will not take away to the Words which God has spoken*"!

The Lord says in the mouth of Isaiah, "*To the law and to the testimony. If they do not speak according to this word, it is because there is no light in them.*" (Isaiah 8 : 20). Without light, there is no truth neither life! In other words, Christ is not within!

O yes, putting aside and forgetting the Word of God, leads to darkness and rebellion. If you would change the Word at one point, you have changed It at all points because God's Word is one. It has an unchanging character. God's Word is not unclear; it is too clear instead: It is not incomplete but the divine fullness is its important character!

Christ, our Pattern, had made the Bible His unique reference in all His teachings and acts. The words such as, *"It is written . . ."* or *"What do you read therein . . ."* were always on His lips. He left to His followers an example and a lesson to make the Book of books, their daily nurture and reference.

For, *"Thus says the Lord"* teaches us in a mighty way, how to know and to obey Him, and how to adore and honor Him according to His greatness.

For, *"It is written"* opens before our eyes the unique path to the righteousness and holiness, and at last to the Life.

For, *"My Word"* is so complete and eternal that it is unnecessary for a finite and mortal creature, so powerful, so learned and wise he may pretend to be, to change, to add or to subtract anything to the divine sayings.

This Great Book is God's voice speaking to us, just as surely if we hear it with our ears. If Adam and Eve would obey their Maker and keep themselves from touching what was forbidden, the Bible in its form today would but exist in form of the sole Ten Commandments. Thus, apart from some historical counts tales from the Jew's or early Christians' life, the centre of the Scriptures is the Ten Commandments explained in divers manners to bring us back to the right of eternal life lost in Eden by our first parents.

Anyway, we should always know that where the Word is, there is division. *"I have come to set division"*, Christ declared. God's Word is a separating word, and as a separating word, those who believe it are duty bound to protect it and defend it against all attacks. We must also recognize the simple historical fact that the Bible's greatest attacks have always arisen from within the Church itself. We are not the first, nor are we alone in the fight; He was betrayed and crucified by His own fellow citizens, Knowing this, He has assured us ". . . *lo, I am with you always, even to the end of the age*".

In light of the plan of salvation, the key to that life to come is the obedience to the Law of God through Christ the King who strengthens us; as He makes it so clear, ". . . *if you wish to enter into life, keep the commandments*" (Matthew 19 : 17).

Hearing powerful words of life preached by Jesus, a woman in the crowd praised Mary His mother just because she gave birth to Him, saying, "*Blessed is the womb that bore You, and the breast which nursed You*". But Christ replied and corrected her immediately to set things aright, "*More than that, blessed are those who hear the word of God and keep it.*" (Luke 11 : 27, 28)

We show our *love* for Jesus and God by keeping and obeying His Word. Let us emphasize it. The centre of the Bible is the Decalogue and in each of its pages, are explained its precepts in different ways that the man of God may be faultless.

The Decalogue is the expression of God's love for us, through the eternal covenant, "*. . . 'I will take you as My people, and I will be your God. Then you shall know that I am the Lord your God which brings you out from under the burdens of the Egyptians. And I will bring you into the land which I swore to give to Abraham, to Isaac, and to Jacob; and I will give it to you as a heritage: I am the Lord'.*" (Exodus 6 : 7, 8)

The obedience to the Decalogue is in return the Christian's response to this infinite God's love that is to love God with all our heart, with all our spirit and with all our might, and love our fellow man as ourselves. Our love to God is seen through what we do toward our fellow man, as Christ states it clearly that how could you love God you do not see, without loving your brother, whom you see!

"*Oh how I love Your law!*", affirms boldly the psalmist, "*It is my meditation all day. You, through Your commandments make me wiser than my enemies; for they are ever with me. I have more understanding than all my teachers, for Your testimonies are my meditation. I understand more than the ancients, because I keep Your precepts. I have restrained my feet from evil way, that I may keep Your word. I have not departed from Your judgments, for You Yourself have taught me*" (Psalms 119 : 97 - 102)

The ultimate purpose of the Word of God, is to bring back to Him the rebellious children of Adam, and spiritually recreate all creature polluted by sin. It is about salvation for mankind and to grant them the eternal life lost in Eden by the sin of our first parents who broke up the Law of their loving Ruler.

Entering into eternal life means to be redeemed, to be a newborn Christian, to be a part of the invisible congregation of saints though still in this earth.

Two parts are involved in the salvation of man.

FORTUNAT TSHIMANGA-MUKADI

God Himself, through Christ, had first done His part on Calvary, and did it with a joyful heart, that the prophet sings, "*The Spirit of the Lord God is upon Me; because the Lord has anointed Me to preach good tidings to the poor; He has sent Me to heal the brokenhearted, to proclaim liberty to the captives, and the opening of the prison to those who are bound; to proclaim the acceptable year of the Lord, and the day of vengeance of our God; to comfort all who mourn.*" (Isaiah 61 : 1, 2)

And man must do his part, that his salvation work may be complete, for "the salvation of the soul requires the blending of the divine and the human strength, God does not propose to do the work that man can do to meet the standard of righteousness" (Signs of the Times, September 25, 1901)

Led by the Holy Ghost, man senses his need, acknowledges his sinfulness, repents of his transgressions, and exercises righteousness by faith in his Savior that stands to the sinner's heart warning, "*Behold, I am coming as a thief. Blessed is he who watches, and keeps his garments, lest he walk naked and they see his shame.*" (Revelation 16 : 15) and the shame of his hypocrisy revealed in the righteous judgment of the Lord!

Then, once as one is born again and becomes a Christian, such one must take seriously this warning on account in his daily life. For, he can no longer be of the world, but a member of Christ's flock that follow Him always; in such a manner that the devil may flee far from this new creature. Therefore, the Lord coverts him or her with the power from above, according to His promises, "*And I will pray the Father, and He will give you another Helper, that He may abide with you for ever*" (John 14 : 16); and ". . . *lo, I am with you always, even to the end of the age. Amen*" (Matthew 28 : 20)

Amen indeed!

IX—THE PIERCED BODY

Then He said to them, "O foolish ones, and slow of heart to believe in all that the prophets have spoken! Ought not the Christ to have suffered these things and to enter into His glory?" (Luke 24 : 25, 26)

PILATE WANTED VERIFICATION that Jesus was dead before allowing his crucified body to be buried. So a Roman guard thrust a spear into Jesus' side. The mixture of blood and water that flowed out was a clear indication that Jesus was dead. Jesus' body was then taken down from the cross and buried in Joseph of Arimathea's tomb. Roman guards next sealed the tomb, and secured it with a 24-hour watch. Meanwhile, Jesus' disciples were in shock. They no longer had confidence that Jesus had been sent by God. They also had been taught that God would not let His Messiah suffer death. So they dispersed. The Jesus movement was all but stopped in its tracks. All hope was vanished. Rome and the Jewish leaders had prevailed, or so it seemed. But it wasn't the end, for, in fact Christianity exists today as the world's largest religion, as proof of Christ's resurrection after the third day of His death! Some skeptics have proposed that Jesus lived through the crucifixion and was revived by the cool, damp air in the tomb. But this theory is contradicted by the scientific researchers that testify that, the spear, thrust between His right ribs, probably perforated not only the right lung, but also the pericardium and heart and thereby ensured His death. Also the reports of non-Christian historians from around the time when Jesus lived, mentioned the death of Jesus:—Lucian (120-after 180 A.D) referred to Jesus as a crucified sophist (philosopher). Josephus (c.37-c.100 A.D.) wrote, "At this time there appeared Jesus, a wise man, for he was a doer of amazing deeds. When Pilate condemned him to the cross, the leading men among us, having accused him, those who loved him did not cease to do so."—Tacitus (c. 56-c.120 A.D.) wrote, "Christus, from whom the name had its origin, suffered the extreme penalty . . . at the hands of our procurator, Pontius Pilate."[15]

Finally, there is no historical account from Christians, Romans or Jews that disputes either Jesus' death or his burial. In light of such evidences and testimonies, Jesus was clearly dead, of that there was no doubt. No serious historian really doubts Jesus was dead when He was taken down from the cross. However, many have questioned how Jesus' body disappeared from the tomb. And what is known historically of Jesus' enemies is that they accused Jesus' disciples of stealing the body, an accusation clearly predicated on a shared belief that the tomb was empty. But the Romans had assigned a 24-hour watch at the tomb with a trained guard unit (from 4 to 12 soldiers). Yet the stone was moved away and the body of Jesus was missing.

If Jesus' body was anywhere to be found, His enemies would have quickly exposed the resurrection as a fraud. But something extraordinary must have happened, that made the followers of Jesus cease mourning, cease hiding, and begin fearlessly proclaiming that they had seen Jesus alive. It passes the bounds of credibility that the early Christians could have manufactured such a tale and then preached it among those who might easily have refuted it simply by producing the body of Jesus.

The resurrection opened the way to the effusion of the Holy Ghost that came to bestow upon the newborn ones the divine nature, to seal them of holiness and eternal life. The outpouring of the Spirit at Pentecost is the fulfillment of Christ's other promise to the apostles not to quit Jerusalem until they be filled of the power from above.

They obeyed and continued to pray earnestly with the same heart, same mind and the same spirit! Putting aside all differences and disagreements!

Then, while they were hiding by fear of the Jews shut up in a room, the Spirit of God pierced the walls and, "*Then there appeared to them divided tongues as of fire, and one sat upon each of them. And they were all filled with the Holy Spirit and began to speak with other tongues, as the Spirit gave them utterance.*" (Acts 2 : 3, 4)

The foreigner visitors in Jerusalem at that time were surprised and amazed, because ". . . *everyone heard them speak in his own language. Then they were all amazed and marveled, saying to one another, 'Look, are not all these who speak Galileans? And how is it possible that we hear, each in our own language in which we were born . . .'"* (Acts 2 : 6 - 9)

The time came for the disciples to *"go and make followers from all people in the world, baptizing them in the name of the Father and the Son and the Holy Spirit and teaching them to obey everything that the Messiah had taught them, for He will be with them always, even until the end of this age."* (Matthew 28 : 19 - 20—New Century Version); and many signs followed those that believed, as token of the presence of the risen Savior among them. In the name of the Nazarene, they cast out devils, they took up serpents that did not harm them and they laid hands on the sick who recovered from all kind of diseases, without surgery or many sophisticated modern drugs, according to His promise. (see Mark 16 : 17, 18)

So was born the Church of Jesus Christ, the Body of the Risen Savior whose members, named since then 'Christians', were of the same accord. People from almost parts of the known world, were taught and trained according the message of Christ; and those who believed in Him as Savior and Messiah, were baptized in water in the name of the Father and the Son and the Holy Ghost, by order of the Messiah

While Peter responding to the Cornelius' call and was preaching in his house, himself was amazed of the outpouring of the Spirit of God upon the Gentiles and he testified ". . . *'In truth I perceive that God shows no partiality. But in every nation whoever fears Him and works righteousness is accepted by Him. The word which God sent to the children of Israel, preaching peace through Jesus Christ—He is Lord of all, that word you know, which was proclaimed throughout all Judea, and began from Galilee after the baptism which John preached: how God anointed Jesus of Nazareth with the Holy Spirit and with power . . . all things which He did both in the land of the Jews and in Jerusalem, whom they killed by hanging on the tree. Him God raised up on the third day . . . And He commanded us to preach to the people, and to testify that it is He who was ordained by God to be Judge of the living and the dead. To Him all the prophets witness that, through His Name, whoever believes in Him will receive remission of sins"* (Acts 10 : 34 - 43)

The preaching of the Good News of salvation through Jesus the Christ went up all around Jerusalem and all the roman empire of the first century. Soon it reached the regions located far away, in witness of His death, resurrection and ascension.

The Lord, through Abraham, specifically chose Israelites to be His special representatives upon the earth in the first covenant. He did not choose a people; He chose a person, Abraham from whom a peculiar people came, that they might be His valued property. A peculiar treasure for His glory. This choice being totally the act of God and an expression of His grace, as unmerited gift, for nothing in them was found that made them worth of that free given-grace.

Yes, from them was asked love for their Creator and fellowmen in obedience to His Law and all His requirements as response to this grace; *'The Lord will establish you as a holy people to Himself, just as He has sworn to you, if you keep the commandments of the Lord your God and walk in His ways. Then all peoples of the earth shall see that you are called by the name of the Lord, and they shall be afraid of you'.* (Deuteronomy 28 : 9, 10)

In the same manner, He made a second covenant through the blood of His Son and made disciples for His Kingdom to come, people that were not Abraham's seed in the flesh. When, under the power of the Spirit of the Lord, Peter had to mingle with the uncircumcised, he had to explain to his Jew brothers his attitude and he said unto them, "' . . . *You know how unlawful it is for a man that is a Jewish man to keep company with or go to one of another nation. But God had shown me that I should not call any man common or unclean . . .* "; and then, ". . . *While Peter was still speaking these words, the Holy Ghost fell upon all those heard the word. And those of the circumcision who believed were astonished, as many as came with Peter, because the gift of the Holy Ghost had been poured out on the Gentiles also".* (Acts 10 : 28 - 45)

A new covenant is so made with a new people of God.

As the Lord had always to complain about the Israelites' unbelief and sinful behavior, so it is the same with the new Israel, and the cycle sin—confession—forgiveness—reconciliation—sin, seen all the walk of the Israelites with their God, continue to be observed in the Christian realm, individually and collectively, through their history.

Indefatigably, the loving God sent from time to time the messages through His chosen messengers to bring back His rebellious children.

The prophet Nehemiah depicts well this continual rebellion of the Israelites, saying: ". . . *they were disobedient and rebelled against You, cast Your law behind their backs and killed Your prophets who testified against* to turn them to Yourself; and they worked great provocations. Therefore You delivered them into the hands of their enemies who oppressed them; and in their time of their trouble, when they cried to You, You heard from heaven; and according to Your abundant mercies You gave them deliverers who saved them from the hand of their enemies. But after they had rest, they again did evil before You. Therefore You left them in the hand of their enemies, so that they dominion over them; yet when they returned and cried out to You, You heard from heaven; and many times You delivered them according to Your mercies, and testified against them, that You might bring them back to Your law. Yet they acted proudly, and did not heed Your commandments, but sinned against Your judgments, which if a man does, he shall live by them . . . Nevertheless in Your great mercy You did not utterly consume them nor forsake them; for You are God, gracious and merciful"* (Nehemiah 9 : 26 - 31)

Which god is like our merciful and longsuffering God Creator!

Though they were one people, which stood before the Lord with Moses at Mount Sinai to conclude a pact that they might be unto the Lord *"a kingdom of priests and a holy nation"* with the Ten Commandments as their unique holy and eternal Law till they entered into Canaan and afterward; at the first coming of Christ however, they were already divided in many sects of Scribes, Pharisees, Sadducees, Essenes, the Zealots and the Nazarenes: each of them flattering himself being the one, which have holiness and divine knowledge.

How many Christian denominations are in the world today and the divisions are still going on, each one always pretending speaking according to the Bible and in the Name of Christ! Other have set customs and catechisms above the sayings of the Holy Book.

The root of this aberration is found in the deceitful and selfish spirit of trying to change or correct the Word spoken by the Almighty God. This attitude will surely lead people to the eternal destruction, unless they put the divine words above all philosophy and human teachings.

Simon Peter warned his contemporaries in terms so clear against the divisions and false teachers, saying *"There used to be false prophets among God's people, just as you will have some false teachers in your group. They will*

secretly teach things that are wrong-teachings that will cause people to be lost.
They will even refuse to accept the Master, Jesus, who bought their freedom.
So they will bring quick ruin on themselves. Many will follow their evil ways
and say evil things about the way of truth." (2 Peter 2 : 1, 2—New Century
version)

X—THE BODY OF THE RISEN

We are of God: he that knows God hears us; he that is not of God hears not us. Hereby know we the spirit of truth, and the spirit of error. (1 John 4 : 6)

KNOWING THAT THE enemy will continue to attack His Church with fierce anger and unceasing effort to destroy it, the Master spent all the night before His crucifixion to pray for the unity of His Church" . . . *I am coming to you; I will not stay in the world any longer. But they are still in the world. Holy Father, keep them safe by the power of your name, the name you gave me, so they will be one, just as you and I are one . . . They don't belong to the world, just as I don't belong to the world. Make them ready for your service through your truth; your teaching is truth . . . I pray for these followers, but I am also praying for all those who will believe in me because of their teaching. Father, I pray that they can be one. As you are in me and I am in you, I pray that they can also be one in us. Then the world will believe that you sent me . . . I will be in them and you will be in me so that they will be completely one"* (John 17 : 11, 16, 17, 20, 21, 23—The New Century Version)

What a powerful plea!

Despite this earnest and faithful prayer and the numerous warnings from the Son of God, as in Matthew 7 : 16, 18, also of the apostle Paul in Galatians 3 : 28; 1 Co. 1 : 10 - 13; 13; Ephesians 1 : 22; 4 : 15; 5 : 23, 30, the disciples show early a tendency to fight one another (refer to Luke 9 : 46 - 48; 20 : 20 - 28), revealing the desire for power and causing disagreements. Some claimed to be Cephas', the other ones to belong to Paul, and so on . . .

Today the Church's unity is doubtful not only by its split into three major branches, Roman Catholic, Eastern Orthodox and Protestant; but amazingly in more and more small groups, claiming each detaining the whole truth which leads to salvation! This division spreads darkness on the work of salvation left to the Church by its Master; for it contradicts the order of the Master who prayed, "... *Holy Father, keep through Your name those whom you have given Me, that they may be one, as We are.*" ... "*that they all may be one, as You, Father, art in me, and I in You, that they also may be one in us ...*" (John 17 : 11, 21)

The so-called theologians, the false apostles and prophets, the masters, the priests, the pastors, the bishops, the teachers, and the like, continue to pierce the Church as they pierced the Body of the Savior! They then invent names more and more sophisticated for their groups, with the purpose of attracting people, in such a way that the prophecies may be fulfilled, "*Then many false prophets will rise up and deceive many . . . For false christs and false prophets will rise and show great signs and wonders to deceive, if possible, even the elect.*" (Matthew 24 : 11, 24) It is certainly understandable that even a very earnest and sincere seeker after the Truth would be confused over the religious situation today, with hundreds of denominations, sects, and cults in Christendom alone, and with new religious movements arising almost every day.

Nevertheless, God has provided adequate instruction for us to enable us to "*know the spirit of truth and the spirit of error*" (I John 4 : 6) if we really want to do so.

As shown below in these charts, the divisions appearing almost every day make the Christian religion the one where the divisions are the most spread:

- On these four columns are given the global statistical totals applicable to each bloc, and at the end of the table, for global church membership.
- Congregations (worship centers) and adult church members are all referring to the year 1995.
- Affiliated church members (total Christian community) for 1995.
- As defined here, world Christianity consists of 5 major ecclesiastical traditions divided into 300 major ecclesiastical traditions, composed of over 33. 000 distinct denominations in 230 countries, these denominations themselves being composed of over 3,400.000 worship centers, churches or congregations.)

2 Name	3 Congregations 1995	6 Affiliated 1995	13 Countries
ORTHODOX Totals	**90,900**	**209,624,000**	**133**
Arabic or Arabic / Greek-speaking Orthodox	1,100	1,380,000	29
Armenian Orthodox (Gregorian)	1,100	5,593,000	47
Bulgarian Orthodox	4,200	6,384,000	20
Byelorussian / Belorussian (While Russian / White Ruthenian)	900	4,854,000	6
Coptic Orthodox	2,500	9,234,000	24
Ethiopic, Ethiopian Orthodox, GoOez-speaking	13,100	21,902,000	15
Georgian Orthodox	600	2,589,000	9
Greek Orthodox	36,000	14,912,000	72
Macedonian Orthodox	1,000	1,259,000	5
Moldavian Orthodox	200	1,303,000	3
Polish/Slavonic-speaking Orthodox	400	1,021,000	2
Romanian Orthodox	8,300	19,271,000	23
Russian Orthodox	11,200	80,451,000	51
Syro-Malabarese (Eastern-Syrian), Syriac/ Malayalam-speaking	1,600	2,251,000	12
Syrian, Syriac-speaking Orthodox or Syro-Antiochian	700	1,018,000	24
Ukrainian Orthodox	3,100	27,121,000	9
Other Orthodox	4,900	90,000	
ROMAN CATHOLIC Totals	**328,000**	**994,154,000**	**235**

Jurisdiction for both Latin-rite and Eastern-rite Catholics	600	1,599,000	9
Latin-roe Catholic	315,300	975,673,000	229
Maronite (Syro-Antiochian, Western Syrian)	1,000	2,978,000	11
Melkite (Byzantine, Greek Catholic; Arabic-speaking)	500	1,116,000	12
Ian Byzantine rite	1,600	2,012,000	2
Syro-Malabarese (Eastern Syrian)	2,600	3,055,000	1
Ukrainian Byzantine rite	3,700	5,093,000	10
Other Catholic	1,700	5,606,000	
ANGLICAN	**91.800**	**74,521,000**	**162**
Anglo-Catholic	5,000	1,965,000	39
Central or Broad Church Anglican	5,500	9,292,000	32
Anglican Evangelical. Evangelical Anglican	18,500	15,345,000	12
High Church Anglican (Prayer Book Catholic)	12,800	7,604,000	30
Low Church Anglican (Conservative Evangelical)	15,800	20,065,000	15
Anglican, of plural or mixed traditions	33.500	20,129.000	41
Other Anglicans	700	121,000	
PROTESTANT Totals	**957,000**	**318,027,000**	**231**
Adventist	34,000	11,011,000	199
Baptist	125,400	48,133,000	163
Christian Brethren (Plymouth Brethren; Open only)	16,700	2,798,000	113

Congregational Congregationalist	11,500	2,438,000	55
Disciple, Restorationist, Restorationist, Baptist, Christian	8,700	1,919,000	18
Anglican Evangelical, independent Evangelical	20,100	5,482,000	89
Holiness (Conservative, Methodist, Wesleyan, Free Methodist)	43,600	7,387,000	117
Lutheran/Reformed united church or joint mission	10,800	15,041,000	22
Lutheran	81,900	60,696,000	122
Mennonite Anabaptist-(Left Wing or Radical Reformation)	9,500	2,009,000	59
Methodist (mainline Methodist United Methodist)	89,500	22,902,000	108
Nondenominational (no church or antichurch groups)	11,800	3,434,000	76
Oneness-Pentecostal or Unitarian Pentecostal; Jesus Only	11,600	2,463,000	74
Baptistic-Pentecostal or Keswick-Pentecostal	232,000	49,420,000	174
Holiness-Pentecostal: 3-crisis-experience	28,800	5,650,000	118
Apostolic or Pentecostal Apostolic (living apostles)	11,600	1,587,000	30
Reformed Presbyterian	97,700	43,902,000	141
Salvationist (Salvation Army)	14,100	2,378,000	84
Other Protestants	87,644	29,387,000	

INDEPENDENT Totals	1,593,100	348,196,000	220
Black American Oneness Apostolic	3,400	1,873,000	3
New Apostolic, Catholic Apostolic (Invingite),Old Apostolic	23,700	8,293,000	149
African independent charismatic	12,400	1,935,000	30
Chinese charismatic	212,400	35,778,000	3
Filipino charismatic	1,700	1,289,000	2
White-led charismatic	111,900	17,478,000	43
Black American charismatic Full Gospel	5,000	1,100,000	1
Filipino Full	3,300	2,050,000	4
White-led Fun Gospel	9,200	2,537,000	6
Latin American grassroots	5,900	2,245,000	15
Brazilian grassroots	3,000	3,000,000	1
Korean cell-based network	100	1,100,000	1
African Independent neo-charismatic	17,800	8,730,000	13
Chinese neo-charismatic	8,600	1,973,000	57
Chinese Oneness Pentecostal	4,000	1,084,000	11
African Independent Pentecostal	55,900	18,943,000	41
Black American Pentecostal	19,100	6,162,000	18
Mono-ethnic Pentecostal	4,800	1,242,000	15
Indonesian Pentecostal	10,700	3,347,000	2
Indian Pentecostal	17,000	2,243,000	12
Latin American Pentecostal	27,300	6,027,000	22

While-led Pentecostal	28,900	8,553,000	55
Brazilian/Portuguese Pentecostal	44,300	15,898,000	6
Chinese radio believers	40,400	2,519,000	2
Indian radio/TV believers	10,500	9,020,000	4
European White radio/TV believers	8,390	5,128,000	11
African Independent Spiritual	8,300	1,186,000	6
White-led Word of Faith/ Prosperity	6,700	1,619,000	7
African neo-charismatic of mixed tradition	4,200	1,500,000	1
Zionist African Independent	12,200	10,140,000	6
schism ex Anglicanism in Protestant direction)	4,500	1,460,000	14
Independent Baptist	97,900	27,547,000	95
Hidden Buddhist believers in Christ	17,100	1,830,000	8
Conservative Catholic (schism ex Rome)	3,000	4,518.000	30
Independent, Disciple, Restorationist, Christian	31,100	4,289,000	96
Anglican Evangelical, Independent Evangelical	6.800	1,357,000	48
Independent Fundamentalist	7,200	1,915,000	31
Hidden Hindu believers in Christ	20,400	10,637,000	7
Holiness (Conservative Methodist non-Pentecostal)	7,700	1,393,000	39
Latin-rite Catholic	18.300	5,828,000	1
Independent Lutheran	4,900	1,690,000	20

Independent Methodist	22,900	6,862,000	46
Nondenominational (no church or anti-church group)	15,200	2,109,000	71
Old Believer, Old Ritualist	3,300	1,957,000	19
Reformed Catholic, retaining Roman Catholic claims	9,500	5,110,000	11
Reformed Orthodox (uncanonical reform movement)	1,800	1,023,000	15
Independent Reformed, Presbyterian	29,200	7,884,000	51
Independent Ukrainian Orthodox	3,400	6,324,000	18
United church (union of bodies of different traditions)	27,200	10,701,000	3
ethnic or mono-ethnic denomination	6,700	1,092,000	2
Marginal Independent Christian (Black third-World indigenous)	4,500	1,211,000	48
single congregation(s): one autonomous congregation	10,600	1,996,000	7
Jehovah's Witnesses (Russellites)	70,500	11,305,000	212
Later-day saints (Mormons), including Mormon schismatics	20,000	7,955,000	102
Metaphysical science, Divine Science, Religious Science	3,600	1,097,000	55
Other independent	485,010	37,233,000	
World Totals	**3,167,000**	**1,769,920,000**	**238**

(Adapted from *"David A. Barrett, World Christian Encyclopedia, 2001, p 16-18"*)

These statistics speak loudly by themselves.

The divisions in the Church can be recommended by conscience and virtue, to separate the wheat from the chaff before the matchless Reaper comes, for '. . . *there must be divisions among you so that you who have God's approval will be recognized*'. (1 Corinthians 11 : 19; Life Application study Bible, New living translation). However, the most of these divisions in Christianity are but from ignorance, boast, selfishness, pride, lust and the search of power for, one of the works of the flesh is to cause divisions among people. (Galatians 5 : 20).

Catholicism began when men, especially bishops, being elders and pastors, desired prominence over other Church members. Eventually, one desired prominence over all. They incorporated many pagan practices into worship. Protestantism began with Martin Luther deciding the Catholics were wrong on many things. Rather than going to God's Word to find out everything to do, he fixed the things they believed to be wrong. This approach left many things not fixed. The same approach has been followed through the ages in the formation of many Christian denominations, whether they split from Catholicism, or from another protestant denomination.

According to the history, in the 1800's, several men, from different denominations, and independent of each other, saw the wrongness of division in accordance with Jesus' prayer for unity. After all, if He prayed for it, could it not be possible? They decided to go back to the Bible, rather than the invented traditions and doctrines of men. They thought if all would take the Bible, and solely the Bible as authoritative above all philosophy and theology, there could be agreement; for, divisions only happen when people speak where the Bible does not speak or are silent when the Bible speaks. They thought they were saved at the time, by being obedient to the revealed will of God, rather than they were saved based on a feeling within themselves. In other words, they trusted God over Man. They became Christians in the exact same way people are recorded as becoming Christians in the first century. God's Word is a seed. Being seed, whenever planted, it will always produce the same fruit. If it produced Christians in the first century, it will produce Christians in the 19th, 20th, and even at the end of time. If another crop comes up, it is not from God's seed, but rather is tares to be rooted up at the Judgement. God's Word is true and the gates of hell could not prevail against the Church, if rooted on the Word. However, after this time of good intention, things continued to go in the way the great Deceiver fought to see them go and divisions spread more and more, both for good and bad!

Since there are so many Christian denominations, the main question is, if unity as claimed by the ecumenism champions is important or possible, would it be based on organization or teaching, the number of members or the beauty of buildings, the high instruction of the leaders or the love of truth, the eternal Word of God or human traditions and catechisms! Ecumenism whose inventors pretend to promote Christian unity throughout the world in putting together Roman Catholics, Orthodox and divers Protestant groups and other Independents, is only a mere bluff, for unity might be found in the teachings based only on the Word of God. The noble purpose would be to put aside all human traditions and philosophy, and remain only on the biblical Truth, for *"Heaven and earth shall pass away: but my words shall not pass away"*, says the Master of the Universe in Luke 21 : 33.

The noble motives are well expressed here and there, "And yet almost everyone, though in different ways, longs that there may be one visible Church of God, a Church truly universal and sent forth to the whole world that the world may be converted to the Gospel and so be saved, to the glory of God" (Second Vatican Ecumenical Council, Decree on Ecumenism Unitatis Redintegratio,). "How indeed can we proclaim the Gospel of reconciliation without at the same time being committed to working for reconciliation between Christians? However true it is that the Church, by the prompting of the Holy Spirit and with the promise of indefectibility, has preached and still preaches the Gospel to all nations; it is also true that she must face the difficulties, which derive from the lack of unity. When non-believers meet missionaries who do not agree among themselves, even though they all appeal to Christ, will they be in a position to receive the true message? Will they not think that the Gospel is a cause of division, despite the fact that it is presented as the fundamental law of love?" (Cf. John Paul II, Letter to the Bishops of Europe on the Relations between Catholics and Orthodox in the New Situation of Central and Eastern Europe, May 13, 1991),

However, in the Catholic Church's point of view, the word 'Church' is the Roman Catholic Church, and the all others are considered as 'the separated brothers and sisters' who should be brought back into the Church.

On the other hand, the World Council of Churches (WCC), the broadest and most inclusive among the many organized expressions of the modern ecumenical movement, is a movement whose goal is Christian unity. The WCC brings together more than 340 churches, denominations and church fellowships in over 100 countries and territories throughout the world, representing some 550 million Christians and including most of the world's Orthodox churches, scores of denominations from such historic traditions of the Protestant Reformation as Anglican, Baptist, Lutheran, Methodist and Reformed, as well as many united and independent churches. While the bulk of the WCC's founding churches were European and North American, today most are in Africa, Asia, the Caribbean, Latin America, the Middle East and the Pacific. For its member churches, the WCC is a unique space: one in which they can reflect, speak, act, worship and work together, challenge and support each other, share and debate with each other. ". . . *from every tribe and tongue and nation . . .*". The churches that make up the WCC live in remarkably different social, economic, cultural and political conditions.

Here comes the important question. What are conditions of membership and lifestyle? It is said, "Churches which agree with the WCC basis are eligible to apply for WCC membership. Applications may be approved at an assembly by two-thirds of the member churches or, between assemblies, by two-thirds of the central committee (unless objection from one-third of the member churches is received within six months.)" A prospective member must evidence "sustained independent life and organization" and "constructive ecumenical relations" with other churches in its country. Ordinarily, member churches have at least 25,000 members (churches with at least 10,000 members may be associate members, eligible to participate in all WCC activities but not to vote in the assembly).

WCC rules state that becoming a member signifies a church's "faithfulness to the basis of the Council, fellowship in the Council, participation in the life and work of the Council and commitment to the ecumenical movement as integral to the mission of the church". There is no membership assessment, but "an annual contribution to the general budget and programs of the WCC, commensurate with their resources", is listed among membership responsibilities.

Where is Christ in such a platform!

Interestingly amazing enough, this kind of Christian unity based, not on the Everlasting Word of God but on the human rules and mere complacency, not on the solid Rock of righteousness but on building size and members' wealth; is but a house built on the sand, which will be destroyed by the rain, the hailstorm and the floods that will accompany the coming of the Lord!

Such Christian structures are not unique in our today world. As long as every denomination and sect remains steadfast on its teachings and doctrine, the idea to build Christian unity for which Christ prayed, is only the hypocrisy and the lie, good to amuse the blind audience.

If the ecumenism was real and sincere, based on the love for the Resurrected Savior, the humble spirit of self-denial and meekness and above all, the search of the saving Truth, different Christian denominations and groups would join in the same mind and in the same judgment on divine things based solely on the Bible! They might fight together in a brotherly spirit to end conflict and killings between Christians still entertained by the leaders in some parts of this world. They might accept in their schools and church pulpits, teachers, evangelists and ministers from other denominations and churches!

Instead, they built and continue to build the walls of separation among believers for whom Christ died; because they fear that, allowing some faithful Bible teachers to their pulpits or 'their' followers to mingle with other believers, they may come to a discernment and discover their errors, malice and falsity, and so they would quit their churches and deprive them the mean of their living!

Listen to this testimony. Paul Bernabee (not his real name), a newcomer qualified teacher in Canada went to a successful interview in school to teach math and the principal and his team were glad to find someone to hold the position and send his application to the school board. Paul was invited to the board to sign the documents for his hiring. Then he was asked,

The Board: Are you a Christian?
Paul: Surely, I am a Christian, he proudly reply
The Board: Good! Are you a Catholic Church member?
Paul: No, I am a Latter-day Saint (*not his real church*).

The Board: Paul, we are sorry not to hire you, because your Church does not collaborate with the Catholic Church and does not recognize papal authority. We are truly sorry that we cannot help you.

In his later search, Paul found that most of his other no-catholic friends hired at that board, have denied their faith to find the job. Does in Canada, Catholic school system whose schools are subsidized by the public funds from all citizen taxes regardless of their religion, have legally the right to discriminate other citizens from working in its schools because of their beliefs? What about Christ's admonition to love even "*. . . your enemies and to give them food . . .*"?

Christ did not take the step toward His disciples to prevent them mingling with Pharisees and other pagans that He might protect them from being deceived; instead He prayed and let them judge themselves of what they had to believe. For, He was sure that His teachings were all true and worthy to give life to those that would live by His Word! '*Behold, I send you out as sheep in the midst of wolves. Therefore be wise as serpents and harmless as doves. But beware of men, for they will deliver you up to councils . . . ,*' (Matthew 10 : 16, 17a)

In many cases, mainly among protestant churches, the issue of organization and doctrine is the most praised instead of the Bible teachings. The question is, against what are we protesting? A glimpse of the multitude Pentecostal organizations will show that the teachings and gestures are fundamentally the same, except some light variations as the form of drums, the ceremonial clothing of the 'prophets' and other leaders; so why they do not form one body?

Why such many divisions even among those that claim to act under the 'power of the Spirit of God' and speaking in so-called new tongues as proof of authenticity and truth? Is the Spirit of our Lord divided? Claiming to act under the power of God and be divided, even opposed and fighting one another, is it Christianity or worldly behavior?

Peter, led by the power from above, gives us some light: "*. . . Those false teachers only want your money, so they will use you by telling you lie. Their judgment spoken against them long ago is still coming, and their ruin is certain*". (2 Peter 2 : 3—New century Bible Version)

The leaders of those unnumbered denominational factions, holding respectfully the Bible in their hands as their well loved book, are confident of themselves and of their doctrine as based on the Word of God. The counsel is, "*Try all spirits*" to make sure that you are on the footsteps of the True Way of Life. For this is the warning of Him who paid such a so high price for His Church: "*Beware of false prophets, who come to you in sheep's clothing, but inwardly they are ravenous wolves. You will know them by their fruits . . . A good tree cannot bear bad fruits, nor can a bad tree bear good fruit.*" (Matthew 7 : 15, 18). And their fruit is the division and strife every morning! "Since the created world is not self-sufficient, every illusion of autonomy which would deny the essential dependence on God of every creature, the human being included, leads to dramatic situations which subvert the rational search for the harmony and the meaning of human life" (Pope John Paul II's Encyclicals, Given in Rome, at St. Peter's, on December 30 of the year 1987, *The Tenth of my Pontificate*.)

It is not different among Sabbath keeping churches, where statistics speak of over 500 different denominations that have discovered the truth about the forgotten fourth commandment lost since the dark ages, and the list of groups still growing larger with time.

There's only one Way to eternal life, which is Christ Jesus. No matter the large size of your church buildings, no matter the level of instruction of your leaders, no matter the great number of the membership in your congregation, if you are out of the Way, your destination is eternal death. Jesus continually referred to Himself in ways that confounded His listeners. He made the audacious statement, "*Before Abraham was, I AM.*" He told Martha and others around her, "*I AM the resurrection and the life; he who believes in me, though he is dead, yet shall he live.*" Likewise, Jesus would make statements like, "*I AM the light of the world*," "*I AM the only way to God*," or, "*I AM the truth*." These and several of His other claims were preceded by the sacred words of God, 'I AM'. What did Jesus mean by such statements, and what is the significance of the term, "I AM"? What was the context of term?

In the Hebrew Scriptures, when Moses asked God His name at the burning bush, God answered, "*I AM*." He was revealing to Moses that He is the One and only God who is outside of time and has always existed. Incredibly, Jesus was using these holy words to describe Himself. The question is, 'Why?'

Since the time of Moses, no practicing Jew would ever refer to himself or anyone else by 'I AM.' As a result, Jesus' 'I AM' claims infuriated the Jewish leaders. One time, some leaders explained to Jesus why they were trying to kill Him: "*Because you, a mere man, have made yourself God.*" The point is that these Old Testament scholars knew exactly what He was saying; He was claiming to be God, the Creator of the universe. It is only this claim that would have brought the accusation of blasphemy upon Him.

Jesus taught that He is God in the way the Jews understood God and the way the Hebrew Scriptures portrayed God, it is why they mocked Him when He was on the cross, "*You have saved others and you cannot save yourself*". Therefore, His resurrection should occur to confirm His divinity. In Him, there is the Truth, the Light and the Life. He is the incarnate Word of God. Only through Him and His Word, we have salvation. All other ways and philosophy are but vain.

Alleluia.

XI—THE PENALITY PAID

Pilate therefore said to him, 'Art You a king then?' Jesus answered, 'You say rightly that I am a King. For this cause was I born, and for this cause I have come into the world, that I should bear witness to the truth. Everyone who is of the truth hears my voice.' Pilate said unto him, 'What is truth?' (John 18 : 37, 38a)

What can we say . . .
They crucified the Savior of the world!
Though He spent all His earthly life
In a loving self-denial, feeding the hungry ones . . .
Always extending His hands to bless,
To heal the sick and devil-possessed ones,
Rising from the dead
And above all, preaching the
Good News for the eternal life!
Were you there when they crucified our Lord, were you there . . . ?
O sometimes it causes me to tremble!

How can we understand that . . . ?
He came to His own but they did not recognize Him.
He did not harm anybody; He never rises up His voice
But they hated Him for nothing . . . .
Betrayed and delivered with a kiss by one of His friends,
One of His zealous disciples denied him three times!
People chosen by Himself by love,

With whom He spent about forty-two months,
All left Him alone in the time He needed them the most!
Were you there when they nailed Him to the tree, were you there . . . ?
O sometimes it pushes me to revenge!

How can we watch such a scene . . . ?
He was arrested by a mob and bound as criminal!
He was beaten and undressed
By those human hands He created and blessed!
They mocked Him and spat on His face!
What! . . . They pierce his hands and feet with nails,
And His side with a spear!
His kingly head crowned of weaved thorns!
And the earth drank the precious blood
Of the beloved Son of God . . .
Nevertheless, they recognized that
He is *"the King of the Jews"*
Were you there when they pierced Him in the side, were you there . . . ?
O sometimes it causes me to hide under the rocks!

"Eli, Eli lama sabachthani . . . !"
Cried the Lord of lords and God of gods!
The sun hided its face and a profound darkness
Fell upon the face of the earth!
Under the burden of anguish, the Temple curtain torn
Itself in pieces to reveal the contents of the Temple.
The earth shook, the rocks broke apart
And the graves opened!
Were you there when the sun refused to shine, were you there . . . ?
O sometimes it causes me to cry!

How not to cry . . . !
The women from Jerusalem, of all His disciples were
The sole witnesses of the sufferings of the Savior;
They followed the mob to Golgotha
To know where their Master would be buried.
In a new sepulcher where no one was put before,
Him who did not need it . . .

FORTUNAT TSHIMANGA-MUKADI

Were you there when they laid Him in the tomb, were you there . . . ?
O sometimes, it causes me to despair!

JESUS' DEATH WAS predicted in Scripture, and was necessary, for it is written, ". . . *thus it was necessary for the Christ to suffer and to rise from the dead the third day, and that repentance and remission of sins should be preached in His name to all nations, beginning at Jerusalem"*. (Luke 24 : 46 - 47)

Herod was exceptionally happy to meet Jesus, thinking that He would work some miracles for him. He asked Jesus many questions, but Jesus didn't answer any of them. Herod felt very angry that Jesus would not answer any of his questions and would not perform miracles for him like a magician or a clown at a theater. However, Christ had nothing to say to the man who had John the Baptist beheaded. The very silence of Christ was the greatest rebuke that could have been given. Herod and his soldiers mocked Christ, dressing Him in one of old robes found there and sent Him back to Pilate. Pilate said that, neither him nor Herod did find any reason to put this 'Man' to death, and concluded that he will therefore punish Him and release Him. But the very chief priest and the scribes and the religious leaders of His nation shouted and instigated people to claim the release of Barabbas the murderer, and to crucify Christ!

It was necessary not just for the Messiah to die, perhaps in a painless way, but to suffer, and to be crucified for our salvation. It was an essential part of Jesus' ministry, and an essential part of the gospel. Jesus had predicted His own sufferings and death, even His death on a cross (see John 12 : 32 - 33). Not only He was sure it had to happen the way it did, but also He accepted it to be that way (Matthew 26 : 54). For it was His purpose, His mission (see John 12 : 27). He had to fulfill the prophecy He gave to Isaiah many centuries before (according to gospel of Luke chapter 22 verse 37 and the prophet Isaiah in chapter 53).

Jesus said that His death would be a ransom to save all people which believe in Him (see Mark 10 : 45). At His Last Supper, He said that He gave His body on behalf of mankind, and He gave His blood to form a new covenant, or a special relationship between the Creator and His creatures, based on forgiveness (read Luke 22 : 19 - 20). He was, as Isaiah had predicted, an innocent person who suffered and died to ransom the guilty ones.

God laid our sins on Jesus, and He was killed for our transgressions to buy our freedom.

Jesus not only predicted His death, He also explained its significance for us, and this is why it means for us good news. He gave His body for us, for our benefit. He allowed His blood to be shed so the Mankind might be forgiven.

Jesus is the mediator between His Father and humans. His death enables us to have a covenant with the Godhead, a relationship of promise and loyalty. Indeed, the death of Christ was the only way for our salvation to fulfill the requirement of the holy unchanging Law of His Father. For, it was said to our first parents in Eden, "*If you eat the fruit, you will surely die*" (Genesis 2 : 17). It is the reason He had come in the flesh to our world.

That is why Jesus, though He knew what pain awaited Him, resolutely set out for Jerusalem to meet with His killers (see Luke 9 : 51). A sepulcher was borrowed for His burial

Fortunately, the burial of the Savior was not the end but the beginning of our history as a peculiar people, born not from the will of men but of God, a people different from all other in the Universe.

For, if the death of Christ was not followed by the resurrection, according to His own sayings and to what was foretold by the holy prophets, you and I could never meet! You and I could not call each other brother and sister, though we may be born in a same village, town or country! You and I were lost forever in sins.

We have all sinned, and the penalty had to be paid in order for God to be just. Christ has paid that penalty. Romans 5 : 6 - 10 says, "*For when we were still without strength, in due time Christ died for the ungodly. For scarcely for a righteous man will one die; yet perhaps for a good man someone would even dare to die. But God demonstrates His love toward us, in that, while we were still sinners, Christ died for us. Much more then, having now been justified by His blood, we shall be saved from wrath through Him. For if when we were enemies we were reconciled to God through the death of His Son, much more, having been reconciled, we shall be saved by His life*". What a wonderful love for God and Christ to have paid our penalty.

Also, we read in I Peter 3 : 18, "*For Christ also suffered once for sins, the just for the unjust, that he might bring us to God.*" Yes, Christ is the just, who had to die for us the unjust, so that it would be possible for us to be brought back to God. Because of the death and sufferings of Christ for us, God can now be just in saving us.

The only way had Man to be saved is through Christ's sufferings and heinous death on the Cross. There was no other way. The apostle John in chapter 14 verse 6 says, *"Jesus said to him, I am the way, the truth, and the life: No man comes to the Father except through Me."* The only way we can get to God is through Christ. We also read in Acts 4 : 12, *"Nor is there salvation in any other, for there is no other name under heaven given among men by which we must be saved."* We cannot be saved by relying on Mohammed, Buddha, Judaism, and Joseph, Paul or Mary, Hindu gods or any other way. Neither can we devise our own system of Christianity as is being done today and expect it to save us. Only Jesus Christ can specify the conditions for our salvation, because He paid our price and is our only Saviour.

Christ went through much suffering for our sins. It is beyond our imagination what He endured. Christ came to this earth for the purpose of dying for our sins. There are many Old Testament prophesies that foretell the inevitable death of Christ. For example, the king David in Psalms chapter 22 and the prophet Isaiah in chapter 53, describe clearly what Christ to go through to make salvation available to us. Christ's death was no accident, because it was in God's eternal plan to redeem Man that way because the offence was great.

Christ in His omniscience, fully knew what was soon going to happen. In Matthew 20 : 17 - 19 we read, *"Now Jesus, going up to Jerusalem, took the twelve disciples aside on the road and said to them, Behold we go up to Jerusalem, and the Son of Man will be betrayed to the chief priests and to the scribes; and they will condemn Him to death, and deliver Him to the Gentiles to mock and to scourge and to crucify. And the third day He will rise again"*. Christ went there willingly to die for us.

Christ was both divine and human. The human part of Christ dreaded His death on the cross as much as we would if we were on death row. He knew that it was going to happen the way it did. Luke in chapter 22 verses 41 - 44 describes Christ in the garden of Gethsemane with His apostles the night before His crucifixion, this way, *"And He was withdrawn from them about a stone's throw, and knelt down, and prayed, saying, Father, if it is your will, take this cup away from Me; nevertheless not My will, but yours, be done. Then an angel appeared to Him from heaven, strengthening Him. And being in agony He prayed more earnestly. Then His sweat became like great drops of blood falling down to the ground"*. Yes, Christ was dreading the horrible death that He was about to endure for you and for me.

Also, we read in I Peter 2 : 24, *"Who Himself bore our sins in His own body on the tree, that we, having died to sins, might live for righteousness: by whose stripes you were healed."* Jesus has personally paid the price for our sins, so that we can be made righteous before God. When a person is made righteous, by obeying God's plan to save man, God will then save him.

The human side of Christ knows how we feel. He had the same feelings, the same sorrows, the same fears, and He experienced pain just like we do. He fully knows what it is to live a human life. On the Day of Judgment, no one will be able to point a finger at Christ and say, "You just don't know what it is to live as a human". Yes He does. The fear, the sorrow, the tears, the mocking, the spitting, the pain of scourging, and the crucifixion were all dreaded by our Lord. It hurt Him as much as it would us. He was the innocent dying for us, the guilty. It is more hurting if you suffer for something you did not do.

Crucifixion on a cross is the cruellest form of torture that has ever been devised by man. There is nothing worse. Our Lord hung there in pain and agony for six long hours in a slow death, enduring punishment, so that God could be just in saving us. What wonderful love beyond description that God and Christ have for us.

The earth of the tomb, either the big stone placed upon it, did not retain Him from rising from death with splendor and power; in such a way that, Joseph, the tomb owner might expect to be laid therein when his time of death would come!

The resurrection meant life for Jesus, but a far better life than what He had on earth, that is the glory which He had with the Father before His incarnation (see John 17 : 5). By His resurrection, He was powerfully revealed as the Son of God (see Romans 1 : 4). The resurrection declared who He had been all along, more than His miracles. To make this a biggest event of salvation, He instituted Communion along with baptism, to emphasize the commemoration of this death and the resurrection to a new life.

The resurrection proves that God will judge the world through Christ (read Acts 17 : 31); it also means life for us that believe in Him. As Paul says, "*. . . we will be saved by His life*" (Romans 5 : 10). If you "*. . . believe in your heart that God has raised Him from the dead, you will be saved*" (Romans 10 : 9) "*And if Christ is not been risen, then our preaching is empty and your faith is also empty*" (1 Corinthians 15 : 14). Our salvation depends not just on Jesus' death, but also on His resurrection (according to 1 Peter 3 : 21).

Now people should know that Jesus grew up to give His life as a ransom for our sins, to bring us forgiveness, to be a light to the Gentiles, to defeat the Devil, and to defeat death itself in His death and resurrection. They can see how Jesus is the fulfillment of God's promises.

O yes, we can see much more than the Jews could more than 2,000 years ago, but we still do not see everything therein: we do not yet see every promise fulfilled; we do not yet see Satan chained where he can deceive the nations no more (see Revelation 20 : 2); we do not yet see all nations knowing God (see Matthew 24 : 14); we do not yet see the end of crying and tears and death and dying (see Revelation 7 : 17).

We still long for the final answer, but in Jesus, we have the hope and the assurance. Hope is energizing!

There is a promise, a promise guaranteed by God, ratified by His Son, sealed by the Holy Spirit. Let us believe that everything else will come true, that Christ will complete the work He has begun. Promise creates hope, guarantied by Him who gives the promise and by what we have known of Him.

Our hope is a beginning to bear fruit, and we can be confident that all the promises will be fulfilled, not necessarily in the way we might expect, but in the way that God has planned.

He will do it, as promised, through His Son, Jesus Christ. We may not see it now, but God has already acted, and God is working even now behind the scenes to bring about His will.

Just as the birth of the Baby Jesus gave to the world a hope and a promise of salvation, so in the risen Jesus we now have hope and promise of completion. That is true of the growth of the Kingdom of God (read Mark 4 : 30 - 32), it is true in the work of the Church (read Matthew 28 : 18 - 20), and it is true in each of our lives according to John 15 : 1 - 4.

As we come to Christ in faith, His work begins to grow in us. Jesus said that we must each one of us be born again, and when we come to believe in Him, the Holy Spirit overshadows us and begets in us a new life. Just as Jesus promises, He comes to live within us.

The promise that Jesus gives to the world does us no good unless we accept Him as our Hope. We need to let Jesus live in us.

However, we do not yet have the fulfillment of all the promises that God has made. We do not yet have all the life and goodness that He offers. What we have is hope, a promise of better things to come. What we have now is just a small grain of mustard in comparison to the glory that God will give us later.

One might look at himself and think: 'I don't see much here. I'm not much better than it was seven years ago. I am still entangled with sin, doubt and guilt. I am not much better at being a godly person than my parents were. Is God really doing anything in my life? It doesn't seem like I've made any progress . . .'. Stop there and remember Jesus. Your spiritual journey may not seem good for much right now, but it is, because God had promised to be with you always. The Holy Spirit promised to be in you is a down payment of glory yet to come.

Even justification, most commonly associated with Jesus' death, is also a result of His resurrection (see Romans 4 : 24 - 25). Our salvation depends on the entire sequence of incarnation: His birth, ministry, death and above all His resurrection. For, without resurrection, Jesus would be compared to any other liar and false prophets like those, in each generation rose up, proclaiming themselves christs and messiahs for a time and then are engulfed in death without return.

Like the Communion, our baptism pictures our participation in Jesus' death and resurrection. In this, the sprinkling of water at the baptism is a human institution, which does not fit in God's plan of salvation. Rising from the water pictures our new life (see Romans 6 : 4) and it pictures our future: "*. . . we also shall be in the likeness of His resurrection*" (Romans 6 : 5). "*. . . when He is revealed, we shall be like Him, for we shall see Him as He is*" (1 John 3 : 2). Our resurrected bodies will be like His (see 1Corinthians 15 : 42 - 49).

By His matchless blood, He recreated a new people, called to be different from all the inhabitants of the world, though living in the world. People who have to put off the old man, which is corrupt according to the deceitful lusts and to be renewed in the spirit of their

FORTUNAT TSHIMANGA-MUKADI

mind, that they put on the new man, which after God is created in righteousness and true holiness (see Ephesians 4 : 22 - 24). For, it is not their worldly comfort and prosperity that matters, but their spiritual peace in Christ, and joy in the Holy Ghost; the enjoyment which depends so much upon their careful and jealous observance of the Law of Christ in their walk and conversation. Paul sets before the minds of those that are born again, the "consolation in Christ," the "comfort of love," the "bowels and mercies," the "fellowship of the Spirit," which they have to experience and rejoice therein. And the clear and delightful doctrine of salvation is always set before them as the ground of all. In the beginning of this chapter, he beseeches them, in consideration of the wonderful things already presented, to walk worthy of the vocation wherewith they are called; exhorting to lowliness, meekness, long-suffering, and mutual forbearance in love, and that they should thus endeavor to keep the unity of the Spirit in the bond of peace. Christ and all His people are one, and this unity is to be made manifest through the work of the ministry by the apostles, prophets, evangelists, pastors, and teachers given to the Church; and the brethren, by walking in the truth in love, do grow up into Christ as the Head, coming into a manifest unity of faith, and showing that they are one body in Christ (see verse 17).

Those who are members of the Body of Christ and are following Him and growing up into Him, do not walk like other Gentiles, in the vanity of their minds, but do and must put off the old man and put on the new; that, by no other course, can they follow Christ and grow up into Him (read Colossians 3 : 9, 10). Those to whom Paul is addressing these things have all been made, without any will or so called free agency of their own, the subjects of two births. In their first birth, they were manifested in the possession of natural life, which is derived from Adam. They are begotten unto an inheritance which is corruptible, defiled and that fades away. In their second birth, they are, (as much without any will or aid of their own) manifested as in the possession of spiritual life, which is derived from God through Jesus Christ, in whom it was from everlasting. The inheritance unto which the heirs of this life are begotten is incorruptible undefiled and fades not away. "Knowing this, that our old man is crucified with him, that the body of sin might be destroyed, that henceforth we should not serve sin;" (Romans 6, 6).

Surely, the old man is to be put off as a ruler and director. The principles and desires of the old or carnal nature are not to be followed, and are not followed when we walk as Christians. All of our natural wisdom and affections are corrupt, and never guide us in the path of holiness. Here should come a renewal in the spirit of our minds. Only the new man, the spiritual understanding and wisdom can lead one to follow the Savior as an obedient child, seeing a spiritual power and beauty in the ordinance, and carefully regarding all of His directions. The new man tells us that this world is not our abiding place, that here we are pilgrims, and that the Lord has taken charge of us, and that while we trust in Him, He will surely protect us, and that He does mean just what He says. In order to contemplate divine things, to speak of them, to act in accordance with them, we must be renewed in the spirit of our minds. The same powers that, under the control of the natural spirit or life, are engaged upon evil or worldly subjects are, when quickened or animated by the Spirit of Christ engaged upon heavenly things.

As no one before Him, Jesus had an amazingly productive ministry, teaching and healing thousands of people. He attracted large crowds and had potential for much more. He could have healed thousands more by traveling to the Jews and gentiles who lived in other areas. However, He allowed such a wonderful work to come to a sudden end. He could have avoided arrest, but He chose to die instead of expanding His ministry. Although His teachings were important, He had come not just to teach, but also to die, and He accomplished more in His death than in His life.

As the prophet Isaiah stressed it: "*Surely He has borne and carried our sorrows, yet we esteemed Him stricken, smitten by God, and afflicted. But He was wounded for our transgressions, He was bruised for our iniquities; the chastisement for our peace was upon Him, and by His stripes we are healed. All we like sheep have gone astray; we have turned, every one, to his own way; and the Lord has laid on Him the iniquity of us all. He was oppressed and He was afflicted . . . For He was cut off from the land of the living; for the transgressions of My people He was stricken . . . Yet it pleased the Lord to bruise Him; He has put Him to grief. When You make His soul an offering for sin . . . Because He poured out His soul unto death, and he was numbered with the transgressors, and He bore the sin of many, and made intercession for the transgressors,* [as you and me]". (chapter 53 verse 4 - 12).

Behold One who suffers not for His own sins, but for the sins of others. Though this Man was cut off from the land of the living, it did not become the end of the story; for He "*will see His offspring and prolong His days*" (verses 11, 10). Because of all this, the Cross is the good news for us: we were redeemed, and our sins received the penalty they deserved. We will not be raised into glory unless our sins are removed

FORTUNAT TSHIMANGA-MUKADI

from the heavenly records, unless in Christ we are made *"the righteousness of God."* Only then can we join Jesus in His glory. The crucifixion followed by the resurrection make it possible.

God loves people and He hates sin, because sin hurts people. Therefore, there will be a *"day of God's wrath"* when He will judge the world (see Romans 1 : 18; 2 : 5). People who reject the Truth, and they are many, will be punished (verse 8). If they reject the truth of God's grace, they will experience another side of God, His anger. God wants everyone to repent according to Scriptures in 2 Peter 3 : 9, but those who don't, will suffer the result of their sins.

Will all people one day believe and get all saved, as some Christians teach? Not so sure; only wait and see! Anyway, by the death of Jesus, our confessed sins are forgiven, and through His death, we escape the wrath of God, the punishment of sin. The Father is just as merciful as Jesus is, and Jesus is just as angry about sin as the Father is. He is angry at sin because sin hurts the people He loves and it put His beloved Son at the Cross. Jesus is the Judge who condemns (see Matthew 25 : 31 - 46), as well as the Judge who loves sinners so much that He paid the penalty for them.

Let us make a move toward our Redeemer!

XII—GOD IS LOVE

Let CHRIST Live In Your ♡

"But God, who is rich in mercy, for his great love wherewith he loved us" (Ephesians 2 : 4)

AS CHRIST PREDICTED that the gospel of the kingdom shall be preached in all the world for a witness to all nations, before the end comes, the message of the three angels in Revelation is preached and obedience to the Law of God emphasized; including the observance of the seventh day of the week as the blessed day of rest, as found in the fourth commandment of the Decalogue!

The fact that the major part of Christianity does not teach these Commandments as it might be, does not diminish their value and their holiness. Why do they call Christ, *"Lord, Lord"* yet they do not do what He says? Not everyone *"who says Lord, Lord"* will enter His kingdom. Merely listening causes no pain, but doing often does. Doing something means you really believe it. Without doing it, you do not believe it at all. Only, interpret it correctly. The devil One quoted Scripture out of its context; Jesus' response was based on His view that Scripture can neither be broken nor self-contradictory. If you can change the Word at one point, you would have changed it at all points because God's Word is one as His will is. The one and the other have an unchanging character.

God, not only instituted the Sabbath, but many times in His Word, He teaches how to keep it according to His will, by the statutes, precepts or principles that explain, complete and make clear the Law for the understanding of the daughters and sons of Man. Because obedience to the Will of the Creator is a matter of life or death, so He explained His Law to prevent all false interpretation and selfish reasoning.

Memorial of creation, the Sabbath reveals the reason why God is to be worshiped.

He is the Creator and we are His creatures.
He is our Father and we are His sons and daughters.
He is the Sovereign Master and we are His subjects.
He is the Redeemer and we owe everything to Him, even our very life.
We were rebels and opponents and He came down to seek and reconcile with us.
By His blood, He set up a bridge over the gulf made by the sin of Adam and of our own.
We were lost and sold to sin and He bought us back from death by His matchless Blood.
Wanderers and without God, we were not a people, yet He adopted us and bestowed His holy name upon us.
What a great love!

Therefore, in lessening one jot, one letter, one point or one line of the fourth commandment or of any other nine commandments, and His statutes and decrees, not only it is an attempt against the divine Law, but also against the Creator Himself and His authority as Legislator, for the Law shows His very character.

Accused falsely by the Jews to break the Law for healing on Sabbath, Jesus insisted, *"Do not think that I came to destroy the Law or the Prophets. I did not come to destroy but to fulfill."* (Matthew 5 : 17)

Many Christians, blinded by the human philosophy, have understood here that Christ had changed the Decalogue and other biblical principles, explaining 'to fulfill the Law' as 'to change the Law or put an end to it'.

Some other ones evoke Paul's writings; such as, *"Blotting out the handwriting of ordinances that was against us, which was contrary to us, and took it out of the way, nailing it to his cross."* (Colossians 2 : 14) or, *"For He Himself is our peace, who has made both one, and has broken down the middle wall of separation, having abolished in His flesh the enmity, that is, the law of commandments contained in ordinances, so as to create in Himself one new man from the two, thus making peace, and that He might reconcile both to God in one body through the cross, thereby putting to death the enmity"* (Ephesians 2 : 14 - 16)

How can we understand what is said in these verses of the "law of ordinances and of commandments"? There are three kinds of laws mentioned in the Bible:

Moral Law of ten commandments, found in the heavenly sanctuary, is unchangeable, eternal, pure, holy, and written by the very Hand of the Creator on two tablets of stone and given to Israel on Mount Sinai amid thunders, lightning and earthquake, as the universal law for Humanity. To show its special and awful character, it was placed in the ark that nobody could watch or touch those two tablets of stone!

Moses wrote ceremonial Laws on the skins, to govern the sanctuary services. They were pointing to Christ's sacrifice on the Cross and had to end with Christ's mission on earth, and are no longer binding to Christians.

Civil Laws that taught Israelites about health, sanitation, disease, court procedures . . .

By the prophecy given to prophet Daniel in chapter 9 from verses 24 to 27, it was predicted that the law related to sacrifices would cease in the middle of the 17th week allotted to the Jewish nation. The first 69 weeks (483 prophetic days understood as 483 years) bring the history to the baptism of Christ in year 27 AD. In the middle of that last seven years of the prophecy, Christ had been crucified at the spring of year 31AD.

As He hung on the hideous cross, Christ ". . . *cried out again with a loud voice, and yielded up His spirit. Then, behold, the veil of the temple was torn in two from top to bottom . . .*" (Matthew 27 : 50, 51). Then the sacrifices ceased, for Christ had come and had fulfilled the law of sacrifices.

The law of ordinances concerning special holy days, religious festivals and annual sabbaths are specifically given in Leviticus 23 and destined to point to Calvary. However, the law of Ten Commandments still points out our sins until He comes.

To obtain victory over sin, we must trust God's Word and rely faithfully upon Jesus the Nazarene. The important thing for the Christian to keep in mind is that the first motivation of the Law is to ". . . *love the Lord your God with all your heart, with all your soul and with all your strength and your fellow man as yourself*. (Deuteronomy 6 : 5; Matthew 22 : 37 - 40) This is a theme song found throughout the book of Deuteronomy: repeatedly, in a number of different ways, this body of legal material declares that its justification is Love, and it asks what it does because the relationship between God and Man is one of LOVE.

Love is the motivation of the Law, not fear, not the promise of reward, although this is certainly present, not even awe.

According to the Holy Scriptures, in the deliverance of the Israelites from bondage in Egypt, God acted first by His grace, without any good work from them; for they were slaves to Pharaoh of Egypt, and the Lord rescued them by His great power . . . (Deuteronomy 6 : 21). The same for us, born in sin, we were enslaved by it, then God sent His Holy Son to rescue us, without any act of obedience of us.

He first acts for us and bestows upon us His grace, showing His love for us openly by what He had done on our behalf on the Cross. O yes, the appeal, the motivation is love, love based upon the experienced, the known, the real grace, the wonderful mercy and goodness of God. Only through love, can we have a little understanding of the path trod by the Savior, who woke up early morning to go forth to seek and save His lost sheep (Genesis 3 : 9), for GOD IS LOVE!

Christ, our pattern, challenged the Pharisees and the Scribes, ". . . *Which of you could convict Me of sin?*" (refer to John 8 : 46). Nobody did lift up his voice to say, "Me!" Because He came, not only to redeem Man but also to vindicate the authority and the holiness of His Law, presenting its magnificence and greatness before the world and giving us an example of obedience to follow(see John 4 : 34). He strongly and clearly stated, "*He who has my commandments and keeps them, it is he who loves Me. And he who loves Me will be loved by My Father, and I will love him and manifest Myself to him.*" (read John 14 : 21), and also, ". . . *if you want to enter into life, keep the commandments . . .*"

Here the relationship between keeping God's Law and salvation is clearly established by Him who came from heaven, got the Man wicked nature and died on the cross to break down the wall that the sin had put between Humanity and the Godhead.

It is important to note that all the biblical records, which mention the 'Book of Life', connect it with the people of God, never with pagans. When it speaks of the hostile powers toward God's Kingdom and His people, it is specified that it deals with those "*whose names are not written in the Book of Life*" (see Revelation 13 : 8; 17 : 8). In the millennial judgment, which considers the fate of those who will be lost, the Book of Life is also opened to prove that none of those who will be *"thrown into the lake of fire"* were there inscribed according to the book of Revelation chapter 20, verses 12 to 15 and chapter 21verse 8).

In this way, it is shown that there is no excuse for the rebellion. And all enormous mass of rebels that will be lost, will die by their own choice, for they had refused to make divine grace their property. They also may have had their names registered in the Book of Life, if they would have been faithful as those that will then rejoice in the presence of God, within the Heavenly City (refer to Revelation 20 : 6, 9).

The records of devotion and good works never appear in the context of self-justice. Moreover, they are evoked in certain situations wherein the divine comprehension (refer to Psalms 56 : 8, 9) and approval are desired, relating to a work done for His cause as the prophet Nehemiah emphasizes it in chapter 13, verses 14, 22, 31.

An adequate example in the Gospels is found in the statement made to the servants in the parable of the talents: *"Well done, good and faithful servant! You have been faithful with few things; I will put you in charge of many things. Come and share your master's happiness!"* (see Matthew 25 : 21, 23—New International Version)

Every work, each positive gesture of human beings, will testify in the millennial judgment to the transforming power of the divine grace, and will contribute to the honor and glory of the Giver of all things.

The doctrine of salvation by faith alone without obedience is not truly consistent with Biblical teachings on salvation, on judgment or on the relationship faith—works. The truth is that we are saved by grace offered to us through a covenant, a two-way contract: God acts first and Man should accept God's offer; then; God holds out His Hand to Man who have to accept the offer! Therefore, if we accept Christ and do our part, following and obeying Him, then Christ does everything else, forgiving us, cleansing us, healing us, and giving us power to return to the presence of the Father, not because we earned it, but because we accepted the terms upon which He offers His infinite grace and mercy. Even in the days of Moses, the Lord proclaimed that God *"shows mercy to those who keep His commandments"* (Deuteronomy 5 : 10), a principle that has not changed, for God does not change.

FORTUNAT TSHIMANGA-MUKADI

To put it clearly, salvation comes through the merits of Christ, not of our own, but we still must choose the life and seek to repent of our sins with faith in Him. When we turn toward Christ, He can perfect us and make us complete. The talents are endowed freely to people, but not all the recipients are found worthy of them if they are unable to use and develop them!

Some teach that we do not really need to strive to obey God's commandments and make our calling and election sure. Some of these false prophets, who have twisted and mingled the Word of God, teach the questionable doctrine of 'once saved, always saved,' even if we commit murder and fight against Christ. They lull people into false security, telling them that they are saved and that no further effort on their part is needed. This is far from the plain teachings of Christ, His prophets and His apostles. We are on a battlefield. Christ had to fight against the Prince of darkness; Peter had the same experience; Thomas did not escape; Judas was assaulted and failed and he was cast out of the way; even Paul recognizes this battle against the foes in this world.

If in a group of twelve with the Saviour besides them in the flesh, Satan succeeded to deceive so many, how could it be for a congregation of one hundred members living in these hard days of the end may have easy life in Christ!

Consider the words of God in Exodus 20 : 6, where God explains that He offers mercy to thousands of them that love their Creator, and keep His commandments. Has that concept changed? Did Christ revoke it? Absolutely no. God continues to offer His grace and mercy to every one of His creatures, but only those that remain in His love by obeying Him and keeping His commandments will be found worthy to be called FAITHFUL AND GOOD SERVANTS and will be bidden to enter in His Kingdom (see Matthew 25 : 21).

God stretches out His Hand to offer His salvation, mercy and life and only the person who manifests his good will to take them will have them.

What has Christ to tell His people about this matter? We read in the beloved disciple's writings, "*I have come as a light into the world, that whosoever believes in Me should not abide in darkness. And if anyone hears my words, and does not believe, I do not judge him; for I did not come to judge the world but to save the world. He who rejects Me, and does not receive My words, has that which judge him—the word that I have spoken will judge him in the last day*" (John 12 : 46 - 48).

Let us listen to Peter in his second epistle, chapter 1, verses 3 through10: "*. . . as His divine power has given to us all things that pertain to life and godliness, through the knowledge of Him who called us by glory and virtue, by which have been given to us exceedingly great and precious promises, that through these you may be partakers of the divine nature, having escaped the corruption that is in the world through lust. But also for this very reason, giving all diligence, add to your faith virtue, to virtue knowledge, to knowledge self-control, to self-control perseverance, to perseverance godliness, to godliness brotherly kindness, to brotherly kindness love. For if these things are yours and abound, you will be neither barren nor unfruitful in the knowledge of our Lord Jesus Christ. For he who lacks these things is shortsighted, even to blindness, and has forgotten that he was cleansed from his old sins. Therefore, brethren, be even more diligent to make your call an election sure, for if ye do these things, you will never stumble*".

These teachings are echoed throughout the Bible. Through Christ's power, we are given all things pertaining to godliness, for we have been called to glory, and by these things, we can become partakers of the divine nature, becoming more like the Lord, a state that we call eternal life or exaltation. To achieve this, Peter teaches us that growth is required, giving us a list of attributes to achieve step by step, giving all diligence.

It is not automatic! Those that do not do this can fall, becoming as if their sins had never been purged. Finally, Peter calls us to diligence to make our calling and election sure: for if we do these things, we shall never fall. Yes, we can fall (see also 1 Corinthians 10 : 12), but not if we give diligence and endure to the end to make our calling and election sure. This is our active part in our salvation.

Let us then approach the Holy Bible as the very Word of God, an inspired, infallible rule of faith and practice! Let us accept its statements of fact and bow before its enunciations of duty! Let us instinctively tremble before its threatening, and rest upon its promises, as we proclaim this Word of life from the pulpit, or in the classroom; as we attempt to give comfort at some bed of sickness, or in a bereaved home; or as we see our fellow men struggling against temptation or weighed down with care, and would give them encouragement and hope for this present world and for the next! In such cases we want to know that we have not merely something that is probable or plausible, but something that is sure. Absolutely clear.

XIII—ONE ETERNAL LEGISLATOR

If ye keep my commandments, ye shall abide in my love; even as I have kept my Father's commandments, and abide in his love. (John 15 : 10, *King James Version*)

HERE ARE THE Ten Commandments written on the two tablets of stone by God's Hand as found in Exodus 20 : 3 - 17 (King James version Bible) and solemnly proclaimed by God Himself at Mount Sinai to Moses in the presence of all the Jewish Congregation and the multitude of holy heavenly beings watching and witnessing.

1. *Thou shalt have no other gods before me. (v. 3)*
2. *Thou shalt not make unto thee any graven image, or any likeness of anything that is in heaven above, or that is in the earth beneath, or that is in the water under the earth. Thou shalt not bow down thyself to them, nor serve them: for I the LORD thy God am a jealous God, visiting the iniquity of the fathers upon the children unto the third and fourth generation of them that hate me; And shewing mercy unto thousands of them that love me, and keep my commandments. (v. 4-6)*
3. *Thou shalt not take the name of the LORD thy God in vain; for the LORD will not hold him guiltless that taketh his name in vain. (v. 7)*
4. *Remember the sabbath day, to keep it holy. Six days shalt thou labour, and do all thy work: But the seventh day is the sabbath of the LORD thy God: in it thou shalt not do any work, thou, nor thy son, nor thy daughter, thy manservant, nor thy maidservant, nor thy cattle, nor thy stranger that is within thy gates: For in six days the*

LORD made heaven and earth, the sea, and all that in them is, and rested the seventh day: wherefore the LORD blessed the sabbath day, and hallowed it. (v. 8-11)

5. *Honour thy father and thy mother: that thy days may be long upon the land which the LORD thy God giveth thee. (v. 12)*
6. *Thou shalt not kill. (v. 13)*
7. *Thou shalt not commit adultery. (v. 14)*
8. *Thou shalt not steal. (v. 15)*
9. *Thou shalt not bear false witness against thy neighbour. (v. 16)*
10. *Thou shalt not covet thy neighbour's house, thou shalt not covet thy neighbour's wife, nor his manservant, nor his maidservant, nor his ox, nor his ass, nor any thing that is thy neighbour's. (v. 17)*

Now let us take a look to the Ten commandments as presented by the Catholic Church in its Catechism (reference to CatholiCity.com):

1. I am the Lord your God you shall not have strange Gods before me (Exodus 20 : 2 - 6, Deuteronomy 5 : 6 - 10)
2. You shall not take the name of the Lord your God in vain (Exodus 20 : 7 - 8, Deuteronomy 5 : 11 - 12)
3. Remember to keep holy the Lord's Day (Exodus 20 : 8 - 11, Deuteronomy 5 :12 - 15)
4. Honor your father and your mother (Exodus 20 : 12, Deuteronomy 5 : 16)
5. You shall not kill (Exodus 20 : 13, Deuteronomy 5 : 17)
6. You shall not commit adultery (Exodus 20 : 14, Deuteronomy 5 : 18)
7. You shall not steal (Exodus 20 : 15, Deuteronomy 5 : 19)
8. You shall not bear false witness against your neighbor (Exodus 20 : 16, Deuteronomy 5 : 20)
9. You shall not covet your neighbor's wife (Exodus 20 : 17, Deuteronomy 5 : 21)
10. You shall not covet your neighbor's goods (Exodus 20 : 17, Deuteronomy 5 : 21)

Notice that not only the language and the terms had been changed, but also the order and the very essence of the commandments:—The second commandment on the tablets which forbids the idolatry, is simply suppressed, and this led to introduce the worship of persons, places, images and statues of gold, silver, gray and wood.—The fourth commandment became the third and the word 'sabbath' is replaced by the term 'Lord's day' that is celebrated not on the seventh day but on the first day of the week.—Then, to keep the original number of Ten Commandments as on the two tablets, the tenth commandment that took the place of the ninth, is broken into two new commandments.

It is not in vain that God explained some commandments more than other. Concerning the 1st, 6th, 7th, 8th and 9th, there is no explanation for they are clear in themselves; but the 2nd, 3rd, 4th, 5th and 10th have more explanations through statutes, rules and decrees to make them clearer for the humans which He loves so much; not willing anybody find reason to deceive themselves.

The Lord finished His work of creation in six days and then set up the Sabbath, rested in it, blessed it and sanctified it, and He commanded His people to remember the seventh day Sabbath, to hallow it, observe it, to honor it and to enjoy it! And when proclaiming His Holy and Eternal Law of Ten Commandments on Mount Sinai, the people were first sanctified to become worthy of approaching their Maker, there were thunders and lightings, ". . . *so that all the people that was in the camp trembled . . . and the whole mount quaked greatly* (Exodus 19 : 16)", certainly to mark the solemnity and the greatness of the event!

The Catholic Church admits openly and bluntly that she is responsible for the change of the day of rest from Saturday to Sunday. From a Roman Catholic book of Creed, we read the following:

"*Question*: Which is the Sabbath day?

Answer: Saturday is the Sabbath day.

Question: Why do we observe Sunday instead of Saturday?

Answer: We observe Sunday instead of Saturday because the Catholic Church, in the Council of Laodicea (A.D.336), transferred the solemnity from Saturday to Sunday.

Question: Have you any other way of proving that the Church (Roman Catholic) has power to institute festivals of precept?

Answer: Had she no such power, she could not have done that in which all modern religionists agree with her, she could not have substituted the observance of Sunday, the first day of the week, for the observance of Saturday, the seventh day, a change for which there is no Scriptural authority.

(Doctrinal Catechism, p. 147 and The Convert's Catechism of Catholic Doctrine, 1977 edition, p. 50)

The Catholic Church doctrines explain this transfer of the holiness of Sabbath from Saturday to Sunday, not by prophecy or some divine inspiration, but by their belief that Christ had given the Church the power to do so, as they wrongly interpret Matthew 16 : 18, 19, *"And I also say to you that you are Peter, and on this rock I will build My church, and the gates of Ha'des shall not prevail against it. And I will give you the keys of the kingdom of heaven, and whatever you bind on earth will be bound in heaven; and whatever you loose on earth will be loosed in heaven"*. Then they conclude, "the pope can modify divine law, since his power is not of man, but of God, and he acts in the place of God on earth" (Lucius Ferraris, "Papa II" in Prompta Bibliotheca—Venice: Caspa Storti, 1772—C. Mervyn Maxwell, God cares, vol. 1, 128)

Most Protestant Churches, if not all, born almost more than a thousand years after this change was already made by the Mother Church (see Revelations 17 : 5), observe proudly Sunday as the Sabbath day, to remember, they explain, the resurrection of our Savior from death!

Interestingly, interpreting some Scriptures in their ways, without taking heed of the warnings of apostle Paul in Galatians 1 : 8 - 9, the Church of Jesus-Christ of latter-day Saints, by the prophecy of Joseph Smith, based on Hosea's prophecy, affirms, "If the law of Moses, therefore, were the schoolmaster to bring us unto Christ, it would seem perfectly reasonable to assume that when Christ came, there would be no further need of the schoolmaster . . . Can we accept the scriptures as the word of God and question that this prophecy of Hosea (Hosea 2 : 11) should be fulfilled and that the Lord would truly cause Israel's Sabbaths to cease? When Hosea's prophecy was fulfilled, the way was obviously opened for the introduction of a new Sabbath . . . Since Jesus came to fulfill the law, why should some still want to retain it? Why should they not prefer to accept that which Jesus brought to take the place of the law, which includes the new Sabbath, the first day of the week or the Lord's day (Sunday), the day upon which Jesus arose from the tomb? 'The Lord's day' is the day he directed his saints in this dispensation to worship him." (A Marvelous Work and a Wonder, p. 331-334).

FORTUNAT TSHIMANGA-MUKADI

This prophecy of Hosea, wrongly referred to by the false teacher, is not dealing with the Sabbath day issue! God, by the mouth of His prophet is warning the infidel wife, the fall-away Church, how He will punish her sinful conduct, as she left her husband to commit adultery with many lovers. Just as the many today so-called Christian churches do by teaching many false teachings for their eternal loss! In this Testimony, we have emphasized that, in the Bible, the weekly Sabbath day is always in the singular, and where it is plural, it is always about many other common sabbaths found in the Bible beside the holy Sabbath day, always in singular! Christ, the Lawgiver, warned His followers not to break the Sabbath day commandment even when crisis would come after His ascension, saying, *"Let him who is in the field not go back to get his clothes. How woe to those who are pregnant and to those who are nursing babies in those days! And pray that your flight may not be in winter or on the Sabbath . . ."* (Matthew 24; 18 - 20). The desolating armies of Rome surrounded Jerusalem first in the fall of 66 A.D. and then three and a half years later in the spring of 70 A.D. (compare the above text with Luke 21 : 20). Jesus told the disciples to pray that their flight from Jerusalem would not take place on the Sabbath. This prophecy was fulfilled years after Jesus' death and resurrection. The question arises when and how the prophecy of Hosea was fulfilled to give away the fourth commandment of the Decalogue according to the above erroneous interpretation. Simply clear that Hosea's prophecy wrongly used by the 'Saints of our troubled time' is not dealing with the Sabbath day, lest the prophet Hosea may have contradicted the Sovereign Son of God, making himself therefore a false prophet; what is impossibility!

Jehovah's Witnesses affirm that all days are alike; no one is more prominent than another is. They have to work every day of the week, as they understand Paul's epistle to Romans, chapter 14, verses 5 and 6, *"One person esteems one day above another: another esteems every day alike. Let each be fully convinced in his own mind. He who observes the day, observes it to the Lord; and he does not observe the day, to the Lord he does not observe it. He who eats, eats to the Lord, for he gives God thanks; and he who does not eat, to the Lord he does not eat, and gives God thanks."*; so making void the divine blessedness of the seventh-day of the week. Here again it is not Paul abrogating the fourth commandment, he had no such authority and Paul's message is not addressing the Ten Commandments neither the fourth.

O Lord, come down and see how your holy Book is partaken that every one splits over its pages to choose but that fits to his philosophy and his doctrine! Please, O Lord, open the eyes of the blind ones, that they may see the wondrous mysteries of your Spirit!

What History is telling us, is that, Jews had come to be loathed in the Roman Empire after the Jewish-Roman wars, and this led to the criminalization of the Jewish Sabbath. Hatred of Jews is apparent in the Council of Laodicea (4th Century AD) where Canon 37-38 states: "It is not lawful to receive portions sent from the feasts of Jews or heretics, or to feast together with them." and "It is not lawful to receive unleavened bread from the Jews, nor to be partakers of their impiety (*The Council of Laodicea*, Web Publication by Mountain Man Graphics, Australia).

In keeping with this rejection of the Jews, this Roman council also criminalized what they called the Jewish Sabbath as it is seen in Canon 29 of the same Council: "Christians must not judaize by resting on the Sabbath, but must work on that day, rather honoring the Lord's Day; and, if they can, resting then as Christians. But if any shall be found to be judaizers, let them be anathema (excommunicated) from Christ." (Idem).

Someone had complained: "When we present God's holy law, and arguments from scripture draw,
Objectors say, to pick a flaw, 'It's Jewish.'
Though at first, the Most High blessed and sanctified His day of rest,
The same belief is still expressed, 'It's Jewish.'
Though with the world this rest began, and thence through all Scriptures ran, and Jesus said "'twas made for man", 'it's Jewish.'
Though not with Jewish rites, which passed, But with the moral law 'twas classed, Which must exist while time shall last, 'It's Jewish.'
If from the Bible we present The Sabbath's meaning and intent,
This answers every argument, 'It's Jewish.'
Though the disciples, Luke and Paul, continue still this rest to call
The 'Sabbath day', this answers all: 'It's Jewish.'
The good news teacher's plain expression, That "Sin is of the law's transgression," Seems not to make the least impression. 'It's Jewish.'
They love the rest of man's invention, But if the LORD's day we mention, this puts an end to all contention: 'It's Jewish.'
O ye who thus GOD's day abuse, Simply because 'twas kept by Jews,
The Saviour, too, you must refuse, He's Jewish.

The Scriptures, then, we may expect For the same reason you'll reject; For if you will but recollect, They're Jewish.

Thus the apostles, too, must fall; For Andrew, Peter, James, and Paul, Thomas, Matthew, John, and all Were Jewish.

So to your helpless state resign Yourself in wretchedness to pine;

Salvation, surely you'll decline, It's Jewish." (by Uriah Smith (mid to late 1800's, *emphasis added*).

Draw near to God and he will draw near to you. Cleanse your hands, you sinners; and purify your hearts, you double-minded. (James 4 : 8)

HUMAN REASONING ASIDE, we need to consider God's opinion about some Christian celebrations; such as Christmas, we need to look into God's Word to see how He views mixing pagan practices and customs to worship Him. Jesus was not born in December. If we examine the Biblical feasts in the Old Testament, we can determine that He was born sometime in September during the feast of Tabernacles. God never said to honor His Son's birthday; to be fair, He never said 'no' to it, either. What is sure is that, Christmas is not a God-ordained Biblical feast, but a man-made holiday inspired by Satan who has skillfully managed to taint the real reason for the season. The true and sure reason Christmas has survived and grown into such a popular holiday to be observed by more than 80 percent of Americans and almost all nations, even atheistic ones, is because of economic factors and commercialization.

Considering such a season's conditions, the big problem with December is that it would be unusual for shepherds to be *"abiding in the field"* (Luke 2 : 8) at this cold time of year when fields were unproductive. The normal practice was to keep the flocks in the fields from spring to autumn. In addition, winter would likely be an especially difficult time for pregnant Mary to travel the long distance from Nazareth to Bethlehem (70 miles). A more probable time would be late September, the time of the annual Feast of Tabernacles, when such travel would be commonly accepted. Thus, it is rather commonly believed, though not certain, that Jesus' birth was around the month of September.

According to other sources, the conception of Christ may have taken place in late December of the previous year. Thus, Christmas celebration may well be recognized as an honored observation of the incarnation of '. . . *the Word made flesh* . . .' (John 1 : 14), coinciding so with the Jewish Feast of Tabernacles, in September. "It would have at least been appropriate for Christ to have been born on such a date, for it was at His birth that '. . . *the Word was made flesh and dwelt among us*'(idem). Thus, it might well be that when we celebrate today Christ's birth at what we call Christmas (i.e., 'Christ sent'), we are actually celebrating His miraculous conception, the time when the Father sent the Son into the world, in the virgin's womb of Mary. This darkest time of the year, the time of the pagan Saturnalia, and the time when the sun (the physical 'light of the world') is at its greatest distance from the Holy Land, would surely be an appropriate time for God to send the spiritual 'light of the world' into the world as the 'Savior, which is Christ the Lord' (Luke 2 : 11)" [Dr. Henry M. Morris, *The Defender's Study Bible* (notes for Luke 2 : 8,13)].

Why do many Christians celebrate 25th day of December, if that is not when Jesus was born? The Roman Catholic Church chose the date. Because Rome dominated most of the 'Christian' world for centuries, the date became tradition throughout most of Christendom. The original significance of December 25 is that it was a well-known festival day celebrating the annual return of the sun. December 21 is the winter solstice, shortest day of the year and thus a key date on the Roman calendar, and December 25 is the first day that ancients could clearly note that the days were definitely getting longer and the sunlight was returning. Therefore, Christmas on the December 25 has the same pagan origin as sanctifying Sunday instead of Saturday! Those that reject Sunday as the day of rest but honor Christ's birth on December 25 are ignorant or hypocrites (see James 2 : 10 - 12)!

The various misconceptions about Christ's birth illustrate the need to always test everything we hear against God's Word, no matter what the source is. The Bible is the final authority. Despite human misconceptions about God and His Truth, the facts about Jesus are more marvelous than words can express. Christ was indeed born of a virgin in the city of Bethlehem exactly as prophesied many centuries before. Jesus was conceived in Mary, not by man, but by the Holy Spirit of God. As the apostle John reveals, Jesus existed before the Creation of the world (read John 1). He is part of the Holy Godhead, Father, Son and Holy Spirit. He exists from eternity to eternity, without a beginning. It is why He did not make His birth in the flesh a special event. The Son of God came in human form for a purpose, which is to die as a willing sacrifice in payment for the sins of humankind, that He may provide eternal salvation as a gift to all who will accept it and follow Him. If there's a day in Jesus' fleshly life worthy of being honored, His birthday should be the least, not only for many reasons given in this Testimony, but also for the importance of His earthly mission, that is to be offered as a sacrifice for Adam's sin. Indeed, between the two events related to this mission, 'crucifixion' and 'resurrection', the first is the most important for two reasons: His death on the cross was prefigured by centuries of sacrifices in Jewish history, and secondly, we are cleansed by the shedding of His matchless blood; even more, resurrection has also an important significance to fulfill the prophecy and make all His life and teachings genuine.

Christmas and its symbols, the days, the seasons and the years made holy by human powers and introduced maliciously in Christian worship in the name of Christ are lies that only the blind ones can follow. They are against the infallible Word of God, which forbids us to add or to take away any jot from it. They are but traditions of men to honor themselves instead of honoring their Creator. Making the holy Word of God to say what it does not, is a sin against the Holy Spirit who inspires it (Matthew 12 : 31). People do not honor their Creator, they slander Him and make Him a Liar, they covet His throne, steal His power and enslave Him by giving Him a false birthday, they tell lie to their followers by making idols to Him . . .

In the Bible, we read about those that carved idols out of wood or stone, and worshipped their own 'creation' as if it were the 'God' of Truth. If many teachers of the Bible affirm that biblical truth is to be determined by our own personal experiences, is this not the same as erecting our own doctrinal 'god' who is the creation of our own hands? Instead of saying, "it must be true because this is my experience, my instruction, the theology I learned . . ." would not truth be better served if the Bible determines whether our experiences were true, than the other way around?

Lie is the first sin that destroyed the relationship between the Mighty and Holy Creator and Man, holiness being the lone tie that binds Him to His creature. Our concept of the holiness of God determines how we view sin. If God is all love and no justice, sin will not be much of a concern to the believer. However, if God is holy, and He is just, He cannot have anything to do with the guilty sinner, except for judgment. This is why the atonement of Christ was so necessary to humanity. The horrible suffering and death of Jesus on the cross, was because of your sin and mine, for the non-repentant sinner will surely die! Then, why is it so easy for Christians to forget the depth and horribleness of sin, even after knowing the graphic detail of what Jesus has suffered! This can only be explained by an astonishingly crass attitude of unbelief and ingratitude. Either to continue in sin is to have a low view of what Christ has suffered, or it is tantamount to unbelief in the atonement of Christ!

By reflecting upon the love of God that is revealed to us in the sufferings of Christ, it makes one wonder why we placidly resign ourselves to sin instead of reeling in horror over the slightest occurrence of sin in us! The very sin that one commits is the very thing that put Jesus on the cross! Sin, that horrible and soul-damning act, is the punctuation mark of unbelief! What is our attitude towards the very thing that has crucified our Lord? Can we love and cherish that which cost Jesus so dearly? Some may say that they dislike sin, yet preach that we cannot be alive without sinning. This, my friends, is a statement of faith and belief in one's personal experience, not the teaching from Scripture!

The question we should be asking is whether this belief reflects the God of Scripture, or whether it reflects an imaginary "god" of our own making. The only way to know is to seek and believe what God has to say about it! What did Jesus accomplish on the cross? Does the atonement of Christ provide hope for freedom from sinning altogether? Alternatively, the believer seeking forgiveness of sins does get only a partial deliverance from sin? What is promised in Scripture, and what is necessary for the Christian? These questions are essential to ensure that we are worshiping and believing the One True God, and not some "gods" of our own invention and created in man's own image. Faith in a false "god" will not save our souls from the torments of hell and eternal death; neither faith in Santa Claus will deliver us from our sins.

The question is whether a believer has to sin or not. What we can infer from this is what God reveals in Scripture concerning sin and humans will indicate what He accomplishes through the atonement of His Son. We do not have to wander in ambiguity over what God wills, and what God does in the believer concerning deliverance from sin. God is not cruel in leaving us clueless about sin and the atonement.

What is our concept of God? What is our attitude towards sin? How do the two relate? Do we have "God," or a "god"? The Book of the books reads, "*Let the wicked forsake his way, and the unrighteous man his thoughts: let him return to the Lord, and He will have mercy on him; and to our God, for He will abundantly pardon.*" (Isaiah 55 : 7). A pungent conviction of sin requires a high conception of God and a pure standard of morals. It is sad for us as Christians to claim to know God but still have sins we are not ready to forsake. The Scriptures tell us that there are those who believe in God, while their iniquities separate them from their God, and their sins hid His face from them, that He will not hear their prayers; for, their hands are defiled with blood, and their fingers with iniquity, while their lips speak lies, their tongue mutter perverseness (read Isaiah 59 : 2 - 3).

It is time to *"Lament and mourn and weep! Let your laughter be turned to mourning and your joy to gloom. Humble yourselves in the sight of the Lord, and he will lift you up"* (James 4 : 9, 10).

Making certain religious days holy by the force of their authority and philosophy is the arrogance for the leaders and ignorance for their followers. There is not one place in the Bible where anything is holy, except that be made holy by the mouth of the 'I AM.' Only Him, as the Creator, can decide which person, place, year, month or day is holy. No matter how hard we try, we cannot make anything or anyone holy, because holiness is not dependent on our actions or decision; but it is God's attribute.

Let us insist here: Holiness is solely dependent on His determination and greatness. In the same way, there is no longer the holy week, the holy month, the holy year since the ancient dispensation had ended. Even some religious people had made themselves 'holy father'! O Lord, have mercy. Listen this complaint, "*Then He said to me, 'Have you seen this, o son of man? Turn again, you will see greater abominations than these'. So He brought me into the inner court of the LORD'S house; and there, at the door of the temple of the LORD, between the porch and the altar, were about twenty-five men with their backs toward the temple of the LORD and their faces toward the east, and they were worshiping the sun toward the east. And He said to me, 'Have you seen this, o son of man? Is it a trivial thing to the house of Judah to commit the abominations which they commit here? For they have filled the land with violence; then they have returned to provoked Me to anger. Indeed they put the branch to their nose. Therefore I also will act in fury, My eye will not spare nor will I have pity . . ."* (Ezekiel 8 : 15 - 18). Have mercy Lord God!

We see here sun worship starting long before Christ's ministry on earth.

XV—SO, KEEP THE LAW!

For he is not a Jew who is one outwardly, nor is circumcision that which is outward in the flesh; but he is a Jew who is one inwardly, and circumcision is that of the heart, in the Spirit, not in the letter; whose praise is not from men but of God. (Romans 2 : 25 - 29)

IT IS A known maxim that 'the Bible, the Bible only', is the religion of Protestants, and in my youth as a student in a Catholic school, I was taught to despise the Bible as a deceitful book of separated Christians; so I did not touch it until I finished University.

According to the sixth article of the Church of England Beliefs, "Holy Scripture containeth all things necessary to salvation"; and in the Westminster Confession, it is in like manner declared that "the whole counsel of God, concerning all things necessary for His own glory, man's salvation, faith, and life, is either expressly set down in Scripture, or by good and necessary consequence deduced from Scripture; unto which nothing at any time is to be added, whether by new revelations of the Spirit, or traditions of men". Moreover, the Bible, as the Word of God is called 'Torah' meaning 'Law' in Jewish culture. On the other hand, the dictionary defines 'law' as 'a rule of conduct or action prescribed or formally recognized as binding or enforced by a controlling authority of a community'.

Let us get an example from daily life: if you drive into a private toll highway, knowingly or not, you are under a law to pay the owner a fee for using his highway. However, if the government purchases the highway use rights and makes your access free, you are no longer obligated under that law to pay a toll. Therefore, God as the Lawgiver is the controlling Authority of His people in every age and generation.

Then, the nation of Israel was given the written laws from the very Hand of God, as their Legislator, laws that no other nation on Earth was given; which laws were given to be kept as long as they were in force according to the controlling Authority. However, Satan suggests first to Israelites and to Christians that 'no one can keep the whole law' to accuse God as unfair and dictator, asking impossible things of His people!

As citizens of the free countries, does your city have laws? How many laws does your state, your province, your country have? It is evidence that we are living with tens of thousands of laws, which we could easily break. However, how many did you break today? We guess none, for everyone affords to keep them correctly for fear of the penalty or to prove one's loyalty to the government and love for the country! Then, if you did make a wrong turn on the road, you knew you did not have to; you could have kept that law too. If you get a traffic ticket, you have to pay the fine in order to be a law-abiding citizen again.

Therefore, the common argument, that no one could keep the law and the only way to salvation is solely by faith in Christ is a bluff set up by the Enemy of Christ to deceive the weak and the blind ones. Yes, it is by the blood of Christ that we gain the entrance to heaven; however, that blood is imputed to men by grace through faith and by the works of the Law of Ten commandments. Many scriptures in the Bible echo this theme: Keep the Law (Matthew 19 : 17; Luke 8 : 15; John 14 : 15, 23).

Could a loving and unchanging God and Father ask of His beloved children something which could not be done? During all His walk and dealings with His chosen people, there was never the complaint "Why Lord, no one can keep the whole Law, so how could you ask us to do such a difficult thing?"; for they understood that the Law could be kept; the Bible asserts that they kept it (read Joshua 22 : 2 Judges. 2 : 17)

The loving Lord Creator does not command to do the impossibility! Keeping the Law given by love is easy to those that love Him. It is why He promises life to those that keep His Law which is not burdensome (Luke 16 : 17).

Keeping the Law in a world under the power of Satan does not mean a person never does wrong; it means that if wrong was wrought, the person should follow the procedure for forgiveness that is in the Law. In so doing, the person has kept the Law and thus he is a law-keeper.

Many Scriptures quoted above in the previous chapters have already given an answer to the question 'why keep the Sabbath?'; nevertheless, let us give more light as it is the purpose of this Testimony. The Sabbath or 'rest' is found in the Word of God in the beginning of Mankind, when God the Creator, on the seventh day of the first week, "*ended His work which He had done, and He rested on the seventh day from all His work which He had done. Then God blessed the seventh day and sanctified it, because in it He rested from all His work which God had created and made.*" (Genesis 2. 2, 3)

Latter, on Mount Sinai, concluding a covenant with the Israelites as His peculiar chosen people according to the promise made to Abraham, Isaac and Jacob, God gave them His Law of Ten Commandments ratified with the blood of the animals. The ceremony was so great and solemn that there were thunders and lightning, and a thick cloud upon the mount, and the voice of the trumpet exceeding loud. The scene there was so dreadful that the people were afraid and asked Moses himself to talk to them instead of the Most High God Himself.

Why did God make all that marvelous display of His power on Sinai before giving the two tablets of Law to seal his covenant with His people? Why did He want that all people to be on the Mount, instead of calling only Moses to Him and then giving him the Ten Commandments? Why did people have to be prepared and purified for seven days before going to meet the Most High? Is the Sabbath worthy to be remembered in a Christian Church? Did the Almighty God need a rest for a six-day work? Even, as we know Who our Maker is, did He really need six days to finish His work of creation? Think about all this and marvel at the message God wanted to send to His people!

In our actual state of finite creatures born in sin, we are unable to understand fully and to answer all our concerns on those questions by ignorance or hypocrisy; but the day will come when every question will be answered! However, the Word of God gives us now whatever we need for our salvation. This is the fourth commandment as written by the celestial Majesty on the first tablet of the Decalogue, "*Remember the Sabbath day, to keep it holy. Six days you shall labor, and do all your work, but the seventh day is the Sabbath of the Lord your God. In it you shall do nor your female servant, nor your cattle, nor your stranger who is within your* gates. For in six days the Lord made the heaven and the earth, the sea, and all that is in them, and rested the seventh day. Therefore the Lord blessed the Sabbath day, and hallowed it." (Exodus 20 : 8 - 11)

Seen too closely and attentively, this commandment is complete and clear enough to be understood by men and women that are well minded. However, to prevent all malicious devices of the Prince of this world and Father of the liars, God explains it more and more through precepts and principles, and through His prophets.

All kind of task must be done and finished in six first days of the week, and then to rest completely on Sabbath which is a holy day. To mark a sign upon His children, which obey Him, God declared: ". . . *Surely My Sabbaths you shall keep, for it is a sign between you and me throughout your generations that you may know that I am the Lord who sanctifies you. You shall keep the Sabbath therefore, for it is holy unto you. Everyone who profanes it shall surely be put to death; for whoever does any work on it, that person shall be cut off from among his people. Work shall be done for six days, but the seventh is the Sabbath of rest, holy to the Lord . . ."* (Exodus 31 : 13 - 15). Here is the fourth commandment put in another way specifying that, as God sanctified the Sabbath, in the same manner His faithful people who keep it accordingly are sanctified and made holy! No other commandment among the Ten bears this mark of sanctity for us!

Exodus 16 : 22 - 26 designs the sixth day, our today Friday, as the day of preparation, as the last day of the week of work for cooking, baking or boiling the food and finishing all kind of work, before the Sabbath starts at sunset: "*On the sixth day the people gathered twice as much food—four quarts for every person. When all the leaders of the community came and told this to Moses, he said to them, 'This is what the Lord commanded, because tomorrow is the Sabbath, the Lord's holy day of rest. Bake what you want to bake, and boil what you want to boil today* [our Friday]. *Save the rest of the food until tomorrow* [Saturday] *morning.' So the people saved until the next morning, as Moses had commanded, and none of it began to stink or have worms in it. Moses told the people, 'Eat the food you gathered yesterday* [Friday]. *Today* [Saturday] *is a Sabbath, the Lord's day of rest; you will not find any out in the field today. You should gather the food for six days, but the seventh day is a Sabbath day. On that day there will not be any food on the ground*" (The everyday study Bible—New century Version, *emphasis added*).

The Creator of all Nature performs here two miracles to put a sign on His holy Day:—no manna was found in the field on Sabbath;—versus to the manna gathered along the week which got worms if kept till the next morning, the manna gathered on the sixth day to be eaten in the next morning on the Sabbath day did not breed worms nor stink.

Does God continue to perform miracles today? O yes, for He is the same forever. Only believe and trust Him!

As it was not enough for Him to forbid cooking and boiling on Sabbath; the Lord, because of His matchless love, not willing any one to perish, took the culinary problem at its roots, and forbade even the kindling of fire on His Day of rest: "*Then Moses gathered all the congregation of the children of Israel together, and said to them, These are the words which the Lord has commanded you to do: Work shall be done for six days, but the seventh day shall be a holy day for you, a Sabbath of rest to the Lord. Whoever does any work on it shall be put to death. You shall kindle no fire throughout your dwellings on the Sabbath day.*" (Exodus 35 : 1 - 3)

Some Sabbath keepers, pushed in disobedience to this rule of cooking or kindling fire on Sabbath by the false teachers among them, justify themselves that the Bible speaks here about the fire only for the blacksmith forge! Though the word 'blacksmith' is not found either in the verses before or in those following this statement!

O Lord, when Satan binds us, your light is but dimmed for us!

The Creator, by the mouth of the prophet Jeremiah, taught the people that, bringing a load on Sabbath was unacceptable, and said: "*Thus says the Lord: take heed to yourselves, and bear no burden on the Sabbath day, nor bring it in by the gates of Jerusalem; Nor carry a burden out of your houses on the Sabbath day, nor do any work, but hallow the Sabbath day, as I commanded your fathers.*" (Jeremy 17 : 21, 22)

There are also the precepts to fix the duration of this holy day, which is from sunset on the sixth day to sunset on the seventh (Mark 15 : 42); long displacements or travel on Sabbath not allowed (Acts 1 : 12); even seeking our own pleasure and speaking out our own words on Sabbath not tolerated (Isaiah 58 : 13, 14).

Foreseeing crisis and trials to come at the end of times, prepared by Satan to molest God's people, Christ advised His disciples what to do in preparation of those hard times. He urged them earnestly, saying: "*And pray that your flight may not be in the winter, or on the Sabbath. For then there will be great tribulation, such as has not been since the beginning of the world until this time, no, nor even shall be*". (Matthew 24 : 20, 21) Imagine someone remaining in his house while his city is under fire of the adverse conquering army! Christ asks us only to pray and wait for deliverance! Only by faith as small as a mustard seed (Matthew 17 : 20), we can speak to the mountain to move into the lake and it will be so! There should not be any compromising act when it comes to obey. In this, the three young Hebrew captives in Babylon have given us a big lesson of trust in God, when they were asked to bow down king Nebuchadnezzar's statue and were facing death in the blazing furnace if they would not obey the king's command (read the story in Daniel, chapter 3, verses 7 through 18.

Do we really take heed to the Lord's warning? Do we pray earnestly to the Lord that the trouble, wars and disasters, hurricanes may not fall upon us on His holy Day of rest, as He recommended us? Are we trustful enough to our God that we may not betray Him if disasters and famine fall upon us? Or, do we think that those promises of God's deliverance are not made for us or they are reported in the Word only as ancient time fables worth to be put in garbage today?

Now it is time to make all our prayer meetings and home worship moments to claim these promises and to be heavenly minded, not only that these calamities could not reach us, but the most important, to accept death of this body that our souls may be saved in the day of judgment (see Luke 9 : 24 - 26)

However, an unpredictable, charitable and unselfish work is tolerated, ". . . *What man is there among you who has one sheep, and if it falls into a pit on the Sabbath, will not lay hold of it and lift it out? Of how much more value then is a man than a sheep. Therefore it is lawful to do good* [for your neighbor's sake] *on the Sabbath.*" (Matthew 12 : 11. 12, *emphasis added*). Today, those that suppress the fourth commandment use selfishly this verse to excuse their wrong doings, even though many of them have never had one sheep of their own to care for!

It makes me laugh when listening to many learned Christians arguing that the Sabbath commandment was a Jewish law and, as freely saved ones by the blood of Christ, they are no longer under such kind of law.

They forget that the Decalogue in its wholeness was given to Jewish people: Christ Himself being born in a Jewish nation and having kept fully His Father's commandments: "*My food is to do the will of him that sent me . . .*", He asserts in John 4 : 34

Inspired by the Lawgiver, Isaiah writes, "*Do not let the son of the stranger who has joined himself to the Lord, speak, saying, the Lord has utterly separated me from His people . . . , everyone who keeps from polluting the Sabbath, and holds fast My covenant, Even them I will bring to My holy mountain, and make them joyful in My house of prayer . . . For My house shall be called an house of prayer for all people.*" (Isaiah 56 : 3 - 7)

Today, the millions of Christians, some of them sincerely, take Sunday, which is the first day of week, as the day of rest instead of Saturday, the seventh day. Who made the change? For what purpose? The preceding chapters have already given the light on these two questions.

XVI—ONE IS THE HEAD

The Christ

For the husband is the head of the wife, even as Christ is the head of the church: and he is the Saviour of the body. (Ephesians 5 : 23)

AFTER HIS RESURRECTION, Christ appeared many times to His disciples for forty days before ascending to heavens, giving them the last instructions and urging them to keep all He taught them before His death, such as, "*. . . till heaven and earth pass, one jot or one title shall in no wise pass from the law, till all be fulfilled*". Moreover, "*. . . if you love me keep my commandments.*"

Moreover, the records of the Bible on Creation, Flood, Israelites wanderings, and on the birth, teachings and life of the Christ and the birth of the Christian Church are not the live reports from the journalists watching and registering these events on cameras and iPads, for "*. . . the prophecy never came by the will of man, but holy men of God spoke as they were moved by the Holy Spirit*". (2 Peter 1 : 21), but writing according to what they were told by the Holy Spirit, about events that had taken place many years or many centuries before the writers were born!

What the Church had to "*bind or loose on earth*" is not what the Sovereign God, as Supreme Legislator, had established and put in Law; but if "*. . . your brother sins against you; go and tell him his fault between you and him alone. If he hears you, you have gained your brother . . . if he refuses to hear them* [the witnesses], *tell it to the church. But if he refuses even to hear the church . . .*" (Matthew 18 : 15 - 17a, *emphasis added*). Then comes the conclusion of the matter, "*. . . let him be to you like a heathen and a tax collector. Assuredly, I say to you, whatever you bind on* earth will be bound in heaven, and whatever you loose on earth will be loosed in heaven." (Matthew 18 : 17b - 18)

Another trick and falsity is taken in the misinterpretation of the Revelation of apostle John, chapter 1 verse 10, "*I was in the Spirit on the Lord's Day, and I heard behind me a loud voice, as of a trumpet*".

I am wondering why so many learned teachers and respected so-called 'theologians' believe that this 'Lord's day' means Sunday!

If there were people which can justify that this 'Lord's day' is a day of the week, they can only be the Sabbath keeping Christians, for the Lord calls the seventh day "*My Sabbath*" or "*My holy day*" (Exodus 31 : 31; Isaiah 56 : 4; 58 : 13; Ezekiel 20; 12, 20). Jesus is Himself the '*Lord of the Sabbath*' but never 'Lord of Sunday'. Yes, the seventh-day Sabbath is His because, as Creator of the Universe, He set it apart, He rested in it, He blessed and He sanctified it.

Nevertheless, when we go meekly and prayerfully through God's Prophecy and Revelation, this 'Lord's day' in the Revelation of John is not Sunday, neither Saturday: it is not a day of the week.

It is simply about the day of the end time, for the events John was shown are about to take place at the second coming of the Lord! The heavens were opened to him and he watched the Seat of the Lord (see Revelation 1 : 19, 4 : 1 - 2, 10 : 1, 2, 17 : 3 - 5 . . .). The Lord's Day in these verses, is the day when the Lord will come to vindicate His Holy Law, which men had despised, to pay to everyone according to his deeds. Apostle Paul stresses it clearly in his First Letter to the Thessalonians, chapter 5, verses 2 and 3, saying, "*For you yourselves know perfectly that the day of the Lord so comes as a thief in the night. For when they shall say, 'Peace and safety'! then sudden destruction comes upon them, as labor pains upon a pregnant woman. And they shall not escape*" Apostle Peter also depicts the soon coming of our Lord in these words, "*But the day of the Lord will come as a thief in the night, in which the heavens will pass away with a great noise, and the elements will melt with fervent heat; both the earth and the works that are in it will be burnt up*" (2 Peter 3 : 10)

Some false teachers had tried to make many calculations to discover and set up that awful day, but in vain! For Christ Himself warned us clearly that nobody, even the holy angels do not know that day!

When God decides to speak to His children the prophets, He does not choose a special day or a day of rest to give His revelations. He needs but a heart sanctified and prepared to bear His messages of life and His testimonies to His beloved ones.

The expression, 'the day of the Lord' is already found many times in the Old Testament, long time before the resurrection of Christ. In Isaiah 13 : 6 - 9, it is written, "*Wail; for the day of the Lord is at hand! It will come as destruction from the Almighty. Therefore all hands will be limp, every man's heart will melt . . . Behold, the day of the Lord comes, cruel, with both wrath and fierce anger, to lay the land desolate; and He will destroy its sinners thereof from it.*" (Read also Zephaniah 1 : 7 - 9)

Praise the Lord that many dictionaries today found in the world still define these two days, Saturday and Sunday, in the same way as in the Bible; even though other dictionaries in different languages found here and there, Sunday has become the seventh day and Monday the first one! This is an intellectual trickery! Fortunately, many churches do not follow yet, this wrong way of counting days of the week, even though many of them do not consider Saturday as a day of rest blessed by the Most High!

It is sad, but a matter of fact, that Church authorities had decided something different from what the Bible teaches. We read: "Sunday is our mark of authority. The church is above the Bible, and this transference of Sabbath observance [to Sunday] is proof of that fact." ("Catholic Record", London/Ontario, 1. Sept. 1923, *emphasis added*) This is another statement confirming the responsibility of the Catholic Church in the change: "Of course the Catholic Church claims that the change was her act . . . And the act is a MARK of her ecclesiastical authority in religious things." (H. F. Thomas, Chancellor of Cardinal Gibbons).

It is startling and at the same time troubling that the Lutheran Church with the many sister protestant churches has united with the Roman Catholic church in breaking this special commandment, and thereby taking part in the falsification of the Testament of Jesus. This is what a few Protestants have to say about this change in the day of rest:—"And where are we told in the Scriptures that we are to keep the first day at all? We are commanded to keep the seventh day, but we are nowhere commanded to keep the first day." (Isaac Williams: "*Plain Sermons on the Catechism*", p. 334,336).—"On the other hand there is no command in the New Testament that establishes or provides for the celebration of Sunday. And of course there does not exist any command that says that Sunday is going to assume the role of the Sabbath (Saturday) for the Christian." (Catechism note (22) "Sabbaten og søndagen" by Odd Sverre Hove. *The Norwegian newspaper:* "Dagen" 7/10-95).

The fact that many Christians hold to the observance of the first day of the week as the day of rest in memory of the resurrection of Jesus (for some of them) is not from the holy Scriptures. The scriptures state that Jesus is the Lord of the Sabbath (Mark 2 : 27, 28). He created this world and He instituted the day of rest. It is even written that ". . . *All things were made through Him, and without Him nothing was made that was made.*" (John 1 : 1 - 3; Genesis 1 : 26) Therefore, if the day of rest was to be changed, Jesus would be the One to make that change, but this He has not done. The Bible says that God blessed and hallowed the seventh day. Where is it written in the Scripture that Jesus has asked us to stop keeping the seventh day holy, commanding us to keep the first day in remembrance of His resurrection instead? Are you able to find anywhere that He has changed the Ten Commandments, including the command to keep the seventh day Sabbath holy, the commandment which Himself wrote with His own finger; or that the Father or the Son has made holy and blessed the first day of the week? And S. V. McCasland says ". . . such a celebration might just as well be monthly or annually and still be an observance of that particular day (as an event of His resurrection)." (From *Sabbath to Sunday*, Samuelle Bacchiocchi, Pontifical Gregorian University Press, *emphasis added*)

The Sabbath was instituted long before the first Jew, Abraham, even existed; in the beginning, at Creation, and Jesus says that it was made for Man (Mark 2 : 27, 28). It was made for you and me, not for the Jews alone. In addition, Jesus says that as long as we see the heaven above our heads and the earth beneath our feet, God's Ten Commandments are valid and unchangeable (Matthew 5 : 17, 18). They are just as valid today in the new covenant through Christ as it was in the first covenant with the Jews. The only change in the new covenant from the old is that we may come directly to Jesus and have forgiveness for our sins without the system of sacrificial offerings that were done away with, since Jesus has come as the true sacrificial Lamb, and He has been sacrificed once and for all, and also all feasts and sabbaths related to that old system were taken away with it (Hebrew 9 : 24 - 28) Therefore, though you are not a Jew according to the flesh, by your second birth in Christ, which was born as Jew, you are spiritually a Jew. It is why Paul regards the Gentiles converted to Christianity as spiritual Jews, even though they are non-Israelite and literally uncircumcised (Galatians 6 : 16); and he states, ". . . *remember*

FORTUNAT TSHIMANGA-MUKADI

that you, once Gentiles in the flesh—who are called Uncircumcision by what is called the Circumcision made in the flesh by hands—that at that time you were without Christ . . ." (Ephesians 2 : 11 - 13). Using the analogy of an olive tree, he explains how converted Gentiles are members of the *'Israel of God'* (Romans 11 : 13 - 21). Because the Law given to the Jewish people is holy and eternal, you are accountable to it. Paul makes it plain showing that God's act of inclusion of Gentiles in His special nation should not be regarded as a favor to the Gentiles over the Israelites, *"For . . ."* he explains, *". . . if you were cut out of the olive tree which is wild by nature, and were grafted contrary to nature into a cultivated alive tree, how much more will these, who are natural branches, be grafted into their own olive tree?".* (Romans 11 : 24) Moreover, out of all the Ten Commandments, only the fourth is not Jewish, for the Creator Himself rested upon it on one hand and on the other, He cannot commit adultery nor lie nor make idols to worship them, as we are able to! God does not favor anybody, for, Jew and Gentile alike have equal access to the promises of their Maker through the Lamb of God (Galatians 3 : 28)

Let us insist to make it clearer! After instituting with splendor and majesty, the seventh-day rest at the end of His six-day work of creation (Genesis chapter 2 verses 2 and 3), the Eternal Legislator set up through His Word, statutes, ordinances and principles, to make everything clearer for our benefit concerning this holy day:

- Exodus 16 : 23 - 29: all work of cooking and baking should be done and finished before the end of the sixth day at sunset;
- Exodus 20 : 8 - 11: the Sabbath is included in the Ten Holy Commandments on the first tablet of stone which shows our love to our Creator; (refer also to Deuteronomy 5 : 12 - 14);
- Exodus 31 : 12 - 17: the Sabbath is a sign between the Creator and His creatures that He is their Maker, that in keeping it faithfully, we testify of His creative power which is the highest of His attributes; (see Ezekiel 20 : 12, 20);
- Exodus 35 : 2 - 3: Death penalty for whoever defiles the holy Sabbath day.
- Numbers 15 : 32 - 36: even a light work as gathering sticks on the Sabbath is forbidden by the Lawgiver, (see also Matthew 28 : 1, Mark 16 : 1; Luke 23 : 54 to 24 . . .):

- Nehemiah 10 : 31: not selling nor buying on the Sabbath, nor doing any business on this holy day; (read again Nehemiah 13 : 15 - 22);
- Isaiah 56 : 1 - 8: Everyone, eunuchs or strangers to Israelite people, who keep themselves from defiling the Sabbath in any sense, are blessed and God will bring them to His holy Mountain;
- Isaiah 58 : 13 - 14: even speaking the vain words on the Sabbath day is forbidden;
- Isaiah 66 : 22 - 23: the Sabbath will be kept and honored in the New Jerusalem;
- In Jeremiah chapter 17 verses 21 to 27, God stresses that bringing any burden on Sabbath is forbidden;
- Amos 8 : 5: rushing to go to work before the end of the Sabbath is a sin;
- Matthew 12 : 1 - 12; Jesus, the Lord of the Sabbath instructed us that doing good on the Sabbath is lawful, refer also to Mark 3 : 2 - 4, Luke 6 : 1 - 9, 13 : 10 - 16, 14 : 1 - 5; John 5 : 9 - 18, 9 : 14 - 15;
- Matthew 24 : 20 - 21: to earnestly pray that no tribulation may fall upon us on Sabbath day; the carpenter Jesus used the holy hour of the Sabbath to preach and heal, see also Mark 6 : 2, Luke 4 : 16, 31; Mark 1 : 21;
- Mark 2 : 23 - 28: the Sabbath was made for the benefit of Man and his offspring ;
- Acts 13 : 14, 27, 42 - 43: the disciples, as their Master, used the Sabbath day to preach and heal, read also Acts 16 verse 13, Acts 17 verses 2 - 3 and Acts 18 : 3 - 4.

These are the implementation measures promulgated to help God's people to understand fully and to comply with the fourth commandment as a whole, that they may be faultless, nor be deceived and tossed to and fro by human philosophy and satanic devices. The psalmist sang,

"Blessed are the undefiled in the way, who walk in the law of the Lord. Blessed are those who keep His testimonies, who seek Him with all their heart."

The Law of God is "manifested not only in 'commandments', but also in wrath of God which ". . . *is revealed from heaven against all the ungodliness and unrighteousness of men, who suppress the truth from unrighteousness"* (Romans 1 : 18). So the special and holy people of God, like Abraham, are obedient people, called from all nations, who have chosen not to live by bread alone, but also, ". . . *by every word that proceeds from the mouth of God"* (Matthew 4 : 4). God's Spirit working in such ones to produce faith and obedience, making them special to God. "It is also the duty of the Church, in the ever-changing situations to interpret the divine Law according to the revelation of God given to the Church" (SDA Bible Students' Source Book—Commentary References Series, Volume 9, p. 565), without changing it nor lessening one letter of the Will of the Creator.

As Almighty God, Jesus would choose any other easy and comfortable way to redeem Man, but He came down to comply fully with the strictness of His Father's Law, for His food was to do the will of His Father, by dying on the Cross on behalf of Adam's sons and daughters.

He left His glorious seat, humbled Himself to death,
and the shameful death on the cross!
What a God!
He took upon Himself the likeness of His creatures and grew up
as a tender plant, to strengthen the weak and heal the bruised.
What a Savior!
As a worm, He was despised and rejected of those He
came to save; and made Himself a man of sorrow that
the ransomed ones might come joyfully to Zion.
What a Creator!
He was stricken and smitten of God, He was afflicted and wounded that
the children of Adam may have peace with the Father in His holy place.
What a long-suffering Man!
Crowned with thorns, He was mocked, undressed and
spat on the face by those He fed and cherished.
What a sacrifice!
In all His sufferings and humiliation, he opened His mouth
but to bless and console the women from Jerusalem.
What a Lord!

XVII—PAUL HAD NO AUTHORITY
TO CHANGE THE LAW

Blotting out the handwriting of ordinances that was against us, which was contrary to us, and took it out of the way, nailing it to his cross; And having spoiled principalities and powers, he made a show of them openly, triumphing over them in it. Let no man therefore judge you in meat, or in drink, or in respect of a holy day, or of the new moon, or of the sabbath days: Which are a shadow of things to come; but the body is of Christ. (Colossians 2 : 14 - 17)

THIS TEXT IS used as one of strong justifications that the sacredness of Saturday as Sabbath is no longer in effect under the New Covenant; and some of our fellow Christians emphasize that observing Saturday as a day of rest is the sign of 'missing the mark', because, they explain, Sabbath day belongs to the old dispensation which is no longer in effect, it is the 'one of the weak and beggarly elements' of the Law, useless in the new dispensation. This is often cited as a direct parallel to the Book of Numbers, chapters 28 and 29, where the Sabbath is described alongside burnt offerings, new moons and all things that have been made obsolete with the first coming of Christ.

Many other scriptures are referred to as proof of the end of the seventh-day Sabbath observance, especially other pauline epistles are often quoted, such as Romans 14 : 5 - 6, which states, "*One person esteems one day above another; another esteems every day alike. Let each be fully convinced in his own mind. He who observes the day, observed it to the Lord; and he who does not observe the day, to the Lord he does not observe it . . . "* and Galatians 4 : 9 - 11. Essentially, they suggest that Paul's claim here is that ritual observance of days, including the weekly Sabbath, is no longer prescribed under the New Covenant. Therefore, they insist, ritual observance of a weekly Sabbath is thus not required, but is optional according to the conscience of each individual Christian. However, Paul is surely referring to the Jewish festivals rather than the weekly Sabbath.

His second letter to the Corinthians, in chapter 3 : 2 - 3, is also often used, *"You are our epistle written in our hearts, known and read by all men; clearly you are an epistle of Christ, ministered by us, written not with ink but by the Spirit of the living God; not on tablets of stone, but on tablets of flesh, that is, of the heart."* They understand here that "Christians should no longer follow a law written *"on tablets of stone"* that is, the Ten Commandments, but follow a law written upon *'fleshy tablets of the heart'"*. The question is 'Which law written on the heart is it'? As we know, on the tablets of stone, there was not only the fourth commandment, but also the nine other Commandments as a whole! No sincere Christian, even the less learned one, can think that in this new law written upon the 'fleshly tablets of heart', adultery is allowed, robbery is praised, murder is permitted! The controversy continues with verses 7 to 11, *"But if the ministry of death, written and engraved on stones, was glorious . . . which glory was passing away . . . For if that which is passing away was glorious, what remains is much more glorious"*. Some non-sabbatarians claim, "this is a direct reference to the Ten Commandments; therefore, they argue, new covenant Christians are no longer under the Mosaic law, and thus Sabbath-keeping is no longer required; the new covenant 'Law' is based entirely upon love, and Love is considered the fulfillment of the Law", according to how they understand Romans 13 : 10.

Finally, other non-sabbatarians frequently use the epistle to the Hebrews, from chapter 3 : 7 to chapter 4 : 11 to dismiss the keeping of the seventh-day Sabbath as being no longer relevant, regular and literal day of rest, but instead, they explain, "is a symbolic metaphor for the eternal 'rest' that Christians enjoy in Christ, which was in turn prefigured by the Promised Land of Canaan".

In addition to the pauline teachings that appear to rescind the Sabbath, Jesus Himself is recorded as redefining the Sabbath law. Some examples of this include Luke 13 : 10 - 17, John 5 : 17, and John 9 : 13 - 16. As Jesus proclaimed Himself to be *'Lord of the Sabbath'* who has *"fulfilled the Law"*, this has been interpreted by many Christians to mean that those who follow Him are no longer bound by the Fourth Commandment, though the verb 'to fulfill' does not mean 'to suppress' or 'give away'. How one could pretend being follower of Christ and in the same time deny His teaching and fight against His unchanging will? Arrogance, blindness or ignorance? God alone knows.

A righteous and unfailing Lawgiver is He who honors His own decisions and, if abolishing them, should do so in the same manner He established them with display, splendor and magnificence and by written decrees, as He did it on Mount Sinai. The Son strongly emphasized saying, not one Jot or spot could be changed in the Decalogue until the end of this sinful world!

We have to notice that the Sabbath was to be kept by the Israelites as a perpetual covenant between them and God forever! Is there any evidence whatsoever those Israelites who became Christians were to forsake that sacred covenant and start keeping another day? Does God have a double standard when it comes to which day to keep as the Sabbath? No. Rather, according to the same Paul, Gentile Christians were to be *"grafted"* into Israel and become spiritual Israelites (reference to Romans 11 : 17, 24 and Galatians 3 : 28 - 29). This same Apostle was inspired to state very clearly that, *"For he is not a Jew who is one outwardly, nor is circumcision that which is outward in the flesh; but he is a Jew who is one inwardly; and circumcision is that of the heart, in the Spirit, not in the letter; whose praise is not from men but from God"* (Romans 2 : 28 - 29). For these reasons, Paul called the New Testament Church, *'the Israel of God'* (Galatians 6 : 16). Therefore, the truly converted Gentiles become part of spiritual Israel and have to obey the Ten Commandments, the great spiritual Law of the Creator. Surely, they must also obey the terms of the perpetual Sabbath covenant that the pre-incarnate Jesus made with Israel. It is a sign between Jesus Christ and His people forever!

In Isaiah 56, we find a remarkable prophecy set right in the midst of end-time prophecies, many of which refer to the time just ahead of us. In this setting, God gives this pointed instruction to men and women of all nations: *"Blessed is the man who does this, and the son of man who lays* hold on it; who keeps from defiling the Sabbath, and keeps his hand from doing any evil" (verse 2). A few verses later, God instructs the Gentiles or foreigners to keep His Sabbath and describes the blessings that would come from doing so: "*Do not let the son of the foreigner who has joined himself to the Lord, speak, saying, the Lord has utterly separated me from His people; nor let the eunuchs who keep My Sabbaths, and choose what pleases Me, and hold fast My covenant, even to them I will give in My house and within My walls a place and a name better than that of sons and daughters; I will give them an everlasting name that shall not be cut off. Also the sons of the foreigner who join themselves to the Lord, to serve Him, and to love the name of the Lord, to be His servants, everyone who keeps from defiling the Sabbath, and holds fast My covenant, even them I will bring to My holy mountain, and make them joyful in My house of prayer. Their burnt offerings and their sacrifices will be accepted on My altar; for My house shall be called a house of prayer for all nations*" (verses 3 to 7).

Jesus said that the Sabbath was made for 'Man', that is, for all humanity. Now notice how Jesus and the Apostles continually kept the seventh-day Sabbath, the same day that all the Jews around them were keeping.

God tells us repeatedly that Christ is the 'Light', the example of how we ought to live. It is amazing how many professing Christian leaders will give lip service to this statement, yet they 'reason' and argue and argue again; they argue against following Christ's perfect example in Sabbath-keeping and other acts of obedience to God's Law! Speaking of Jesus, the Gospel of John tells us that in Him was Life, and the Life was the Light of men. Moreover, the Light shines in the darkness, and the darkness does not comprehend it (John 1 : 4 - 5). It is sad and awful that many of us today really do not comprehend that 'Light' any more than did those in Jesus earthly days.

Later, Christ said, "*I am the light of the world. He who follows Me shall not walk in darkness, but have the light of life*" (John 8 : 12). Can a person reject Jesus' teaching, refuse to follow His example and the entire way of life He exemplified, and still claim to be His follower, pompously bearing His Name? God inspired Peter to instruct us, "*For to this you were called, because Christ also suffered for us, leaving us an EXAMPLE, that you should follow His steps: 'who committed no sin, nor was deceit found in His mouth.'*" (1 Peter 2 : 21 - 22, *emphasis added*)

Acts 20 : 7 says that, on the first day of the week, they came together to break bread, where Paul preached until midnight. This text arrogantly used as proof of the change of sacredness from Saturday to Sunday. One must remember, however, that according to Jewish tradition referring to Genesis 2 on creation and as described in Leviticus 23 : 32, a day begins when the sun goes down and it is counted from sunset to the following sunset. Then this meeting apparently gathered in the evening or went from noon until sunset. Therefore, those who believe that the early Christians kept the Sabbath on the seventh day understand clearly and justly, that this meeting (Acts 20 : 7) would have begun on Saturday and went on in the night, part of the first day (our today Sunday). Because the Jewish writers of the Bible, called 'Sunday night' what we call today 'Saturday evening or Saturday night', after the sun went down at around our 6: 00 PM!

Paul would have been preaching on Saturday night until midnight and then walked eighteen miles from Traos to Assos during Sunday hours: he would not have done so, if he had regarded Sunday as the day of rest, much less boarding a boat and continuing to travel to Mitylene and finally on to Chios. The Biblical evidence suggests that Paul was a lifelong Sabbath keeper for the sake of his background and profession of faith; and if Sunday were now the Sabbath for him on the sake of the new change of sacredness from Saturday to Sunday, then this journey would have been contrary to his character of faith and obedience. Therefore, those who claim that the practice of keeping Saturday holy had been abolished at Paul's time, and thus would have no impact on Paul's actions, have no solid proof to sustain this false assumption.

Anyway, the focus of the story is about Eutychus, his accident, and his resurrection, not the changing of the holiness of the days of the week from the seventh to the first. It is worth to be emphasized that no disciple, prophet, teacher, even the Son of Man had the power to change so easily, what the Mighty Creator has established with majesty and power!

Also it is referred to Acts 2 : 45 as a proof of the change, as the apostles went to the Temple in Jerusalem and broke bread from house to house 'daily'. There is no mention of the Sabbath, and it is debatable whether this is a reference to Communion. There are many instances of the Gospel being taught and preached on non-specific days as well as daily. There is one example in Mark 2 : 1 - 2 and another in Luke 19 : 47 - 20 : 1, where Jesus Himself taught and preached daily. Even breaking bread daily, which is our communion service today, could not be understood as an abolition of the sacredness of Saturday as day of rest; for, communion service is not related solely to the day of rest; as we know well that the first communion service officiated by Christ Himself was not done on a day of rest! The breaking of bread and the preaching of the gospel are merely mentioned as events that might take place on any day of the week and they confer no sacredness to any day of the week in which they are organized.

The majority of Christians, who sanctify Sunday, suggest these actions are indicative of a new reverence for God's acts in Christ, in connection with the first day of the week; and such ones believe that Sunday is a Sabbatical day, a resting day set aside for worship of God through Jesus Christ, the resurrected Savior, and they see no continuing obligation to keep Saturday ordinances in their 'Jewish' form. It is often argued by some Christian groups that the loss of special reverence for Saturday was due to a Great Apostasy in connection with the Constantinian shift; and most of the groups holding this belief see seventh day sabbatarianism as a mark of the restored church.

The issue over the name of the seventh day is actually a cultural question. Canada, United States, and England and some other few English-speaking countries, are actually a minority in calling Sunday the first day of the week and Saturday the last. In most of Europe and its ancient colonized countries in Africa and around the word, Monday is the first day, and Sunday indeed the seventh. Here are the Names of the Days of the Week in major European cultures (adapted from Information Please® Database, 2007, Pearson Education, Inc.)

Latin	English	German	French	Italian	Spanish
Dies Solis	Sunday	Sonntag	dimanche	domenica	domingo
Dies Lunae	Monday	Montag	lundi	lunedì	Lunes
Dies Martis	Tuesday	Dienstag	mardi	martedì	martes
Dies Mercurii	Wednesday	Mittwoch	mercredi	mercoledì	miércoles
Dies Jovis	Thursday	Donnerstag	jeudi	giovedì	jueves
Dies Veneris	Friday	Freitag	vendredi	venerdì	viernes
Dies Saturni	Saturday	Samstag	samedi	sabato	sábado

The seven-day week originated in ancient Mesopotamia and became part of the Roman calendar in A.D. 321. The names of the days are based on the seven celestial bodies (Sun, Moon, Mars, Mercury, Jupiter, Venus, and Saturn), believed at that time to revolve around Earth and influence its events. Most of Western Europe adopted the Roman nomenclature. The Germanic languages substituted Germanic equivalents for the names of four of the Roman gods: Tiw, the god of war, replaced Mars; Woden, the god of wisdom, replaced Mercury; Thor, the god of thunder, replaced Jupiter; and Frigg, the goddess of love, replaced Venus.

In fact, the majority of the countries who today call Sunday the seventh day of the week are those who speak Latino-roman languages (Italy, France, Spain and their ancient colonies) and are Roman Catholic, while on the other hand, they affirm that their sanctification of Sunday in memory of Christ's resurrection which occurred, not on the seventh day but the first day of the week. Thus, in most other countries around the world, such as in central Africa, Latin America, in Asia, . . . it's a challenge to convince people, even the learned ones, that Monday is the second day of the week of the Creation, that Sunday is the first; for dictionaries and calendars have been modified to blind the learned ones.

I grew up in such a Catholic church-minded environment and was taught and trained to call Sunday 'Day of rest' and Monday 'First Day'. As I was not accustomed to the Bible teaching until I finished the high school and entered University, I started searching and bought my first bible. Then I began to be interested in Protestant beliefs and attended some services at the Presbyterian Church, which translates the biblical Sabbath as 'Jewish Day of rest' in our local languages, to hide the truth about this holy day of rest. The problem is that many learned persons are not ashamed to put confusion on things clearly established in the Word of God, which they claim to stand for! How many people, less fortunate than I was, are perishing by lack of knowledge!

Then here arises the enigma: if Sunday is 'sanctified' to the honor of Christ's resurrection by becoming the seventh day of the week, according to the Protestantism, this supposed to honor the resurrection of the Savior becomes a bluff, for Monday becoming the first day, it should then bear logically the honor of Christ's resurrection! Then, Christ being resurrected on the first day according to biblical logic, Monday would bear the honor of Christ's resurrection and so on! This is a very proof that, in God's business, the high instruction is sometimes only infancy! It is the so-learned teachers of the Law in Jesus' time that were astonished and confused by the wisdom and knowledge of Him who was but taught by the heavenly Teacher!

In this debate, Catholic Church leaders are more consistent and honest than are the Protestant philosophers and teachers for they always consider Saturday as the seventh day of the week and Sunday the first, affirming they have changed the sacredness of the seventh day from Saturday to Sunday by their own power, as the pope has the authority to do so!

XVIII—HOLY DAYS AND HOLIDAYS

"But now, after that you have known God, or rather are known by God, how is it that you turn again to the weak and beggarly elements, to which you desire again to be in bondage? You observe days and months and seasons and years. I am afraid for you, lest I have labored for you in vain." (Galatians 4 : 9 - 11)

O YES, IN Church history, people, bringing their customs and traditions therein, had kept certain days as holy! However, Christ says in His Word that if He did not come to this world, everyone would be right to decide whatever seems to him good to be saved.

Paul exhorts, *"Be transformed by the renewing of your mind"* (Romans 12 : 2). Our new self *"is being renewed in knowledge after the image of its Creator"* (Colossians 3 : 10). Both heart and mind are involved in this renewal. Behavior is, too. These three work together in those who are being transformed by Christ.

The mind alone is not enough. If only the mind is involved, we may be like demons that know truths about God but do not obey Him. Simply knowing the truth is not enough. We must not only hear, but we must also do (Matthew 7 : 24).

Behavior alone is not enough. If we go through the motions without really believing in God, we are play-actors. Again, if we but believe in God and do the right actions, if our heart is far from Him, our worship is in vain. If we sing God's praises without really feeling any affection for Him, we are hypocrites.

Thus, we need right beliefs, right actions, and right emotions.

If the heart is right and our beliefs are right, then right behavior will be the result. We want right behavior, but we need to remember that it is the result of other things; even it is not the ultimate goal. We have to become unceasingly transformed and thus become more like Christ in righteousness and holiness!

We are one people and we have one faith and one Savior, and we form Christ's Body. If Paul is really telling us to have everyone his own day to rest and to hallow (see Romans 14 : 5 - 6), we would no longer be one people, for everyone would have his own beliefs and faith. We do not have to live everyone to himself, for we are the Lord's. Paul indeed is not asking us to behave in the Church according to our feelings, by following what 'seems right' to us, or what we 'feel good in our heart'; instead, we should also ask ourselves, 'What says the Lord?', for "*There is a way that seems right to a man, but its end is the way of death*" (Proverbs 14 : 12).

Our feelings are not a safe guide, but only the Bible is; for, on the Day of Judgment, we are going to be judged only by what the Lord had said in His Word. That is going to be the only standard for judgment. For our Lord says, ". . . *the word that I have spoken will judge him in the last day*" (John 12 : 48). So, if I or anyone else cannot point to what he is standing for in the Word of God, then please do not believe Him, because there is too much at stake, your very soul!

Our soul is worth more than the whole world and everything in it, "*for what profit is it to a man if he gains the whole world, and loses his own soul? Or what will a man give in exchange for his soul?*" (Matthew 16 : 26). Our soul is the part of us, which represents our whole being that is going to continue to live on forever throughout all eternity. We cannot afford to lose it into eternal punishment, which is death.

In today's Christian world as in the time before Christ's earthly ministry, pagans and Jewish people alike have set up days, months and years as holy, in which they were calling assemblies gathering to enjoy life or to worship their 'God or gods'.

While every effort is made to undermine the sanctity of the Law and thus explain the nullity of the seventh-day Sabbath, Christianity had also adopted in various ways and symbols many festivals and holidays, which many of their followers do not understand their meaning or their origin.

Here are some more popular festivals in the western world.

Valentines Day is the day for love in American culture, when sweethearts buy cards, candy, flowers, and romantic dinners to prove their devotion to the one they 'adore'. It has roots in the ancient festivals of the European ancestors, with roots in an ancient Roman fertility rite known as the 'Lupercalia' celebrated on Feb.15th, in honor of the gods Lupercus, Faunus and the founders of Rome, Romulus and Remus. During the festival, young men would draw the names of eligible girls from an urn. These couples would be paired up until the next Lupercalia, often in intimate ways: the young man would wear the slip bearing his Valentine's name on his sleeve, and attend to the lady with flowers, gifts, and words of affection. This drawing of Valentine lots continued into the Middle Ages in Europe. As Christianity became more prevalent, the celebration of love became associated with the patron saint of love and couples in Roman culture; and in AD 496 Pope Gelasius declared February 14th sacred in honor of St. Valentine.

Halloween or the Forces of Darkness celebrated on October 31st, is a day of ghosts, witches, goblins, and grotesque creatures. It is also a day of orange and black, of candles and jack-o-lanterns. Costume parties and strange customs occupy the minds of western civilization, and all of this seems to be intensifying every year. Children wearing every kind of costume imaginable, and some unimaginable, have been going door to door for years at the end of October saying "trick or treat" and collecting bags full of treats. In recent years, many people have been decorating their yards as cemeteries and making their houses look spooky. Even churches have Halloween parties and set up "haunted houses" as fund raising projects. The history shows that Halloween has its origin in the British Isles about 1300 years ago. In those days, there were many men and women who practiced a so-called "nature religion" known as Wicca or Witch. The female Wiccan was known as a witch, and the male Wiccan was known as a wizard. The Wiccans were worshippers of the "Earth Mother", the sun, the moon, and stars. The full moon is sacred to witches, especially if it is on a Friday; even greater if the Friday is the 13th day of the month. Witches have special ways of celebrating their 'sabbath', and even though they do not believe in Satan, it is Satan who gives them the experiences they have and deceives them into thinking it is the forces of nature they are tapping into. It is believed that on that night, the barrier between this world and the next, known as the astral plane, becomes very thin; thus this allows spirits of departed ones to travel freely back and forth between the earth and the spirit realm. In the early days in

England, the Druids would walk until they came to a house or a village where they shouted the equivalent of "trick or treat." The treat was a slave girl or any female to be given to the Druids which, if given, was taken to a place where she was raped and killed and then sacrificed on the sacred bonfire until only glowing embers were left. The "bonfire" is the origin of the modern day bonfire.

As we can clearly see, Halloween is not harmless, though many Christians believe the contrary.

Easter originated as the worship of the sun goddess, the Babylonian Queen of Heaven or Astheroth who was later worshipped under many names including Ishtar, Cybele, Idaea Mater (the Great Mother), or Astarte for whom the celebration of Easter is named. Easter is not another name for the Feast of Passover and is not celebrated at the biblically prescribed time for Passover. This pagan festival was supposedly "Christianized" several hundred years after Christ. History records that spring festivals in honor of the pagan fertility goddesses and the events associated with them were celebrated at the same time as "Easter". Easter was not considered a "Christian" festival until the fourth century. Early Christians celebrated Passover on the 14th day of the first month and a study of the dates on which Easter is celebrated reveals that the celebration of Easter is not observed in accordance with the prescribed time for the observance of Jewish Passover.

Roman emperor Constantine the Great convoked the Council of Nicaea in 325. After much debate, the Nicaean council decreed that 'Easter' should be celebrated on the first Sunday, after the full moon, on or after the vernal equinox. Why was so much debate necessary if 'Easter' was a tradition passed down from the Apostles? The answer is that it was not an Apostolic institution, but, an invention of Man! They had to make up some rules. The truth is that Easter has nothing whatsoever to do with the resurrection of our Lord and Savior, Yeshua, or with the Biblical feast of Passover with which it often coincides! In Western Christianity, Easter is celebrated on the first Sunday following the first full moon after the vernal equinox. Thus, for Western churches the earliest possible date of Easter is March 22 and the latest possible date is April 25. In Eastern (Orthodox) Christianity, Easter is celebrated on a Sunday between April 4 and May 8, often following the date of Western Easter by a week or more.

Instituted centuries ago by the Catholic church, *Ash Wednesday* is the first day of Lent and occurs forty days before Easter, a six-week season of preparation for Easter. Many Christians, mostly Protestants and independents, had never given Ash Wednesday a thought until 2004, when Ash Wednesday became a huge day in American Protestant consciousness. Why? Because on that day Mel Gibson released what was to become his epic blockbuster, *The Passion of the Christ*. For the first time in history, the phrase "Ash Wednesday" was on the lips of, not just Catholics and other "high church" Protestants, but also of millions of evangelical Christians,. In the earliest centuries, Catholic Christians who had fallen into persistent sin had ashes sprinkled on their bodies as a sign of repentance, even as Job repented "in dust and ashes" (Job 42 : 6). The custom started around the tenth century when many believers began to signify their need for repentance by having ashes placed on their foreheads in the shape of the cross. Even this sign of sinfulness hinted at the good news yet to come through its shape. Today, celebrations of Ash Wednesday vary among churches that recognize it.

In Roman Catholic tradition, the *Holy Week* or the week of Lent, is the week immediately preceding Easter Sunday. It is observed in many Christian churches as a time to commemorate and enact the passion and death of Jesus through various observances and services of worship. While some church traditions focus specifically on the events of the last week of Jesus' life, many of the liturgies symbolize larger themes that marked Jesus' entire ministry. In Roman Catholic tradition, the conclusion to the week is called the Easter Triduum, a space of three days usually devoted to special prayer and observance. Some liturgical traditions, such as Lutherans, simply refer to 'The Three Days.' The Easter Triduum begins Thursday evening of so-called Holy Week with Eucharist and concludes with evening prayers on Easter Sunday. Increasingly, evangelical churches that have tended to look with suspicion on tradition of observing the 'Holy Week' are now holding Holy Week services, especially on 'Good Friday'. This special Catholic week starts with 'Palm Sunday' and ends in the 'Holy Saturday' and some church traditions have daily services during the week.

Palm Sunday observes the triumphal entry of Jesus into Jerusalem that was marked by the crowds, who were in Jerusalem for Passover, waving palm branches and proclaiming Him as the messianic King. Sometimes this is accompanied by a processional into the church. In many churches, children are an integral part of this service since they enjoy processions and activity as a part of worship. In many more liturgical churches, children are encouraged to craft palm leaves used for the Sunday processional into crosses to help make the connection between the celebration of Palm Sunday and the impending events of Holy Week.

In most Protestant traditions, the liturgical color for The Season of Lent is purple, and that color is used until Easter Sunday. In Catholic tradition (and some others), the colors are changed to Red for Palm Sunday. Red is the color of the church, used for Pentecost as well as remembering the martyrs of the church. Since it symbolizes shed blood, it is also used on Palm Sunday to symbolize the death of Jesus. While most Protestants celebrate the Sunday before Easter as Palm Sunday, in Catholic and other church traditions it is also celebrated as Passion Sunday anticipating the impending death of Jesus.

Friday preceding Easter Sunday is called *Good Friday* because it is the day that Jesus died on the cross for all of our sins. In Latin countries, it is called 'Holy Friday; In Germany, it is called 'Mourning Friday' or 'Friday of Mourning.' And Norway refers to it as 'Long Friday', a reference to the length of the day's services. The Orthodox Churches call it 'Holy Friday' and 'Great Friday.' All of these names are instructive and understandable. So how did it come to be called 'Good Friday' in English-speaking lands? The reality is that we do not know for sure.

However, it was recognized that the evils of that day led to the greatest good, the salvation of humanity. Thus, despite the bad, the day was truly good; despite the evil of that day, God evoked the greatest good from it. On this day Christians commemorate the passion, or suffering, and death by crucifixion of the Lord, Jesus Christ. Many Christians spend this day in fasting, prayer, repentance, and meditation on the agony and suffering of Christ on the cross. The big question remains: who instituted the day and conferred the sanctity to it? As we know, praying and fasting is a matter of need of a Savior at any time in any year!

Among all those so-called Christian holidays, one is the most popular and is celebrated in various ways even by those that do not have anything to do with Christ as their Savior; its popularity continues to grow as the pleasure seeking affect the multitude. This is the feast of *Christmas*. We read, ". . . *while they were there, the days were completed for her to be delivered. And she brought forth her firstborn Son, and wrapped Him in swaddling clothes, and laid Him in a manger, because there was no room for them in the inn.*" (Luke 2 : 6, 7). In December, thousands of Christians of different faiths from all over the world gather in Bethlehem, the town of Jesus' birth, to witness annual rituals at the Catholic church of the Nativity. On Christmas Eve, a horseman bearing a large cross leads a procession of church members and dignitaries into the church. They continue down steep stairs and enter the Grotto of the Nativity, a long, narrow underground cavern. Carrying an ancient image of the baby Jesus, which they wrap in swaddling clothes, they place the figure in a manger at what is believed to be the actual birthplace of Christ.

Although the Gospels describe Jesus' birth in detail, they never mention the date; so historians do not know on which date the Messiah was born. The Roman Catholic Church chose December 25 as the day for the Feast of the Nativity in order to give Christian meaning to the existing pagan rituals. Thus, the Church replaced festivities honoring the birth of Mithra, *'the god of light'*, with festivities commemorating the birth of Jesus, whom the Bible calls the 'Light' of the world. By so doing, the Catholic Church hoped to draw pagans into Christianity by allowing them to continue their revelry while simultaneously hoping to honor the 'unknown' birthday of Jesus. The Eastern Orthodox Church took a slightly different course by celebrating Christmas on or around January 8; but, around the end of the fourth century, the Eastern Church in Constantinople had also begun to acknowledge December 25 as Jesus' birthday, with emphasis on the celebration of Christ's baptism on January 6 as the more important holiday.

People almost everywhere observe Christmas. How did Christmas come to be observed, even by those that do not know Jesus? How did the customs and practices associated with Christmas make their way into traditional Christianity's most popular holiday?

William Walsh (1854-1919) summarizes this holiday's origins and practices in his book *'The Story of Santa Klaus'*, 1970, p. 58 in this way, "We remember that the Christmas festival . . . is a gradual evolution from times that long antedated the Christian period . . . It was overlaid upon heathen festivals, and many of its observances are only adaptations of pagan to Christian ceremonial". How could pagan practices become part of a major church celebration? What were these 'heathen festivals' that lent themselves to Christmas customs over the centuries?

During the second century before Christ, the Greeks practiced rites to honor their god Dionysus (also called Bacchus or Bacchanalia). It spread from the Greeks to Rome, center of the Roman Empire. In addition to the Bacchanalia, the Romans celebrated another holiday, the Saturnalia, held in honor of Saturn, the god of time. These celebrations also often ended in riot and disorder. ". . . Hence the words Bacchanalia and Saturnalia acquired an evil reputation in later times," according to Walsh, (p. 65). "Both of these ancient holidays were observed around the winter solstice, the day of the year with the shortest period of daylight".

Many of the other trappings of Christmas are merely carryovers from ancient pagan celebrations. Santa Claus comes from Saint Nicholas, the "saint whose festival was celebrated in December and the one who in other respects was most nearly in accord with the dim traditions of Saturn as the hero of the Saturnalia" (idem, p. 70).

According to legend, the Christmas tree tradition began with the founder of German Protestantism, Martin Luther around year 1500. While walking through the forest on Christmas Eve, Luther was so moved by the beauty of the starlit fir trees that he brought one indoors and decorated it with candles to remind his children of God's creation. German immigrants took the Christmas tree to other parts of Europe and to the North America, where it soon became a popular tradition. To give to the feast much splendor, Blown-glass ornaments, tin angels, paper chains, candles, cornucopias filled with sugarplums, and other decorations made the simple evergreen tree into a beautiful parlor centerpiece were added to the scene at Christmastime.

Christmas gifts themselves remind of the presents that were exchanged in Rome during the Saturnalia. In Rome, the presents usually took the form of wax tapers and dolls, the latter being in their turn a survival of the human sacrifices once offered to Saturn. Christmas is thus a diverse collection of pagan forms of worship overlaid with a veneer of Christianity.

During the days of the apostles in the first century, the early Christians had no knowledge of Christmas, as we know it today. Nevertheless, as a part of the Roman Empire, they may have noted the Roman observance of the Saturnalia while they kept their customary 'feasts of the Lord' (listed in Leviticus 23). The *Encyclopaedia Britannica* tells us: "The sanctity of special times was an idea absent from the minds of the first Christians who continued to observe the Jewish festivals, though in a new spirit, as commemorations of events which those festivals had foreshadowed" (*11th edition, Vol. VIII, p. 828, 'Easter'*).

In the beginning, Christians were opposed to Christmas. Some of the earliest controversy erupted over whether Jesus' birthday should be celebrated at all. "As early as A.D. 245, the Church father Origen was proclaiming it heathenish to celebrate Christ's birthday as if He were merely a temporal ruler when His spiritual nature should be the main concern. Of all times of the year suggested as the birth of Christ, December 25 could not have been the date". Indeed, "If Jesus Christ was born in Bethlehem, and his purpose in coming was anything like what is supposed, then in celebrating his birthday each year Christians do violence, not honor, to his memory. For in celebrating a birthday at all, we sustain exactly the kind of tradition His coming is thought to have been designed to cast down" (Tom Flynn, *The Trouble With Christmas*, 1993, p. 42).

Except for those who realize the 'reason for the season', Christmas is a holiday that doesn't include Christ at all, which automatically makes it a big shameful lie. Then, without Christ, what is the purpose? Yet practically everyone in the Western World 'celebrates' Christmas, even the atheists! Christmas to the world is a holiday to throw parties, get together with family and friends, and exchange gifts that, if truth be told, should not probably have been bought, because many people end up going deeply into debt to buy gifts they can sorely afford. One of the most important passages in Scripture that should help us in the matter is, II Corinthians 10 : 3 - 5: "*For though we walk in the flesh, we do not war according to the flesh. For the weapons of our warfare are not carnal but mighty in God to the pulling down strong-holds, casting down arguments and every high thing that exalts itself against the knowledge of God, bringing every thought into captivity to the obedience of Christ . . .*" And apostle James to emphasize in his epistle, chapter 1, verses12-14: "*Blessed is the man who endures temptation; for when he has been approved, he will receive the crown of life which the Lord has promised to them those who love him. Let no one say when he is tempted, 'I am tempted of God'; for God cannot be tempted by evil, nor does He Himself tempt anyone: But each one is tempted, when he is drawn away by his own desires and enticed.*" Add those two texts together, and the primary battlefield is man's mind.

Yes, Satan exists, but all that Satan does is to play upon what we already have in mind, our natural desire to defy and rebel against God and to elevate and worship ourselves in God's place. All Satan does is to present the lust of the flesh, the lust of the eyes, and the pride of life, and we react according to our own internal desires to pleasure ourselves. The battle should not be so much against Satan but first against our own heart. Jeremiah 17 : 9 reads "*The heart is deceitful above all things, and desperately wicked; who can know it?*" One of the things that our deceitful heart does is to tell us that things are not sins when they are, and that we are honoring God when in fact we honor ourselves. While the Holy Spirit is trying to convict us regarding our sin, our heart is trying to tell us that we are inherently good and righteous, and that we can honor God in our own way and He will accept our ways, for He is Love.

So, how can we win this battle? Read our Bible, and compare the Truth in the Bible with the lies in our mind and around us. If we reject the lies in our mind, then Satan will have nothing to grab hold of; and that is the key to becoming a spiritual warrior. It is only when we succeed in driving Satan out of our head by first becoming aware of, exposing, and opposing our own delusions and vanities that we are able to win the fight over Satan ourselves, with the help of the Holy Spirit.

Many encyclopedias plainly reveal that the source of the celebration of December 25 is the birthday of Mithra, the pagan sun god. Sun worshippers since the time of Babel recognized this time of year in honor of their gods: first century believers, taught personally by Christ, did not celebrate His birthday; second century theologians condemned the thought. Only after severe persecution, destruction and inaccessibility to biblical scriptures and the blending of pagan doctrines with the worship of God that was the Mithraic celebration of December 25 proclaimed to be 'Christian' in nature.

XIX—HOW TO KEEP THE SABBATH?

Therefore submit to God. Resist the devil and he will flee from you. Draw near to God and He will draw near to you. Cleanse your hands, you sinners; and purify your hearts, you double-minded. (James 4 : 7, 8)

A S NOT ONLY physical creature, but also most importantly an intelligent and responsible being, Man was made in his heavenly Father's image, and the main benefit of the Sabbath day in God's plan is to provide this special creature with an opportunity to develop a special, high and moral communion with the One in whose image he had been created. Such a special communion being different but more efficient than that which is expected in daily routine Christians' worship, if any.

It may be said to be the opinion of the whole Jewish people and Christian Church, that the sanctification of the Sabbath required by God, consists not merely of cessation from worldly avocations, but also in the consecration of the day to the offices of religion; that this correct view is proved not only by the general consent of the people of God under both dispensations, but also by the constant use of the words such as '*to hallow*', '*to make holy*' or, '*to keep holy*' and '*to sanctify*' used repeatedly in the Scriptures. The uniform use of such expressions shows that the day was set apart from a common to a sacred use and is to be religiously observed.

From the design of the institution, which from the beginning was religious, is the commemoration of the work of Creation, and after the advent, of the resurrection of Christ, as our Mediator. In Leviticus 23, is a list of those days on which there had to be 'a holy convocation' of the people; on which the people were to be called together for public worship, and the Sabbath is the first and the most important one given.

The command is constantly repeated that, during these convocations, the people should be faithfully instructed out of the Law, which was to be read to them on all suitable occasions. To give opportunity for such instruction was evidently one of the principal object of these 'holy convocations' (Deuteronomy 6 : 6, 7, 17 - 19; Joshua 1 : 8). This instruction of the people was the special duty of the Levites (Deuteronomy 33 : 10); and of the priests (Leviticus 10 : 11, compare with Malachi 2 : 7). Let us insist that the reading of the Law was doubtless a regular part of the service on all the days on which the people were solemnly called together for religious worship. Thus in Deuteronomy 31 : 11, 12, we read, "*when all Israel comes to appear before the LORD your God in the place which He chooses, you shall read this law before all Israel in their hearing. Gather the people together, men and women and little ones, and the stranger who is within your gates, that they may hear and that they may learn to fear the LORD your God and carefully observe all the words of this law*". Such was the design of the convocation of the people. Moreover, we know from the New Testament that the Scriptures were read every Sabbath in the synagogues.

The place of the fourth command in the Decalogue; the stress laid upon it in the Old Testament; the way in which it is spoken of in the prophets and the Psalms chapters appointed to be used on this special day, as for example the ninety-second one; the apostles' behavior on the Sabbath; all this shows that the day was set apart for religious duties from the beginning and through all salvation processes till "*all be fulfilled*".

This may also be argued from the whole character of the old dispensation that all its institutions were religious; they were all intended to keep alive the knowledge of the true God, and to prepare the way for the coming of Christ. It would be entirely out of keeping with the spirit of the Mosaic economy to assume that its most important and solemn Holy Day was purely secular in its design.

For all these reasons and other not shown here, it is clear that the precepts of the Decalogue bind God's people in all ages. There are two rules by which we are to be guided in determining how the Sabbath is to be observed, or in deciding what is, and what is not lawful on that holy day. The first is, the design of the commandment: what is consistent with that design is lawful, and what is inconsistent with it, is unlawful. The second rule is to be found in the precepts and example of our Lord and of the Apostles. Thus, the design of the command is to be learned from the words in which it is conveyed and from other parts of the Word of God. From these sources, it is plain that the design of the institution, as already remarked, was in the main twofold. First, to secure rest from all worldly cares and avocations, to arrest for a time the current of the worldly life of men, as not only their minds and bodies should be overworked but also that opportunity should be afforded for other and higher interests to occupy their thoughts; secondly, that God should be properly worshipped, His Word duly studied and taught, and the soul brought under the influence of the things unseen and eternal; the third design is to evangelize the world and to care for and help the sick and the needy ones.

Any man who makes the design of the Sabbath as thus revealed in Scripture his rule of conduct can hardly fail in its due observance. The day is to be kept holy to the Lord. In Scriptural usage, to 'hallow or make holy' is to set apart to the service of God. Thus, the tabernacle, the temple, and all its utensils were made holy. In this sense, the Sabbath is holy; it is to be devoted to the duties of religion and whatever inconsistent with such devotion is contrary to the design of the institution.

Therefore, people must cease all ordinary pursuits and abstain from the intrusion in this holy day, of the physical and material consideration and the common activities of the workday week. It is to be devoted exclusively to the nurture of the intelligent and moral aspects of the man through a spiritual communion with the Most High; that by the power of His Spirit, God's people may be true worshipers who ". . . *will worship the Father in spirit and truth; for the Father is seeking such to worship Him. God is Spirit, and those who worship Him must worship Him in spirit and in truth*". (John 4 : 23, 24).

The Sabbath is thus a special day for worship in the home, in the church or places chosen for this purpose. It is a day of joy to the saved ones and to their children and their children's children that obey the Most High; not that joy of careless ease and fantasy, of joking and speaking vain words and organizing entertaining pleasure, nor of appetite and lust,; but a joy for the salvation found in Christ. A day to learn more about our God and His blessings, to better know the truth that makes us free from deceitfulness, to sing and praise His holy Name, to marvel at His perfect works of creation and salvation and to reach out to the dying world in love for spiritual nurture and physical healing.

Therefore, the Sabbath hours are the Lord's and must be used according to His requirements.

FORTUNAT TSHIMANGA-MUKADI

Friday at dawning of the day, when "the holy hours of the Sabbath approach, it is well for the family members or groups of believers to gather together just before the setting of the sun . . . to sing, pray, and read God's Word, thus inviting the Spirit of Christ as welcome Guest" (Seventh day Adventists believe . . . , p.263), thus putting an end to our work week and opening the time dedicated to the Lord.

The Sabbath is the sign of our obedience, of our election and of our sanctification. Therefore, a soul is elected "who will work out his own salvation with fear and trembling. He is elected who will put on the armor, and fights the good fight of faith. He is elected who will watch unto prayer, who will search the Scriptures, and flee from temptation. He is elected who will have faith continually, and who will be obedient to every word that proceeds out of the Mouth of God. The provisions of redemption are free to all; the results of redemption will be enjoyed by those who have complied with the conditions" (Ellen G. White— Patriarchs and Prophets, p. 208)

Ellen G. White warns and insists to those that pretend to be faithful Sabbath keepers, saying ". . . can you claim the seal of the living God? Can you claim that you are sanctified by the truth? . . ." Then she explains, "We have not, as a people, given the Law of God the preeminence as we should. We are in danger of doing our own pleasure on the Sabbath day." (Selected messages—III, p. 258). Her statement continues in another place, "I was shown the conformity of some professed Sabbath-keepers to the world . . . They give lie to their profession. They think they are not like the world, but they are so near to them in dress, in conversation, and actions, that there is no distinction". (Ellen G. White—Testimonies for the Church—1, p. 131)

These words were written at the mid nineteenth century; imagine what is Sabbath-keeping Christians' behavior in our days, less than two hundreds years latter in the Church, in their workplace or in the street! No longer a sanctified people in the world, but the world in the Church. Everything is done to imitate what is popular, what is drawing crowds, what pleases but men not God. More and more, it is difficult to distinguish the world and the Christians, in praises, in songs, in dress, in words . . . even when they come to worship the Most High!

David advises to *"trust in the Lord, and do good; dwell in the land, and feed on His faithfulness. Delight yourself also in the Lord, and He will give you the desires of your heart. Commit your way to the Lord, trust also in Him, and He shall bring it to pass. He shall bring forth your righteousness as the light and your justice as the noonday"*. (Psalms 37 : 3 - 6)

Except otherwise clearly stated in Scriptures, no statute, precept nor commandment of the Decalogue, was given to be kept only in the wilderness, or for the ancient Israel alone, but for eternity. In the same manner, *"You will not kindle the fire in all your dwellings . . ."* was not only for the illiterate, wild and wandering people in the wilderness, or for those living in the far old time without modern technology, but it is also for the spiritual Israel today which has much knowledge in many sciences, living in the era of satellites, robots and airplanes . . . and for all those that trust in their heavenly Legislator. For the mouth that spoke these words cannot lie or be mistaken. The everlasting One, the Lord God, Creator of the end of the universe, is the same yesterday, today and forever; thus are also His requirements.

We are asked not to kindle fire on Sabbath by divine decrees; let us do our part and by faith let us wait upon the Lord, Who knows the number of hair on his head of each of us, the accomplishment of His promises; let us honor Him by taking Him at His word and worship Him in truth and spirit.

As He cared for ancient Israel in their wandering in the wilderness, He is near to each of His faithful children who honor Him. He knows what we are made of; He remembers that we are but dust and knows better our problems, our difficulties and our weaknesses, more than our fleshy fathers know.

Yes, not only each of our steps in this life is guided by Him, but also "each of our breath and pulsation of our heart, is an evidence of the care of Him in Whom we live and move and have our being . . . From the smallest insect to man, every living creature is daily dependent upon His providence" (Ellen G. White—Education, p. 130,131); o yes, not by our bank accounts though full they may be, neither by our life insurance companies though so sure they seem to be!

The same almighty Hand that kept in the wilderness the sixth-day manna unpolluted on the seventh day morning, is still able to keep our sixth-day food today unspoiled and healthy for use on Sabbath; for, thus says the Lord, *". . . if you have faith as a mustard seed, you will say to this mount, 'Move from here to there', and it will move; and nothing will be impossible for you . . ."* (Matthew 17 : 20)

FORTUNAT TSHIMANGA-MUKADI

Though the food is necessary for our life, the life and the health we have are not solely of the abundance and the best quality of our food, but by every Word that proceeds out of the Mouth of God.

Faith teaches us that God exists. He is a living and a personal God who is involved in His creatures' life as Provider and Sustainer. He does not leave us on our own to do the best we can, to spare our own life by our own strength and wisdom. On the contrary, He knows very well about all our needs. He cares even for the lilies of the field and the sparrows in the air; how much does He the same toward those that are created in His own image! We have but to cherish His principles and allow His Spirit to control our life, by relying upon Christ as our personal Savior.

People sustain many fallacious reasons suggested by the Enemy of God, such as,—'we do not cook, we but warm the food to be healthy',—'our fire is not made of wood as in the time of the Israelites in the wilderness, we but turn on/off buttons of the stove, that's it',—'Sister Ellen G. White advices us to warm our food in cold seasons',—'kindling fire is not among the Ten Commandments',—'we cannot make the Sabbath a burden for the believers',—'doing good on Sabbath is lawful' . . . All these reasonings are but the same answers given to God by Adam (Genesis 3 : 12), Eve (Genesis 3 : 13), Cain (Genesis 4 : 9), Abram (Genesis 17 : 17 - 21), Moses (Number 20 : 10 - 12), and so on, when they were caught doing their own will, instead of God's.

When the seventh day arrives, we must stop pursuing our *'own ways'*, which are the things we normally do; seeking our *'own pleasure'*, meaning just trying to have fun; and speaking our *'own words'*, the everyday things we talk about that do not involve God. This last one is often very hard to follow because we like speak of everything done during our workweek, and *"out of the abundance of the heart the mouth speaks"* (Matthew 12 : 34).

To truly keep the Sabbath in the spirit of God's Law, we must focus our minds on God and those things He wants us to be concerned about during His holy time. Then, as God promises, we will be truly blessed.

Furthermore, in addition to worship on this weekly Holy Day, we should remember Christ's approach that *"it is lawful to do good on the Sabbath"* (Matthew 12 : 12). So, this is a day we can use for making encouraging phone calls or writing letters to the sick, the 'shut-ins' or fellow Christians who are lonely. It may also be possible to visit the sick or others in need on the Sabbath, or to have them over for a Friday evening meal (cf. Matthew 25 : 34 - 36; James 1 : 27).

So we should not think of the Sabbath as the day we 'cannot do' this or that! Rather, we should approach this very special day as a period when we can and should really take time to deeply study and thoughtfully analyze the Bible. It is a time when we can sit quietly, meditating over and thinking through the truly big issues of life: Why were we born? What is the purpose of life? What is the way to achieve that purpose? How are we personally doing in moving toward that objective? Why am I here in this place in this very time? Which message does God send to me in such a particular situation? Why did God put me in connection with such ones? . . . In addition, the Sabbath is the perfect time for unhurried, thoughtful, heartfelt prayer to our Father in heaven, to 'commune' with our Creator, to worship Him, to get to know Him intimately.

Of the Ten Commandments, it is worth to insist, the fourth one, concerning the Sabbath day, is and always has been the real 'test' commandment (cf. Exodus 16 : 4). Many can accept the other nine, "*do not worship other gods*", "*honor your father and your mother*", "*do not murder*", "*do not commit adultery*", "*do not steal*", "*do not lie*" . . . But the fourth commandment is different. To keep it means visibly living quite differently from the society around you, perhaps even being looked upon as odd or weird. Because, in breaking one of the nine, your friends, your parents, the society and the government will judge and condemn you even though they do not know God and His commandments; in the contrary, in keeping the fourth earnestly, you are special and will be looked upon as a foolish or legalist! Yet Jesus said, "*If anyone comes to me and does not hate his father and mother, wife and children, brothers and sisters, yes, and his own life also, he cannot be My disciple. And whoever does not bear his cross and come after me cannot be My disciple*" (Luke 14 : 26 - 27, Today's English Version).

Do you love the '*praise of men*' more than the praise of God? Or do you have the faith and the courage to obey God's commandments, even if you were to lose your job, your friends and perhaps some of your relatives and family members? It needs courage and earnest prayers and matchless love for your Creator and Saviour!

On this seventh day of each week, we should cease from our own work and allow God to work in us, building and nourishing our relationship with Him. "*Remember the Sabbath to keep it holy*" is full of meaning today. Yes, indeed, for many people and professing Christians in particular might be shocked to learn that the seventh-day Sabbath, God's commanded day of rest and communal worship, is not abrogated for the Christian today. It remains very much in force, as shown throughout this Testimony. It is full of meaning and supremely relevant to the lives of all humanity. We are missing some of God's most wonderful blessings if we ignore the observance of His commanded day of rest. True worshiper of God honors God's command concerning the Sabbath. In contrast, Sunday observance does not rest on God's authority or that of His Word, but on the authority of men. The hard question must be asked whether God accepts such worship when His clear precepts regarding His Sabbath are ignored.

God created the Sabbath for Mankind (Mark 2 : 27); therefore, it is obligatory for all men and women and their children to keep God's Sabbath, as they have to do for the other nine commandments. The Sabbath must be kept by 'gentiles' and by all those who were never a part of the physical nation of Israel. "*Thus says the LORD: 'Keep justice, and do righteousness, for My salvation is about to come, and My righteousness to be revealed. Blessed is the man* and the women too *who does this, and the son* and the daughter too *of man who lays hold on it; who keeps from defiling the Sabbath, and keeps his hand from doing any evil . . . To the eunuchs who keep My Sabbaths, and choose what pleases Me, and hold fast My covenant, even to them I will give in My house and within My walls a place and a name better than that of sons and daughters; I will give them an everlasting name that shall not be cut off. 'Also the sons* and the daughters too *of the foreigner who join themselves to the LORD, to serve Him, and to love the name of the LORD, to be His servants—everyone who keeps from defiling the Sabbath, and holds fast My covenant—even them I will bring to My holy mountain, and make them joyful in My house of prayer*" (Isaiah 56 : 1, 2, 4 - 7, *emphasis added*).

Many people make mistake to believe that God will overlook their unfaithfulness in the minor affairs of life, far from Him to do so; He will in no wise sanction or tolerate no confessed and then abandoned sins. If one attempts earnestly to excuse or conceal his or her sin and permits it to remain no confessed and unforgiven, such one will be overcome by the Enemy, and may deserve but the eternal death; for, ". . . *if we sin willfully after we have received the knowledge of the truth, there no longer remains a sacrifice for sins, but a certain fearful expectation of judgment, and fiery indignation which will devour the adversaries"*. (Hebrew 10 : 26, 27)

People must, or better, people need as individuals, ". . . to take heed as they have never done before to a *'Thus says the Lord'*. There are men who are disloyal to God, who profane His holy Sabbath, who cavil over the plainest statements of the Word, who wrest over the Scriptures from their meaning, and who at the same time make desperate efforts to harmonize their disobedience with the Scriptures". (Ellen G. White— Selected Messages—1, p.213). Such ones constitute the army of the Devil and we must be careful to listen to their philosophy and advices, though they pretend being highly learned people and God's ambassadors!

No one who delays an earnest preparation for the day of the Lord cannot make it at time of trouble, distress and anguish that is slowly but really taking place in these last days, as we watch calamities and disasters dogging our generation, while discoveries and technology amaze people and governments take decisions and make laws against the order established by the Most High! Let no one expect to be kept innocent by the heavenly just Judge and be in peace with Him through the merits of His Son, while such one continues to sin willingly. Stop it and then bring your burden to the sin-Bearer to be freed from the Enchanter's power.

FORTUNAT TSHIMANGA-MUKADI

XX—STILL SINNERS!

This is a faithful saying and worthy of all acceptance, that Christ Jesus came into the world to save sinners; of whom I am chief. (1 Timothy 1 : 15).

SOME PEOPLE ASSERT that no matter how much grace one has received from the Lord, yet he can never get beyond the place where he is reckoned a sinner wrongly a sinner wrongly quoting the above verse. They argue, "If Paul said he, was the chief of sinners", they argue, "then how dare we, with so much less grace and salvation, lay claim to anything higher?"

If Paul meant here that he, at this time, was the chief of sinners, let us see how this statement harmonizes with the rest of his teachings and testimonies.

Paul was an apostle called and consecrated by the Messiah Himself. He wrote upon one occasion that he supposed that he is ". . . *not at all inferior to most eminent apostles.*" (2 Corinthians 11 :5). It is true that in his humility he said on another occasion that, he was "*less than the least of all the saints*" (Ephesians 3 : 6) when he considered what a sinner he had been, and how the Lord had saved him and exalted him to 'preach the unreachable riches of Christ'; but even in this humble statement he confessed that he is a saint, which means a holy person, and, even though he says 'the least', it is above being a sinner; and that is far beyond being a chief of sinners!

It is why he boldly affirms that he has "*been approved by God to be entrusted with the gospel . . .*" (1 Thessalonians 2 : 4). We cannot understand how God could choose a man to be an apostle and commit to him the Gospel to preach, knowing that he was still the chief of sinners.

He wrote on another occasion that ". . . *how that by revelation He made known to me the mystery . . . which in other ages was not made known to the sons of men, as it has now been revealed by the Spirit to His holy apostles and prophets . . .*" (Ephesians 3 : 3 - 6); this, of course, included himself, as he was an apostle. Here is a profession of holiness from Paul. It sounds somewhat different from being the chief of sinners.

Paul told the Thessalonian Church, "*You are witnesses, and God also, how devoutly,* holily, *and justly and blamelessly,* without fault, *we behaved ourselves among you who believe*" (1 Thessalonians 2 : 10, *emphasis added*). Suppose that he had added to complete the idea the words, 'me the chief of sinners', how would they have reconciled the statement?

In another place, Paul invites Christians to join him to move forward to the prize set before them: "*I press toward the goal for the prize of the upward call of God in Christ Jesus. Therefore let us, as many as are mature, complete in Christ, have this mind . . .*"(Philippians 3 : 15, *emphasis added*). Paul thus not only classes himself among those who had obtained this perfection to get the prize, but also invites as many as possible those who focus on the same high objective. The chief of sinners would hardly harmonize in such a piece.

He wrote to the Romans and said, "*But I know that when I come to you, I will come in the fullness of the blessing of the Gospel of Christ.*" (Romans 15 : 29). How can one be in the fullness of the blessing of Christ, and at the same time be the chief of sinners? No, night and day cannot cohabite!

In another place, he writes that he is crucified with Christ, and that Christ is living in him. (Galatians 2 : 20). This is one of the strongest expressions of full salvation. Is the chief of sinners crucified with Christ, and possess Christ's life?

He won hundreds to Christ and led many into the baptism of the Holy Ghost. How could one continually succeed in raising men to a higher level of sanctity than himself? How could one, as chief of sinners, succeed in getting other sinners to God, and then in getting them filled with the Holy Ghost, while remaining himself on the throne of sinfulness? God trusted Paul to write a portion of the inspired Word; committed unto him a 'dispensation of the Gospel' and through him wrought miracles of different kinds. Can we imagine a Holy God committing such sacred works to the chief of sinners? No, light and darkness cannot mix!

The very next year after Paul wrote this text about the chief of sinners, he emphasized, "*For I am already being poured as a drink offering, and the time of my departure is at hand. I have fought a good fight, I have finished the race, I have kept the faith. Finally, there is laid up for me the crown of righteousness, which the Lord, the righteous Judge, will give to me on that Day, and not to me only but also to all who have loved His appearing.*" (2 Timothy 4 : 6 - 8). How could the chief of sinners, as he was facing death, have '*fought a good fight*', and '*kept the faith*', that then he was expecting a crown of righteousness? Is a crown of righteousness laid upon sinners' heads?

Paul encourages his readers to, "*Awake to righteousness, and do not sin . . .*" (I Corinthians 15 : 34). And then he fixes their mind, "*What shall we say then? Shall we continue in sin that grace may abound? Certainly not! How shall we who died to sin, live any longer in it?*" (Romans 6 : 1 - 2). It is strange that Paul should exhort others to stop sinning and at the same time keep right on sinning himself. How could he be found consistent?

We read in the Word that sin is the transgression of the law; also, that to him who knows to do 'good', and does not do it, to him it is sin". Now, if Paul was the chief of sinners, then he was a transgressor of the law. This would prove hypocrisy in him; teaching others what he himself did not live up to. If he knew to do 'good' and did it not, as a chief of sinners, then how could he be holy, and just, and blameless, as he declared about himself? This would certainly brand him as false, if he were then the chief of sinners.

Long before Paul wrote the text in question on his 'sinfulness', he repented and was cleansed of his sins when Christ met him on the road to Damascus, struck him down under a mighty load of conviction; therefore he was a gloriously saved man. Every sin he ever committed was blotted out to be remembered against him no more, forever. Now, the question arises, if he was the chief of sinners at the time he wrote this text, did God give him a license to go back into the heinous business again, or did he deliberately take things into his own hands and go to sin again? If he were the chief of sinners, he was not abiding in Christ as he unceasingly claimed it in his epistles.

Notice carefully what the apostle John says about sin: "*Whoever abides in Him* (Christ) *does not sin. Whoever sins has neither seen Him nor known*

Him. He who sins is of the devil, for the devil has sinned from the beginning. For this purpose the Son of God was manifested, that He might destroy the works of the devil. Whoever has been born of God does not sin, for His seed remains in him; and he cannot sin, because he has been born of God." (1 John 3 : 6, 8, 9, *emphasis added*).

If the apostle Paul was, at the time of that writing, the chief of sinners, then, according to the apostle John, he was not abiding in Christ, had not seen Him, nor known Him. But Paul declares to the contrary in all these three things: *"I know a man in Christ who fourteen years ago . . . such a one was caught up to third heaven"* (2 Corinthians 12 : 2, . . .). This man that Paul refers to is himself; see the context of, *"Have I not seen Jesus Christ our Lord?"* in 1 Corinthians, chapter 9 verse 1 and of, *"I know whom I have believed."* (2 Timothy 1 : 12). Thus, we see that Paul was in Christ: he had seen Him, and he knew Him. Again, if the apostle John was correct, and Paul was the chief of sinners, then he was of the devil, and has not had the works of the devil destroyed out of him. However, to say this of such a man would be hard indeed. Yes, he that would make out Paul as saying that he was at this time the chief of sinners, flies in the face of reason, of the Word of God, of Paul's own testimony and experience. He would make him to be not only false and hypocritical, but a deceiver.

We know the concerned statement means something else when he wrote, 'Christ Jesus came into the world to save sinners; of who I am chief'. That Christ came to save sinners there is no dispute in orthodoxy. That he saved Paul is not a mooted question. That he was at one time of his life the chief of sinners, all are willing to admit that in his humility he felt in what he had done in the past. However admitting that, at the time of this epistle writing, he either was of such a character, in thought or in reality, is the 'bone of contention'. One may say that it was simply an expression of humility on the part of Paul in using the phrase, but there is too much at stake for one to make use of such an expression, so far out of the bounds of all truth, for humility's sake.

What, then, does he mean? He means just what he says. He is speaking of two things that came into his life, one was sin, and the other was salvation. He calls attention to the fact of him being the chief of sinners, and as the chief of sinners Christ saved him, thus giving hope for others. If Christ could save the chief of sinners, for what Paul did against Christ's followers, that all might have hope to be saved, no matter how much guilty they may feel. The word 'chief' is mentioned simply to show the power of Christ's salvation and of His atonement for sins as many as they may be. Notice the verse below: "*However, for this reason I*, the chief of sinners!, *obtained* mer*cy* . . ." (1 Timothy 1 : 16 a, emphasis added); and he gives the reason of the emphasis, ". . . *that in me first Jesus Christ might show all longsuffering, as a pattern*, here is the key, *to those who are going to believe on Him for everlasting life*" (verse 16 b, emphasis added).

This power, which acted long years in the past at his conversion, was brought to bear upon one who was the chief of sinners, as a testimony for those that will come to Christ to have the assurance of salvation. Then the expression 'chief of sinners' must apply to the time when the power of salvation was exerted. Hence, we see it was not at the time of that writing, but at the time of his conversion; not the chief sinner now, but the chief sinner saved then.

One of the great delusions is that one may be a Christian, and at the same time be a sinner. If one is a sinner, he is not saved. Of course, the majority may understand what one means by it, but the fact is, salvation and sin do not mix, they do not coexist in the same person. To say, that I was a sinner, but I am now saved by grace, would be the truth. Surely, '*If we say that we have fellowship with Him, and walk in darkness, we lie and do not practice truth*', for '*He who says 'I know Him' and does not keep His commandments, is a liar, and the truth is not in him*' (1 John 1 : 6; 2 : 4) If we stick to the Word of God, there is no possible way to harmonize the two states, the one of sin and the other of salvation? The Word of God does not mix things. It puts them where they belong. If one is a sinner, he is not saved; he is of the devil, out of Christ and not born again. All of this, apostle John makes plain.

Why do people want to hide behind some wrested Scriptures to their soul's destruction, when there is so much light shed on the pathway? Such an attitude is a mystery indeed.

May the Lord save the people from being Christian sinners.

We are now new creation, and this has the implication of having the Holy Spirit in us, walking by the Spirit, and living a life that is Christ-like (Romans 3 : 21 - 24). In addition, while this process is very decidedly a supernatural work of God, the believer can and should cooperate in it by a diligent use of the means which God has placed at his disposal. Is our old nature eradicated by God through faith and baptism? What is it about eradication of sin and sanctification, according to the Bible?

Before our death or Christ's return, whichever comes first we have to be found holy and perfect as He is, that we may meet Him in the clouds. Sanctification denotes that "act of God whereby the pollution and corruption of human nature that results from sin is gradually removed. The old structure of sin is gradually torn down, and a new structure of God is reared in its stead. With the gradual dissolution of the old, the new makes its appearance. It is like the airing of a house filled with pestiferous odors. As the old air is drawn out, the new rushes in. This positive side of sanctification is often called '*being raised together with Christ;*' (Romans 6 : 4, 5; Colossians 2 : 12; 3 : 1, 2). The new life to which it leads is called '*a life unto God;*' (Romans 6 : 11; Galatians 2 : 19)." (C.K. Barrett, A Commentary on the Epistle to the Romans; Harper's New Testament Commentaries; Henry Chadwick, Editor; Harper and Brothers, 1957)

Sanctification, applied to man as born in sin, then by a gracious act, God purifies man who is a sinner from the darkness of ignorance, from indwelling sin and from its lusts or desires, and imbues him with the Spirit of knowledge, righteousness, and holiness, that, being separated from the life of the world and made conformable to God, the new man may live the life of God, to the praise of the righteousness and glorious grace of God and to his own salvation. It consists of the death of the 'old man' and the quickening of the 'new man'. This is why, in many Scriptures, the disciples of Christ are called 'Saints', more often in the Pauline writings. "Sanctification, then, is a process of dying to sin and rising to new life, and it is coextensive with the life of faith. This sanctification is not completed in a single moment; but sin, from whose dominion we have been delivered through the cross and the death of Christ, is weakened more and more by daily losses, and the inner man is day by day renewed more and more, while we carry about with us in our bodies the death of Christ, and the outward man is perishing. According to Scripture there is a constant warfare between the flesh and the Spirit in the lives of God's children, and even the best of them are striving for perfection. Paul gives a very striking description of this struggle in Romans 7 : 7 - 26, a passage which certainly refers to him in his regenerate state. In Galatians 5 : 16 - 24, he speaks of that very same struggle as a struggle that characterizes all the children of God." (G.C. Berkouwer, *Faith and Sanctification*; Eerdmans, 1952)

When Jesus speaks of holiness in the gospel, He gives us what seems to be an impossible task in human point of view: "*Therefore you shall be perfect, just as your Father in heaven is perfect*" (Matthew 5 : 48). How can Jesus command perfection to us 'as it is in our heavenly Father', when we experience the effects of original Sin and struggle against sin daily? We often misunderstand what Jesus truly said. Scripture is God's Word in human language, and human language is often misinterpreted. Statements in the Scriptures must be taken in the context in which they were written and spoken. Why would Jesus ever demand of us something impossible? The perfection is not based on self-justification or self-righteousness, but on our relationship with God. Only God has absolute perfection, and we cannot become perfect or holy on our own. Perfection and holiness are based on the life of God in us. The perfection in Man is through Christ living in us, according to His promise (see John 15 : 4 - 7).We look at Jesus, God in the flesh, since He helps us understand holiness translated into our own human experience, through His grace, without using this grace as a license to sin. The perfection in Man is through Christ living in him.

O yes, a righteous and loving God cannot accept sin or can He allow us, given our natural sinfulness, to set our own standards of righteousness and holiness to become perfect and holy as the Father is. As there will be a judgment, and if there is pardon for sins, surely a loving God would show us beforehand by what measure we will be judged, and for what act we need forgiveness. And He has done this through His Holy Book, the Bible.

How do we live, called to His perfection, but knowing we cannot be perfect as He is while still in this world? Between what we are and what we are called to be spans the glorious arch of God's grace. It is both a covering over us, and a bridge to the Father; still we have to stand up for Jesus and walk like Him. This is our part in the plan of redemption. For we nevertheless sense the risk that we could use God's grace as license to sin. We know that we could presume upon God's grace, even to the point of taking lightly what that grace cost God, thus falling into an even deeper sin than the sin for which we were consciously appropriating that grace. This is a practical and real problem for those of us who struggle with any type of prevailing and persisting sin. How many times can we sin and repent? *'Do not offend the Holy Ghost'*, says the Lord!

What then? In his epistle to the Roman Christians, Paul encourages us, saying, "*There is therefore now no condemnation to those who are in Christ Jesus, who do not walk according to the flesh, but according to the Spirit. For the law of the Spirit of life in Christ Jesus has made me free from* the law of sin and death . . . Because the carnal mind is enmity against God; for it is not subject to the law of God, nor indeed can be. So then, those who are in the flesh cannot please God . . . For if you live according to the flesh, you will die; but if by the Spirit you put to death the deeds of the body, you will live. For as many as are led by the Spirit of God, these are the sons of God" (Romans 8 : 1, 2, 7, 8, 13, 14). Why then, every Sabbath, some of local church leaders in many [if not all] churches, encourage their followers (sic) to organize parties, receptions . . . and for this, they make them kindle fire, cook and warm food, talk of their own business, even travel from cities or provinces to the other! So permitted by the ministers, the weak believers do not think this is sin and have no need to seek forgiveness. Therefore, repeated sins, repeatedly forgiven become trivialized or even accepted as abnormal sin. If we allow the voice of the Holy Spirit become muted, we might even come to deny that a sinful behaviour is sin. What a terrible situation; for, to deny our sin is to miss being the recipients of God's wonderful grace!

A life in the Body of Christ with real accountability is the best protection from such deception. After Peter healed a widely known beggar who had been lame since his birth (Acts, chapter 3 verses 1 to 10), he advised the astonished crowd, saying, "'Repent therefore and be converted, that your sins may be blotted out, so that times of refreshing may come from the presence of the Lord" (verse 19). There are in this verse three important worthwhile commands to help everyone of us: Repent—be converted—sins blotted out. 'To repent' meaning 'to perceive afterwards' conveys the idea that one must recognize and admit he has sinned and should recognize the need to change his or her mind, heart and behaviour. 'To be converted' meaning 'to turn about, to turn towards' indicates that, in addition to recognizing and acknowledging sin committed, one is taking the necessary action to turn away from it by turning toward the forgiving God; this requires doing what is right, not just acknowledging what is wrong. 'To be transformed' implies 'major or total change as the metamorphosis of a caterpillar into a butterfly'. And Paul to conclude, "And do not be conformed to this world, but be transformed by the renewing of your mind, that you may prove what is that good and acceptable and perfect will of God." (Romans 12 : 2)

God expects a profound spiritual change of His newborn children. For this, He had promised us His Spirit to bring us about such a transformation if we earnestly, faithfully and trustfully ask Him. "Behold what manner of love the Father has bestowed on us, that we should be called *children of God! Therefore the world does not know us, because it did not know Him. Beloved, now we are children of God; and it has not yet been revealed what we shall be, but we know that when He is revealed, we shall be like Him, for we shall see Him as He is. And everyone who has this hope in Him keep purifies himself, just as He is pure. Whoever commits sin also commits lawlessness, and sin is lawlessness. And you know that He was manifested to take away our sins, and in Him there is no sin. Whoever abides in Him does sin. Whoever sins has neither seen Him nor known Him. Little children, let no one deceive you. He who practices righteousness is righteous. He who sins is of the devil, for the devil has sinned from the beginning. For this purpose the Son of God was manifested, that He might destroy the works of the devil."* (1John 3 : 1 - 8)

Praise the Lord and let His holy Name be blessed to have made everything so clear and complete!

XXI—REPENT AND SIN NO MORE!

"As many as I love, I rebuke and chasten. Therefore be zealous and repent. Behold, I stand at the door and knock. If anyone hears My voice and opens the door, I will come in to him and dine with him, and he with me." (Revelation 3 : 19, 20)

BECAUSE THE FOURTH commandment is for all times and all people, so are all statutes and precepts related to it, for ". . . *as the new heavens and the new earth which I will make shall remain before Me,*" says the Lord, "*so shall your descendants and your name remain. And it shall come to pass that from one New Moon to another, and from one Sabbath to another, all flesh shall come to worship before Me . . .*" (Isaiah 66 : 22 - 23)

When worshiping our Creator and Saviour, let everyone have in mind that God is present among His people and His angels are watching over them, therefore, let everyone tremble and be filled with fear and awe and revere Him with their faces covered as did Moses; for the holy angels veil their faces in His presence, the mighty cherubim and the bright seraphim approach His throne with solemn reverence. How much more should we, finite and sinful beings saved by grace, come in an awful and reverent manner before our Maker! We should behave before Him in order, harmony and discipline, as do heavenly beings, working ". . . harmoniously. Perfect order characterizes all their movements. The more closely we imitate the harmony and order of the angelic host, the more successful will be the efforts of these heavenly agents in our behalf. If we . . . are disorderly, undisciplined and disorganized in our course of action, angels, who are thoroughly organized and move in perfect order, cannot work for us . . . for they are not authorized to bless confusion, distraction and disorganization" (Ellen G. White, *Testimonies to Ministers*, p. 28). Therefore, the very consecrated ministers of the Gospel have to ". . . encourage order, discipline and union of action, and then the angels of God can cooperate with them". (*Idem*) Our Creator is a God of order, does not accept needless noise and fanfare, and boastings, and He has commanded, ". . . *all you of Judah who enter in at these gates to worship the Lord! Thus says the Lord of hosts, the God of Israel: 'Amend your ways and your doings, and I will cause you to dwell in this place. Do not trust in these lying words, saying, The temple of the Lord, the temple of the Lord, the temple of the Lord are these.* (Jeremy 7 : 2 - 4); behaving otherwise, there is lack of fear for God's greatness and majesty on behalf of those who pretend to come before Him to worship and honor Him. For, "to fear God, is to hold Him in reverence for Whom He is in contrast to who we are. To reverence God, to fear Him, is simply to acknowledge how we, as fallen beings, stand in relationship to Him. It is simply to acknowledge the Creator—creature relationship, as it should be acknowledged. It is understanding how great, how powerful and how holy He is in contrast to how small, how weak, and how unholy we really *by nature* are . . . With this sense of the Unseen, every heart should be deeply impressed. The hour and place of prayer are sacred, because God is there." (Ellen G. White, *Prophets & Kings*, p. 48, 49, *emphasis added*). "The place of worship may be very humble, but it is no less acknowledged by God. To those who worship in spirit and in truth and in the beauty of holiness, it will be as the gate of heaven. The company of believers may be few in number, but in God's sight they are very precious." (Ellen G. White— *Testimonies for the Church—6*, p.363)

Our petition, 'MAY YOUR WILL BE DONE ON EARTH AS IT IS IN HEAVEN" should not be a mere and vain repetition. In this, the Master warns, ". . . *every idle word that men may speak, they will give account of it in the day of judgment. For by your words you will be justified, and by your words you will be condemned.*" (Matthew 12 : 36, 37). Ellen G. White advises, ". . . When one sees clearly a duty, let him not presume to go to God with prayer that he may be excused from performing it. He should rather, with humble, submissive spirit, ask for divine strength and wisdom to meet its claims". (*Patriarchs & prophets*, p. 441)

Idle words are heard more and more among those that are assembling 'in the name of Christ'. The pulpit is used and the time spent in vain discourses of preacher's familial and scholar stories; or to seek and provoke the applause and the laughter in the assembly, to draw the hearers' attention on men and their diploma and international journeys and preaching success instead of directing their attention to the Cross and marvel more at Father's love for us. Sometimes the joke and similar things take place, so that it becomes like a theater or cinema, to flatter the interest of people.

Born again Christians' salvation is so important and its price so high, the time so short and the foes so fierce that the message and warnings must always fully delivered with earnestness, fear and tears, and this for all the time allowed to this purpose. Earnest effort must also be made that Christ the Savior, Him alone, and His work be the sole center of the message. If not, shut up and be seated, for the ground where you are standing is holy and the Lord is among His people.

People make 'their' miracles performance the center of the message; forgetting that miracles, if any, are the Lord's, according His own will and purpose; not for the glory of the evangelist which is but a mere tool in the hands of the Master. "Let none cherish the idea that special providences or miraculous manifestations are to be the proof of the genuineness of their work or of the idea they advocate. If we keep these things before the people, they will produce an evil effect, an unhealthy emotion. The genuine working of the Holy Spirit on human hearts is promised, to give efficiency through the Word." (Ellen G. White—Selected Messages—2, p. 48)

Seemingly, shouting, making noise and even dancing are taking place more and more in the Christian worship. Where did you find Christ, the apostles or those that came directly after them doing such shameful things! Whose example are you followers! In the contrary, kneeling before the Lord is regarded by many as unnecessary, preferring to remain seated while they call upon the holy Name of the Lord. Watch the same people speaking to their boss in their workplace!

So, in every Church gathering where pleasure is the center, where pride is fostered or appetite indulged, there the assemblers are to forget God and lose sight on eternal interests; there Satan is binding his chains about the souls; thus, many turn away from the light, provoked because a word of caution is given, and then wonder, ". . . may we not do as it pleases us ourselves?".

We have to gather to the glory of the Deity and not occupy our mind with worldly things and vile behavior! The true communion with our Savior and Lord is to pray and *"worship Him in spirit and in truth"*.

If not so, thus says the Lord, ". . . *'Inasmuch as these people draw near with their mouths and honor Me with their lips, but have removed their hearts far from Me, and their fear toward Me is taught by the commandment of men, therefore, behold, I will again do a marvelous work among this people, a marvelous work and a wonder; for the wisdom of their wise men shall perish, and the understanding of their prudent men shall be hidden . . .'"* (Isaiah 29 : 13, 14) And again, *"And in vain they worship Me, teaching as doctrines the commandments of men."* (Matthew 15 : 9)

A rightly directed program of worship in harmony with the spirit of true Sabbath keeping will make this blessed day the happiest and the best of all the week, for the church members and their families; a veritable foretaste of our heavenly rest to come, that *"the righteous requirement of the law might be fulfilled in us who do not walk according to the flesh, but according to the Spirit. For those who live according to the flesh set their minds on the things of the flesh, but those who live according to the Spirit, the things of the Spirit."* (Romans 8 : 4, 5)

One wrong step makes another one easily worse. When God called Abram, He said, ". . . *'Get out of your country, from your family and from your father's house, to a land that I will show you"* (Genesis 12 : 1). The same call that had been heard yesterday is heard today and will be heard tomorrow until the coming of the Lord, God willing to make for His honor a people that are called after his holy Name. Whoever hears this Savior's call and does not harden his heart, will join the Church, and let us say, the spiritual Body of Christ.

As heirs of Abram, God calls each and everyone individually from his family, from his particular customs and style of life, from his background and culture to make to Himself a holy Nation, separated from the world and its mirth and noise, to organize them in a Body and to make them fitted for a new Homeland unknown to their parents and ancestors, to abide the houses which they had not built and call each other 'brother and sister' not they were born in the same earthly family, but those of the new birth through the blood of the Lamb. Through faith in Christ, they are members of the royal family, heirs of God and joint heirs with Christ, in Whom they are one.

Therefore, the gathering of such a people has but one purpose, which is to worship and honor the heavenly Father, Ruler and Redeemer whose Name is YAHWEH, to study His Word and to strengthen each other, without "man-made separations between classes and races or countries: men of every class become members of one family, children of the heavenly King, not through earthly power, but through the love of God . . ." (Ellen G. White, *Selected Messages—1*, p. 258). To such ones, God teaches that the place of worship, His house, must be called the house of worship for all people made one in Christ.

However, as the end of time approaches and, the conclusion of this world and the coming of the Lord draw near, the false Christianity is building the walls of separation between those that are supposed to be one. The main reason is that many Christians are not convinced of their state of sons and daughters of the Most High, that they remain, after baptism, attached to their culture, race, life style . . .

Here you will see an Iranian Catholic church in Montreal in Canada; there a Black Seventh-Day Adventist church in Oklahoma in USA; a Chinese Presbyterian church in Bosnia in Yugoslavia, and so on . . . As it was not enough, some people worship under their national flag floating beside the pulpit or wrapping the cross, while a message is heard calling people of all nations to join the Church of Christ! These same flags are those that the conquering armies plant on the conquered enemy land! Where is the place of such flags sometimes tainted with innocent blood where the loving Creator of all nations is honored and worshiped? Are we really born again and transformed at the image of Christ? Did we leave, as did Abram, our nation, family, our customs and worldly behavior to join Christ's Army? Is Christ divided? In this matter, Jehovah Witnesses' point of view is the best and biblical when it comes to not honoring the political and national emblems in the place or time of worship.

I read somewhere, ". . . as a father, while playing his drum, was giving some important instructions to his little boy, this latter replied, 'what you do, prevents me to do what you say'"! Let us speak and behave as them that will be judged by the just and unchanging "LAW OF FREEDOM".

We know by the History that many Christian Denominations, even those that claim detaining all truth, were and are somehow involved in racism, inter-ethnic wars, in heinous slavery, in genocides . . . but it is time to change radically and teach Good News of the Savior to all people without walls of separation, as we come to worship and ". . . come in sight of Calvary and view the royal Sufferer who in man's nature bore the curse of the law in his behalf, all national distinctions, all sectarian differences are obliterated; all honor of rank, all pride of caste is lost". (Ellen G. White, *Selected Messages—1*, p. 258)

If we fail to represent rightly the Creator of the universe as His peculiar people, He is able to arouse a holy and faithful people from the '*stones*'. Let a Greek Pentecostal church be found in Greece; a Sudanese Neo-Apostolic church in Sudan, or an Indonesian United Church in Indonesia; and let all Catholic church members in Bangkok feel free and glad to belong to the Chinese Catholic church where they live, all Seventh-day Adventists in Paris feel likewise happy to belong to the French SDA church down there, no matter where the members are from or what are their backgrounds, no matter how many there are in that congregation. That is it. If not, such churches are but castes organized and named under Satan's instigation to divide and weaken the Body of Christ, they are but the towers of Babel in purpose to make to their builders 'a name for themselves', not for the Savior's glory; thus they destroy the unity of the saints for which Christ prayed all the night long. Let us ask ourselves, how does He look upon castes, upon society distinctions, upon divisions of man from his fellow man because of hair color, eyes dimension, political or clerical position, wealth, birth background or attainment?

Are we not, by baptism, made one new people whose Lord is Yahweh and the country the New Jerusalem to come, for here below, we are strangers! Why do we then tend to desire Sodom as did Lot's wife, which reaped the fruits of her double-minded heart! Abram, our father in faith and our pattern left his country, his kindred and his father's house to go into a land that the Lord had showed him, without taking with him the name 'Haram' of his native country, but the Lord's Name!

As we are in the era in which people are moving to and fro, to mix to others in divers parts of the world, we must find Christians in a town or a city worshiping their God without frustration or discrimination. They move not in the large hordes but individually to settle and espouse customs, language and technology of their new city, which are not contrary to the will of their God! How could we have the arrogance to name the place of worship after our native country or nation or tribe?

Although the time is coming for the true worshipers to worship the Lord not in Horeb, nor in Jerusalem, nor in the churches made by men's hands, for fear of the tribulations to come, but "IN SPIRIT AND IN TRUTH", the Church buildings are still places appointed to encounter our Creator, Lord of the lords. Now these church buildings are still our training fields, that by spiritual sermons, right Bible studies, mutual encouragements . . . we may be fitted for the great Day of trouble and trial predicted by Christ, saying that you will be arrested and handed over to be punished and to be put to death.

Nobody for any reason has the right to divide those that Christ had bought, united and consecrated for His kingdom and bring them back to the world! For nobody can serve two masters in the same time, he will love one and hate the other, because ". . . the world to which we belong by birth is hostile to God and under condemnation; therefore, in order to save us, the cross must deliver us from the world and place us in the church, the Body of Christ the Crucified. Every other aspect of salvation is based upon this fact. The gospel delivers us not primarily from hell to heaven, not from death to life, but from the world to the church . . . Tragically, we see much of the world creeping into the church today. In contradiction to the gospel of Christ, the church is copying the world's fashions, accepting its philosophy, and depending on its resources. All this is happening because the church has lost sight of the true meaning of the doctrine of salvation." (Jack Sequeira, *Beyond Belief*—Glad Tidings Publishers, 1999, p. 115)

In the Seventh-day Adventist church Manual, we read this interesting text, "It is the divine purpose to gather out a people from the far corners of the earth to bind them into a body, the body of Christ, the church, of which He is the living head . . . No distinction on account of nationality, race, or caste, is recognized by God. He is the Maker of all humanity. All men are of one family by creation, and all are one through redemption. Christ came to demolish every wall of partition, to throw open every compartment of the temple, that every soul may have free access to God . . . In Christ there is neither Jew nor Greek, bond or free. All are bought nigh by His precious blood." (*SDA Church manual, Revised 2000*-16th Edition, p. 3, 4)

These affirmations are not particular to the Adventist church, but there are found in many Christian church manuals and professions of faith, even though differently expressed. The problem is that the reality in daily living is so far from the written doctrine, in every church built on culture and traditions of men.

It is sad that the church teachers proudly justify and explain this wrong philosophy instead of being covered of shame. For "*Every kingdom divided against itself is brought to desolation, and a house divided against a house falls*" (Luke 11 : 17). No wonder the church ". . . is so weak and so indistinguishable from the world! When Christ was here on earth, He was a stranger and a pilgrim. He was in the world and witnessed to it of the truth, but he was not of the world. The same must be true of the Christian and of the church . . . to be saved means that we say goodbye to everything that belongs to the world and become a vital part of the Church' *the true and invisible one* (Jack Sequeira, Beyond Belief—Glad Tidings Publishers, 1999, p. 116, *emphasis added*)

Let no one be licentious in God's presence, because the time is running out and the foes so many. Now is the right time to change our worship behavior accordingly to the will of Christ the Savior. It is said that to him that is much given, to the same much will be asked. Fear the Lord!

For a repentant sinner, which divine grace transforms, there is a sincere desire to live in harmony with all divine requirements, not in order to be saved by his works, but he has already found salvation by faith in the infinite love of and for Christ. Then the divine principles exercise their authority upon, not the mere outward, but the inner man by the presence of the Holy Spirit that, when He comes, convicts the individual of what sin is.

We must be taught that sanctification is not the work of a moment, an hour, a day, or is obtained suddenly, but it is ". . . of a lifetime. It is not gained by a happy flight of feeling, but is the result of constantly living for Christ. Wrongs cannot be righted nor reformations wrought in the character by feeble, intermittent efforts. It is only by long, persevering effort, sore discipline, and stern conflict that we shall overcome. We know not one day how strong will be our conflict the next. So long as Satan reigns, we shall have self to subdue, besetting sins to overcome; so long as life shall last, there will be no stopping place, no point which we can reach and say, I have fully attained. Sanctification is the result of lifelong obedience". (Ellen G. White—*Acts of Apostles*—5, p.273)

We are created for God's glory. We cannot say, ". . . *We glorify thy name . . .*", while we do not obey His statutes or we tend to lessen them. If we really love our Redeemer as we unceasingly claim it, we have to obey His commandments that He may ask the Father to send to us another Helper to dwell with us forever, teaching and remembering us all things that were taught by the Son of Man.

For "those who will dishonor God's image and defile His temple in their own persons will not scruple at any dishonor to God that will gratify the desire of depraved heart". (Ellen G. White—*Patriarchs & Prophets*, p. 458)

Unless the heart be renewed by divine grace through the Spirit by obedience and love of Him who lives forever, it will be in vain to seek for spiritual purity of life. "*Let all the earth fear the Lord; let all the inhabitants of the world stand in awe of Him. For He spoke, and it was done; He commanded, and it stood fast*" (Psalms 33 : 8, 9). Allow not ". . . an unchristian trait to live in the heart. One cherished sin will debase little by little, the character, bringing all its nobler powers into subjection to the evil desire. The removal of one safeguard from the conscience, the indulgence of one evil habit, one neglect of the high claims of duty breaks down the defenses of the soul and opens the way for Satan to come in and lead us astray. The only safe course is to let our prayers go forth daily from a sincere heart". (Ellen G. White, *Patriarchs & Prophets*, p. 452)

Therefore, we should reform the habits in our life, right now; not an outward reformation, but a steady one. This is especially needed at this time, in order to fit a people for the coming of Christ. The Savior Himself warns the church, saying," . . . *take heed to yourselves, lest your hearts be weighed down with carousing, drunkenness, and cares of this life, and that Day come on you unexpected*" (Luke 21 : 34)

All the workers of the Gospel must do this, right now.

XXII—BE PREPARED TO MEET HIM

Then the Lord said to Moses, "Go to the people and consecrate them today and tomorrow, and let them wash their clothes. And let them be ready for the third day. For on the third day the Lord will come down upon Mount Sinai in the sight of all the people. You shall set bounds for the people all around, saying: 'Take heed to yourselves that you do not go up to the mountain or touch its base. Whoever touches the mountain shall surely be put to death. (Exodus 19 : 10 - 12)

A S HUMANS, WE embrace the idea of loving others as ourselves but remain blissfully unaware of how the Bible defines love. As a result, we do not understand the necessity of putting into practice the biblical principles that determine the success or failure of our relationships. Apostle John declares, *"Beloved, let us love one another, for love is of God; and everyone who loves is born of God and knows God. He who does not love does not know God, for God is love"* (1 John 4 : 7 - 8). Jesus Christ founded the Christian faith on the principle of love, Christians wholeheartedly loving God and each other. John, one of Christ's disciples and closest friend, penned these words near the end of his life: *"And we have known and believed the love that God has for us. God is love, and he who abides in love abides in God, and God in him"* (1 John 4 : 16).

What is love? Wouldn't it be wonderful if we could use a consistent definition of love, especially when we are speaking about the love God has for us and the love we should have for each other? Sadly, such consistency is lacking in the world. Most people will acknowledge that love, or at least some degree of respect, is essential for personal relationships. The Ten Commandments define love and the purpose of God's law is to teach us how to apply the two great principles of loving God and loving each other. He made this clear in Matthew, chapter 22 verses 35 - 40 when someone asked Him.

Love is the centerpiece of all the Scriptures, of both the Old and the New Testaments. Every commandment of God is for our good. This is because the commandments define the love that is the foundation for all godly relationships. Love simply summarizes the intent of the Ten Commandments. Paul wrote: *"The commandments, 'You shall not commit adultery; You shall not murder; You shall not steal; You shall not covet'; and any other commandment, are summed up in this word, 'Love your neighbor as yourself"* (Romans 13 : 9, New Revised Standard Version).

From the beginning, God's interaction with human beings has been motivated by His love for us. As Jesus said: *"For God so loved the world that He gave His only begotten Son, that whoever believes in Him should not perish but have everlasting life. For God did not send His Son into the world to condemn the world, but that the world through Him might be saved"* (John 3 : 16 - 17). God wants us all to live forever, to attain eternal life. First we must learn how to get along with each other, how to love one another. That is why love is so important.

Peace and harmony are impossible without respect and love. If God was to grant us eternal life without teaching us how to love each other, He would be committing us to live forever in confusion and chaos. It is why He cannot allow resentments, jealousies, hostilities, hatred and selfish desires of human nature to carry forward into eternity. We must learn the real meaning of love or we cannot receive eternal life. Apostle John wrote, *"He who does not love his brother abides in death. Whoever hates his brother is a murderer, and you know that no murderer has eternal life abiding in him"* (1 John 3 : 14 - 15). So we come again to the question: What is love? John gives us the answer. *"This is love, that we walk according to His commandments . . ."* (2 John 1 : 6). The apostle Paul tells us *"love is the fulfilling of the law"* (Romans 13 : 10, King James Version).

When love lacks, confusion and sin prevail. Here is the story.

It is in that way of love for the Creator and for each other that Moses prepared the people to meet with their Supreme Legislator and receive His holy Oracles, the Ten Commandments. Three days were given to the Israelites to clean themselves and to wash all their garments. A tough preparation to meet the Creator and receive His ordinances and statutes destined not only to them, but also to all Mankind. Nobody had to touch the mountain where He stood. God's power and presence did manifest themselves impressively in the culminating account of the Covenant at Mount Sinai. The people, forewarned by God through Moses, agree beforehand to carry out the terms of the Covenant that is to be revealed, because God has liberated them from Egypt and promised to make them His special holy people; they purify themselves for the ensuing Covenant.

We know through their history how the Israelites rebelled against God from time to time. Even more, mixed to other nations and espoused their customs and lifestyle in such a way they came to forget their Maker and His holy Law. However, this mixture was allowed by their Creator to attain His purpose of salvation for the entire Humanity, by allowing them to be deported and to become slaves and servants in foreign countries. By hardening their hearts, they lost sight of the promise of Messiah and His redemptive mission, in such manner that their leaders and teachers did not recognize Him when He came to them in a manger as an Infant, in spite of all prophecies and signs given to them for their instruction through the prophets!

Jesus, by His matchless and infinite love left His heavenly throne, and as a Baby, came down and grew as a tender plant, obeying to His earthly parents. When the time for His heavenly Father's mission came, He chose His disciples and preached the Gospel of divine love. Therefore, in the accomplishment of the Lord's command to the twelve, "*Go ye therefore, and make disciples . . . teaching them to observe all things I have commanded you; and lo, I am with you always, even to the end of the age*", the gospel went on through all the known parts of the world and reached the New World.

As far as it reached different nations, divisions became multiple and Church leaders got it all mixed up more and more biblical teachings and human philosophy, popular traditions and national cultures.

The confusing work started by the Devil in the Church since the fifth and sixth century, invaded even the churches born off the Reformation in the sixteenth century. Indeed, though they considered the Bible as their references for their teachings, some chose therein what pleased them according to the course of their life or their background. The Law of God was made obsolete and many teachers and leaders became "*the blind that lead other blind*"; while others made the study of the Bible their daily bread and helped the faithful ones to recognize the validity and invariability of the Word of God.

The unchanging character of Scripture as authoritative means that the people, no matter how learned and intelligent they may be, should allow Scripture itself to tell them how to regard it. Anyone who denies the authority of Scripture at one point has denied it at all points. Certain Christian groups profess today that the Bible is the sole reference of righteousness given to men by their Maker. Others believe in its main teachings, such as faith in the redeeming blood of Christ, baptism by immersion, salvation through Christ alone, the sacredness of marriage between a man and a woman, the work of the Holy Spirit in the Church, the Ten Commandments as eternal Law of God, foot washing during the Communion service . . . While some other groups place the temperance rules in the center of their teachings to protect themselves from polluting the body which is the Temple of the Holy Spirit . . . Other Christians teach temperance concerning alcohol and tobacco consumption, ignoring all about the meal and the insane animals as the books of Leviticus (chapter 11) and Acts of Apostles (chapter 10 : 10 - 17) stress this doctrine.

Though Protestants still praise Martin Luther to have brought back the Bible into the hands of Christians, unfortunately, they have not all taken it at the level of its true value. Each one has chosen the part of the Bible which is suitable for them, to build up their profession of faith and doctrine, neglecting or rejecting those parts that do not fit in the course of their life; so that the prophecy may be fulfilled, "*They are those who rebel against the light; they do know not its ways nor abide in its paths.*" (Job 24 : 13); and "*The way of a fool is right in his own eye, but he who heeds counsel is wise*" (Proverbs 12 : 15).

If one can assert that he or she can set aside the six-day creation doctrine, the same has asserted his or her supremacy over Scripture: his or her mind and convenience now have a higher authority. Clearly, therefore, the question of authority is at stake in Genesis chapter 1: to determine whose word is authoritative and final, God's or Man's word. Who has the last, as well as the first word? God's Word should be most valuable and authoritative in any circumstance for every human being! This is also part of our love toward Him as our Creator, Father and Redeemer.

In the book of Hebrews chapter 12 verse 1, apostle Paul wrote, "*Therefore we also, since we are surrounded by so great a cloud of witnesses, let us lay aside every weight, and the sin which so easily ensnares us, and let us run with endurance the race that is set before us*". Paul compares himself and his readers as competitors, who, as they contend for the faith in the arena of life, are surrounded by a great cloud of witnesses.

Who are these witnesses that are so interested in our daily war against the evil? They are the holy angels, which had triumphantly resisted the device of Lucifer; also by the saints that have finished their course and are living in heaven as first fruits of the redemptive work of Christ. The witnesses are also the living beings connected to us by natural or spiritual birth or other relationship, that know our profession of faith as followers of Christ!

So, our Christian race is made difficult by the snares set on our way by the Enemy of our eternal life such as misery, wealth, sickness, pleasures, honor, biased philosophy . . . By the order of the Master, the holy angels help us to fight for our victory; also by following the example of those saints that were before us and thus, restraining from deceiving ourselves or our fellow runners in the arena of this life. Thanks to you, Blessed Captain, for you have promised to be always with your faithful ones and you are mightier than the Prince of darkness and his army! You know yours, they hear your voice and they follow you always, no matter how hard the race is!

Therefore, beside the multitude blinded by the honor, privilege and tradition, some faithful ones continued to study diligently the Word of God, hoping to get from it the needed light and knowledge, which bring strength and victory. Among them were the Anabaptists who soon realized that the Ten Commandments as received from Catholics were obliterated and modified in comparison to what is found in the Bible and then one commandment was missing among the Protestant teachings. They set up the remembrance of the seventh day of the week as the day of rest for God's redeemed people, by realizing that the Law of God is a holy, eternal and perfect one, opening the eyes to blind and spreading the light on the path of God's people. They understood that there is not commandment too many, there is not one too few; as Christ puts it clearly, "*For assuredly, I say to you, till heaven and earth pass away, one jot or one title will by no means pass from the law, till all is fulfilled. Whosoever* [philosophers, popes, theologians, writers, apostles, prophets, teachers, pastors, bishops, mighty doctors . . .] *therefore breaks one of the least of these commandments, and teaches men so, shall be called least in the kingdom of heaven . . .*" (Matthew 5 : 18, 19, emphasis added)

As Church history shows, the most prominent leader of this group was Oswald Glait, who along with Andreas Ficher and Hans Bünderlin was active in Silesia about 1528. When Glait published his '*Entschuldigung*' at Nikolsburg in 1527, he was not yet a Sabbatarian, and there is no clue to indicate why he became one. So W. L. Emmerson, in his book entitled 'The Reformation and the Advent Movement p. 74, wonders, "Whatever led Oswald Glait to search the Scriptures to find the truth about the Sabbath, it seems clear he was the first in post-Reformation times to point out that the true Sabbath was the 'seventh' and not the 'first' day of the week. And as Glait was already an Adventist as a result of his association with Hans Hut, he can very proudly be described as the first 'Seventh-day Adventist' of reformation times, in doctrine and practice if not in name."

What a history, therefore, has the Sabbath of the Lord!

It was instituted in Paradise, honored by several miracles each week for the space of forty years, proclaimed by the great Lawgiver from Sinai, observed by the Creator, the patriarchs, the prophets, the apostles, and the Son of God! It constitutes the very heart of the law of God, and as long as that law endures, so long shall the authority of this sacred institution stand fast.

Such being the record of the seventh day, it may well be asked, How it came to pass that this day has been abased to the dust, and another day elevated to its sacred honors? The Scriptures nowhere attribute this work to the Son of God. They do, however, predict the great apostasy in the Christian church, and that the little horn, or Man of sin, the lawless one, should think to change times and laws . . . It is the object of this testimony for which I am indebted toward my Redeemer who gives strength and to His faithful sons and daughters who wrote the similar testimonies.

Nevertheless our heavenly is all about the fourth commandment concerning the Sabbath, written by the divine Hand on the first of the two tablets of the Decalogue, intended to call the believers to "*love their God with all their heart, all their spirit and all their strength*".

Nevertheless our heavenly Father so loves His creatures that at any time He sends, at a due moment, the warning messages calling to repentance and reformation, because, "our salvation is God's object in all his dealings with us. He has chosen us from eternity that we might be holy. Christ gave Himself for our redemption, that through faith in His power to save from sin, we might be made complete in Him." (Ellen G. White—Our high Calling, p. 213).

Only a few accept the divine call and react positively: they confess their sins, change the course of their living and put on the garments of righteousness. They keep His commandments and afford, by God's grace, to be loyal, obedient and steadfast; versus those that are backslider, disloyal and disobedient! They accept to get out of darkness into His marvelous light and show forth His glory to a dying world. The high price set before them calls for endurance on the part of God's people, ". . . *those who keep the commandments of God and the faith of Jesus*" (Revelation 14 : 12)

Christ expresses it clearly, when He taught and prayed, "*For I have come down from heaven, not to do my own will, but the will of Him who sent Me*", "*Abba, Father, all things are possible unto thee; take away this cup from me; nevertheless not what I will, but what thou wilt.*" (John 6 : 38; Mark 14 : 36). There is only one will of God, and it is good, pleasing, and perfect. Yes, truly, there is but one will of God for any creature at any given time. How could it be otherwise? Therefore, either we are doing God's will or we are not doing God's will! There is no middle ground. Our problem as human beings is that of rebellion against His will and lack of love for Him. Lucifer opened the way and became the first rebel, and he has spread the virus of disobedience. Adam and Eve disobeyed God and sin dominates now over their descendants. All sins spring from the one sin of disobedience.

The great Deceiver has filtered into Human consciousness the concept that, no one can do God's will and so, we must be saved by 'grace alone'. By this, he suggests that God recognizes we cannot do His will and so He pardons us only if we will confess the name of Christ, no need to keep His commandments.

God's perfect will is always practical and possible, whatever our motives and circumstances of life. His commandments are not grievous, because they are of love. In addition, professing our faith in Christ cannot be an alternative to doing God's will, for, the very demons believe also and they tremble.

Rather, receiving Christ is the beginning of the program of redemption that leads us to the place where we always do God's will from the heart. No temptation has taken us except that which is common to Man. The idea that no person can do God's perfect will is a lie inspired by the father of the liars to keep God's people from drawing close to the Saviour in love and obedience.

If grace alone is enough for us to be saved, the Messiah would not warn us, "*Strive*, we are on battle field, *to enter through the narrow gate; for many, I say to you, will seek to enter and will not be able*" (Luke 13 : 24, *emphasis added*). The way and gate that lead to salvation would be straight and largely opened if we do not have to do anything for our salvation. Yes, the gate is narrow because, as human beings, mortal, weak, wanting, we do not have, by ourselves, the power to overcome the difficulties set on the way by the life circumstances and the prince of darkness.

"O son of man, say to the children of your people: 'The righteousness of the righteous man shall not deliver him in the day of his transgression; as for the wickedness of the wicked, he shall not fall because of it in the day that he turns from his wickedness; nor shall righteous be able to live because of his righteousness in the day that he sins". (Ezekiel 33 : 12)

ALL THROUGHOUT THE Scriptures, Our heavenly Father is very concerned about the hearts of Adams' children. Figure it out: 200 years before Messiah came down for the first time, a gentile who had come to know Yahweh as Elohim the Creator and repented of his wrong ways of living, then began to make a sincere and earnest effort to walk in His Commandments; at what point would such a person be judged as obedient to God and made perfect? Would it be after he had observed five commandments of the Decalogue, or would it be after he observed eight of them, or might it be solely by the observance of 600 laws and precepts and commandments of Jewish economy for him to achieve salvation according to the order, *"If you want life, keep my commandments"*? The truth is that Yahweh knows the pursuits and motives of the human heart and can meet everyone where they are, without contradicting Himself; for this has always been true: Yahweh sees the hearts of all men and He pays everyone according to the motives of his heart . . . *"Because I will do this to you, prepare to meet your God, O Israel!* (Amos 4 : 12) . . . *Take My yoke upon you, and learn from Me; for I am gentle and lowly in heart, and you will find rest for your souls. For My yoke is easy and My burden light"* (Matthew 11 : 29, 30). Surely, *"Let this mind be in you which was also in Christ Jesus, who . . . but made Himself of no reputation, taking the form of a bondservant, and coming in the likeness of men . . . He humbled Himself . . .* (Philippians. 2 : 5 - 8).

If Scripture is clear on any teaching, it is clear on this: there will be a judgment. It is hard to imagine how a God who repeatedly refers to Himself as Just (Deuteronomy 32 : 4; Isaiah 45 : 21; Jeremy 23 : 5; John 14 : 15, 21 - 24; 15 : 14 . . .), will not execute judgment at the end of the age. In every of its pages, the holy Word of God urges us to fear God and to keep His commandments: for this is man's all duty. For God will bring every work into judgment, including every secret thing, whether good or evil (2 Corinthians 5 : 10, Matthew 12 : 36, Romans 1 : 32, John 8 : 16). Moreover, from Eden to Babylon, we have many examples of what that judgment would be, for our instruction.

"*. . . I AM WHO I AM*", says the Lord. O yes, for "*. . . the everlasting God, the LORD, the Creator of the ends of the earth, neither faints nor is weary. His understanding is unsearchable. He gives power to the weak, and to those who have no might He increases strength.*" (Exodus 3 : 14; Isaiah 40 : 28, 29)

Too much sin, too much iniquity, too much evil has been wrought upon the earth for a God of justice not to manifest that justice, at some point and in some manner. Indeed, how could a Just God be God and not execute His justice.

If the law of your Maker seems to be burdensome to you, pray earnestly that His Spirit may help you to overcome. Then leave yourself in His mighty Hands, so you will surely succeed in whatever you face: any yoke and burden will become lighter than a dry leaf. Then return to the Lord with your heart and mind and strength and He will return to you to save you and your children and your children's children. In the same manner, "*Let your light so shine before men, that they may see your good works and glorify your Father in heaven. Do not think that I came to abolish the Law or the Prophets; I did not come to destroy but to fulfill . . .*" (Matthew 5 : 16 - 18). And Luke stresses it clearer, "*. . . You are those who justify yourselves before men, but God knows your hearts. For what is highly esteemed among men is an abomination in the sight of God. 'The Law and the Prophets were until John. Since that time, the kingdom of God has been preached, and everyone is pressing into it. And it is easier for heaven and earth to pass away than for one title of the Law to fail'.*" (Luke 16 : 15 - 17)

Paul never taught that being under grace was a license to continue breaking Yahweh's Law; this is another perversion of the so-called modern 'Good News Message' often proclaimed today. Rather, the fact of being now of the Body of the Messiah should demonstrate that we live as He lived, we walk as He walked and we love as He loved. He kept the Torah perfectly, and if He now lives in us by the Spirit and if really we are who we pretend to be, we should be living as He did when He was in the world. Also our aim to turn away from Torah breaking and to receive Him in our heart for our salvation is evidence that He lives in us. Paul stresses clearly: '*What then? Shall we sin because we are not under the law but under grace? Certainly not! Do you know not that to whom you present yourselves servants to obey, you are that one's slaves whom you obey, whether of sin leading to death, or of obedience leading to righteousness?*' (Romans 6 : 15 - 16)

Let us look once more to Paul's message to the Galatians, "*I say then: Walk in the Spirit, and you shall not fulfill the lust of the flesh. For the flesh lusts against the Spirit, and the Spirit against the flesh; and these are contrary to one another, so that you do not do the things that you wish. But if you are led by the Spirit, you are not under the law. Now the works of the flesh are evident . . . of which I tell you beforehand, as I also told you in time past, that those who practice such things will not inherit the kingdom of God . . . If we live in the Spirit, let us also walk in the Spirit. Let us not become conceited, provoking one another, envying one another*" (Galatians 5 : 16 - 26). This is so plain for a warning! Notice, it says that we will not be under the law if we are led by the Spirit. There are two ways that we can find ourselves '*under the law*'. One is by refusing to acknowledge that our righteousness and our salvation come from God alone. The other is by refusing to be led by His Spirit which causes us to walk in His statutes, to keep His judgments and to do them! So Paul advises the Galatians to walk in the Spirit and never use their liberty as an occasion or excuse to disobey Yahweh.

So God's plan is to grant to all of us eternal life through Abraham's Seed, which is Christ who came down here to fulfill the law and to show us the path of righteousness which is in His Law and then to redeem us from the curses that came from our first parents' disobedience. Therefore, the standard of righteousness does not change when we accept Jesus, but our standing before Yahweh does, as being covered by His Son's righteousness!

It is a total distortion of Holy Scriptures to believe that everyone else in this life is expected to refrain from the transgression of the Law and will be condemned for their failure to keep it, while those who receive Jesus as their Saviour are free to purposely transgress the law all their lifelong! If we walk in the Spirit, we will be 'subject to the law of Yahweh' and we will not misuse the law of Yahweh to make it fulfill a function that it was never able to fulfill, that is to bring us righteousness and salvation. It is this misuse of the Torah that Paul is addressing in Galatians chapter 5, verses 16 and 17. Let nobody misuse his writings to say something that he never meant to say. Those who do so are in a lot of trouble. Because Paul's writings are most time misunderstood, the Holy Spirit made Peter speak of the same matter in clearer way, *"Nevertheless we, according to His promise, look for new heavens and a new earth in which righteousness dwells. Therefore, beloved, looking forward to these things, be diligent to be found by Him in peace, without spot and blameless; and consider that the longsuffering of our Lord is salvation, as also our beloved brother Paul, according to the wisdom given to him, has written to you, as also in all his epistles, speaking in them of these things, in which are some things hard to understand, which untaught and unstable people twist to their own destruction, as they do also the rest of the Scriptures. You therefore, beloved, since you know this beforehand, beware lest you also fall from your own steadfastness, being led away with the error of the wicked"*. (1 Peter 3 : 13 - 17).

Nevertheless, let us be found by Him in peace, without spot and blameless; let us not be among the unlearned and unstable who twist God's Word to their own destruction, that in the end, the Son of Man would not be saying to us, "Depart from me, you that keep My commandments! *(sic)*" Rather, as Paul said, those who walk in the flesh, meaning the former ways of sin, will not inherit the Kingdom of Christ. Therefore, let us walk in the Spirit . . . Not because of our own righteousness, but because of His indwelling in us. If He dwells in us, then He will cleanse us of the former things and give us the power to walk as He walked and live as He lived, that we may be where He is, when time comes. This is the good news! For *"To him who overcomes I will grant to sit with Me in My throne, as I also overcame and sat down with My Father on His throne . . . He who overcomes shall inherit all things, and I will be his God, and he shall be My son"* (Revelation 3 : 21; 21 : 7). The verb 'overcome' has an important meaning here, to stress that we are in a battle and we have to defeat the opponent. Let us gain the victory over the Deceiver that we may be among the inheritors, ever faithful to trust in Christ's righteousness for our salvation, ever seeking to walk in His Spirit, ever cleaving to the One who is the same yesterday, today and forever.

The eternal principles of love as given in the Law have not changed and they never will. Let's seek to walk in those eternal principles that we may likewise remain in Him; that His living Word, Christ, would abide in us forever.

A good tree cannot bring forth evil fruits; neither can a corrupt tree bring forth good fruit. Therefore the tree which brings not forth good fruit will be cut down, and be burnt in the fire. So we will know them by their fruits, say the Scriptures! What is meant by good fruit? Is it performing many miracles and signs and wonders to prove that what we are teaching is true? Will this prove that our fruit is indeed good, and not evil? Here is the answer, "*Not everyone who says to Me, 'Lord, Lord', shall enter the kingdom of heaven, but he who does the will of My Father in heaven. Many will say to Me in that day, 'Lord, Lord', have we not prophesied in Your name, cast out demons in Your name, and done many wonders in Your name? And then I will declare to them, 'I never knew you; depart from Me, you who practice lawlessness!*" (Matthew 7 : 21 - 23). Some wolves in sheep's clothing would be calling Him Master, Master, but their deeds deny their words!

There is that so awful word, 'lawlessness' which means iniquity! So here we have a group of people who profess to preach Christ. They even think that they are casting out demons; healing all kind of sickness, prophesising, even doing many other wonderful works. Sadly, they were apparently false teachers and deceived by the 'strong delusion'! What will Jesus say to them? "*Depart from me, you who work iniquity!*" What was their true work? In the Greek, it is that word again, 'Anomia' which is 'illegality or violation of the law' or 'without law'! Look it up, you will see. We can know them by their fruits, by their works! "*What shall we say then? Shall we continue in sin, that grace may abound? Certainly not. How shall we who died to sin, live any longer in it? Or do you not know that as many of us as were baptized into Christ were baptized into His death? Therefore, we were buried with Him through baptism into death, that just as Christ was raised from the dead by the glory of the Father, even so we also should walk in newness of life . . .* (Romans 6 : 1 - 6)

Today and in generations past some folks have taught that, being 'under grace', there is no need to keep the holy Law anymore. But the Redeemer Himself says otherwise. He says that those who are without the law have no salvation. Now let us look at more instances of this word "Anomia". Apostle John says, *"Whoever commits sin transgresses also the law, for sin is the transgression of the law. And you know that He was manifested to take away our sins, and in Him there is no sin. Whoever abides in Him does not sin. Whoever sins has neither seen Him nor known Him"*. (1 John 3 : 4 - 6) Again, this verse deals with 'Who Yahweh's people truly are', just what Jesus had revealed in Himself when He came to take away the original sin! So, whoever abides in Him will not sin; therefore, they will not 'transgress the law', for sin is transgression of the law. Indeed, Christ spoke the Truth when He said that 'transgression of the law' or "Anomia" would abound in the last days. He is saying that, just as surely as a dead person does no works; so a faith, a religion that does not include works as proof of a regenerated heart is also dead. Therefore, a true converted person in whom living and saving faith exists will surely produce good works, *". . . Not by might, nor by power, but by my Spirit, saith Jehovah of hosts."* (Zechariah 4 : 6)

One must also consider Ephesians chapter 2 verses 8 and 10, which tell us that salvation is by grace through faith, and that the Father created us for good works, which He prearranged for us to perform. Therefore, how can a person with a dead faith, one that produces no works, be in God's Kingdom, since he would be failing to do the very thing for which God is creating him in Christ? Furthermore, we are to be in God's image and to imitate Christ who, as our High Priest, continues to work toward our salvation.

To each church in the letters of Revelation 2 and 3, Christ says, *"I know your works."* People with an incomplete knowledge of Christianity will argue almost endlessly and quite vociferously that no works are needed for salvation. As said above, salvation is indeed a free gift; it cannot be earned by anyone's works. But that does not mean Christianity does need no works. If so, why would Christ say, *"I know your works"*, if He did not expect people to have them as part of their way of life, as part of Christianity!

Christianity does have works as a major part of its makeup.

Obviously, it is not about an amount of work, nor degree of quality of work to earn that gift for us. The essential is to obey and do God's will clearly expressed in His Word. We do not have immortality inherent in us, for immortality is something that must be given as a gift, and then accepted by the receiver by stretching out his hand to handle it: this is man's response to the Giver by the receiver's good works. Do you catch it! This is what God offers us. He offers us the opportunity to be born again into His Kingdom, thus receiving the gift of eternal life. It must be given and received as a gift. However, it is given on the conditions of faith, repentance, and remaining loyal to Him and to His way. The Master explained this clearly in the parable of three servants found in Matthew 25 : 14 - 30.

It is in the area of loyalty that works play a major role. We show our loyalty by the way we talk, what we talk about, who we fellowship with, and what we do with our time, our knowledge, our means and our energy. In short, we show our loyalty by our works, that is, by our conduct, and what we produce with what we have been given.

The book of Revelation is designed to focus attention on what is of greatest concern to Christ for His people. He wants to ensure that they do not give up or become weary due to the awful pressure of the times, and that instead, they may endure and persevere and be obedient to the very end. Let us put it in a clearer way. This great prophetic Book pursues the purpose which is not merely to give an insight of what is coming, but it is also to convince the Christian that his loyalty, his devotion, his steadfastness, his suffering, and perhaps even his martyrdom for Christ's sake, is not in vain: he should be assured of a wonderful future.

The reason for the stress on works is that character is not formed merely by knowing something, but by knowledge combined with putting it to work until it becomes a habit. Over time, habit becomes character, and character follows the person right through the grave!

If we are not working, emphasizing loyalty to the Person of God and to His way, making every effort to overcome Satan, the world and the self-centeredness within us, resisting with all of our being the temptations to do what is natural, carnal; if we are not expending our energy, and spending our time in working out our own salvation with fear and trembling, according to what Paul is asking us in Philippians 2 : 12, it is very likely, then, that we are not going to have the character necessary to go through the grave with hope; for the wrong works will follow us, and we will not be prepared for the Kingdom of God. Thus, what a person has done, that is, what he has worked out in his lifetime, follows him through the grave, either into the Lake of a destructive Fire or into the eternal life in the Kingdom of God, when the judgment is set.

God's Word tells us that His commandments are not meaningless or arbitrary. They were given to humanity in love from a God of infinite wisdom, knowledge and love. They were given to be a benefit to Mankind, bringing blessings when obeyed, not to burden them. These commandments include God's holy Sabbath. It is a day of rest and refreshing, given to man by the One who designed and created a perfect Man. It is a time for physical, emotional and spiritual renewal. God knew that we would need this time to nurture and strengthen a right relationship with Him. Part of the Sabbath command reads, "*Six days you shall labor and do all your work . . .*" God tells us to take care of our ordinary work and concerns on the other six days, leaving our time and our minds free to properly worship and obey Him by keeping the seventh day holy. When we are free to focus our minds and thoughts on God's way and purpose, the Sabbath truly becomes the blessing and delight God intends it to be, according to Isaiah 58 : 13, 14.

Sabbath observance is specifically mentioned as a part of the covenant God had made with all peoples then. Nevertheless, for many of us, it is a problem! Why? It is matter of habit. Have you ever had difficulty trying to change a habit? This is worth to be repeated and emphasized: as Human beings, we are creatures of habit. We tend to continue acting as we have acted in the past. Like a river flowing through a canyon, the longer a habit continues, the more deeply it becomes ingrained, and the harder it is to be changed. This is true of all habits, good or bad. However, Paul in Ephesians chapter 4 verses 22 to 24 shows that major changes must occur when we are converted to serve God. New good ones must replace old wrong practices and attitudes. Christians must learn good habits like Bible study, prayer, love, faith, patience, attending church meetings, giving to needy and caring for each other, teaching others to know and follow the Truth, and so on. We must also eliminate bad habits like foul language, uncontrolled temper, gambling, drugs, smoking, drinking, gossip, lying, pornography, sexual promiscuity, breaking God's Law as a whole . . .

Knowing what changes to make is not enough. We should know how to make them, for changes do not come easily. For our benefit, the Scriptures alone give us all the guidance we need; there are the best source of guidance for self-help and motivation for self-improvement.

FORTUNAT TSHIMANGA-MUKADI

They teach us that 'love' is one of the strongest forces in existence. Love had moved our Heavenly Father to send His begotten holy Son to the Cross to save us, and if we love Him, we must keep His commandments and above all, to be like Him. In so doing, we certify truly that we know Him. Indeed, the desire to be like someone we admire is a powerful motivation for us to change our bad habits. We are called to be like Jesus. We should follow His steps because He left us a powerful example of living (1 Peter 2 : 21, 22).

As we face each decision in life, we should ask, 'What would Jesus do in such a situation?' This will give us strong motivation to change our lives. (See also Galatians 2 : 20; Matthew 16 : 24; Colossians 3 : 10). For, by experience, we know that in this life, everyone should stand for a cause, for some valuable principles, for something higher, regardless of challenges and adversity: in this, only God the Creator is the Most High on Whom we should focus! For, people we love would forsake us, life circumstances may change and trails and challenges may entice us, but He alone stands as an unshakable Mighty Rock! Having an even big motive in our life, which is the crown of eternal life (James 1 : 12; Revelation 2 : 10), we have to set our minds on our eternal reward, not on earthly things (Colossians 3 : 1 - 6; 2 Peter 1 : 10,11; 2 Thessalonians 1 : 8,9). Lack of motivation is a major reason why it is so difficult for people to change with the purpose to please God, instead they want to please themselves or their friends and their family members; being too concerned with the things of this life. However, if one is determined that serving God is his most important purpose in this life; he will find the means to make the necessary changes. The Scriptures in Proverbs 4 : 23 teach to keep the heart with all diligence, for out of it are the issues of life. Yes, the way we act is determined by our attitudes and intentions. People and circumstances may have influence upon us, but we do not have to give in; we have to do what is for God's will and glory (refer to Matthew 15 : 18, 19; 12 : 34 - 37).

Apostle Paul in Philippians 4 : 13 emphasizes that we can do all things through Christ who strengthens us. This includes changing our ways that we may please God. We should not trust our own strength; we have to use Christ's strength for our success, because Satan can never defeat Him.

From time to time, I have heard some friends and relatives uttering these curses upon themselves 'I just cannot change . . . It is too late for me at the present time . . . I'm only human . . .' In this, they are denying

God's Word and power; they will fail simply because they will give up instead of persisting to use the promise, "*If you commit yourself to the Lord and trust Him, He will accomplish His will for you.*" (Psalms 37 : 5). No matter how strong a temptation you face, no matter how long you have practiced a sin, if God says to change, you can change if you want to: only do your part and He will do His (See Ephesians 6 : 10 - 18; 3 : 20, 21; 2 Corinthians 9 : 8; Joshua 1 : 5 - 9.).

Meditating daily on God's Word is very important in our battle against the evil. For this, we should be accustomed with this Book of books to understand the very essence of its teachings and admonitions (Psalm 1 : 2; 119 : 11; Matthew 4 : 1 - 11). Sadly, too many people grow up with Sunday worship as their custom, it had become a strong mindset and they are very reluctant to accept change or alter their lifestyle. Another reason is that Saturday is a day that is not convenient for most Christians and so sadly, most would rather not know Truth but go into denial. Therefore, even when a sermon is presented on the Sabbath truth, it becomes difficult to such ones to accept this truth, even to search the Scriptures and investigate for themselves to make sure of such a truth. The Enemy of Truth so takes the opportunity to just whisper in their mind, ". . . The day does not matter . . . If it mattered everyone would know about it and would be keeping Saturday . . . Do not bother yourself for the day, everything is OK with your faith . . ."

The TV popular preacher Billy Graham was quoted to have acknowledged the Sabbath truth but stated, "If I were to teach this truth, I would lose most of my listeners." Indeed, here is what we read on his BGEA (*Billy Graham Evangelistic Association*) web site: "God told us to set aside one day out of seven for a very good reason: He knew we needed it. If we work all the time, not only will we wear out physically, but we'll also neglect our relationship with God. This is why one of the Ten Commandments says, 'Six days you shall labor and do all your work, but the seventh day is a Sabbath to the Lord your God' (Exodus 20 : 9 - 10) . . . And then it emphasis "This also is why we observe the Sabbath best when we use it for both rest and worship. Our bodies need rest, and that's why the Old Testament decreed, 'Six days you shall labor, but on the seventh day you shall rest' (Exodus 34 : 21). But our souls also need renewing, and that's why the Sabbath also should be a time for worship and instruction in God's Word. Jesus regularly attended worship on the Sabbath (e.g., Luke 4 : 14 - 16). I'm afraid we're in danger of forgetting this commandment today, but when we do, we pay a price both physically and spiritually. Instead, God loves us, and He wants to bless us by giving us rest and restoring our souls. May this be true every week for you, and every day . . ." Then comes the confusion, "When we know Christ, every day is an opportunity to love Him and serve Him more".

This deception is not isolated among today evangelists; many Bible teachers today follow the same wrong way. Jesus said we are to both obey and teach the law and one cannot sacrifice Truth at any cost. The Enemy has gone to extreme lengths to make sure the Sabbath truth is not taught or believed as it should and he continues to go to extreme lengths and deceptions to keep people ignorant of this Truth, regardless of their high instruction and their numerous diplomas in what they call 'Theology'. It is not surprising for it was the same in Christ's time with His earned rabbis and other teachers!

Never underestimate the Enemy's ability to slowly and subtly bring heresy into the Church and make those with the most Biblical truth to get labelled falsely as cults or legalists. It should be obvious that Satan will always attack Truth the hardest and fiercest way that he has no trouble finding those he can deceive to accomplish his task very convincingly. The fact of the matter is that what is popular is not always true and what is Truth is not always popular. Since the Sabbath is one of the Ten Commandments that defines what sin is, why would not Satan attack it as it appears to be the easiest to attack among them and he does everything in his power to ensure that it should not get recognized or correctly taught. As many of us do not earnestly study the Word and check it with unbiased mind, Satan has achieved his goal and the falsity continues to perpetuate and to blind many.

XXIV—FOLLOW THE WAY!

. . . These things, says He who is holy, He who is true, He who has the key of David, He Who opens and no one shuts, and shuts and no one opens. 'I know your works. See, I have set before you an open door, and no one can shut it; for you have a little strength, have kept My word and have not denied My name'. (Revelation 3 : 7, 8)

THE SABBATH COMMANDMENT, along with all the other nine of the Decalogue, exists since Eden and emphasizes the most important nature of God as Creator of all things, and above all, Man's Maker. To You, O our God, all glories be, for "*You alone are the Lord: You have made heaven, the heaven of heavens, with all the host, the earth and everything on it, the seas and all that is in them, and You preserve them all. The host of heaven worships You.*" (Nehemiah 9 : 6). "The Sabbath therefore, lies at the very foundation of divine worship, for it teaches this great truth in the most impressive manner than no other institute does. The true ground of divine worship, not of that on the seventh day merely, but of all worship, is found in the distinction between the Creator and His creatures. This great fact can never become obsolete, and must never be forgotten." (Seventh-day Adventists believe—A Biblical exposition of 27 Fundamental doctrines, p. 245)

There is no other purpose for the Sabbath day meetings, but to worship and honor the Lord God with all our heart, all our mind and all our strength; to pray and praise His holy Name according to His greatness, to learn of Him and be prepared for the crisis to come.

While we gather for private or public worship, we have to keep in mind that God is present among His people. Because of this presence, we must be more reverent and have all our minds focused on spiritual and heavenly things. The warning addressed to Moses by God on Mount Sinai, ". . . *Draw not nigh hither: put off thy shoes from off thy feet, for the place whereon thou standest is holy ground.*" (Exodus 3 : 5), must be taken on account when children of men come in presence of the Most High. Gathered for worship, people have to know that they come to worship the same unchanging God before Whom Moses, assured of the Almighty God's presence, covered his face and the holy angels bow in praise; people have to be careful of what they say or do and how they behave in His presence.

God is holy and He blessed and made the Sabbath day holy among all seven days of the week. Moreover, wherever He manifests His presence, that place is made holy (read Genesis 2 : 3). Whichever people, time or place dedicated to His service according His will, all these ones become holy (refer to Exodus 3 : 5; 12 : 16; 19 : 6; . . .)

Moses was asked to remove his sandals off his feet to mark reverence of the presence of the Divinity in that wild ground. How much could we do so in our worship assemblies? Surely not removing the physical sandals off our carnal feet, but cleansing our heart and our spirit of the worldliness!

For, the true reverence for God "is inspired by a sense of His infinite greatness and a realization of His presence. With this sense of the Unseen, the heart of every child [and every adult], should be deeply impressed. The hour and place of prayer and the service of public worship, the child [also the adult], should be taught to regard as sacred because God is there. And as reverence is manifested in attitude and demeanor, the feeling that inspires it will be deepened" (Ellen G. White—*Education*, p. 242, *Margin added*).

From the Standard Desk Dictionary by Funk & Wagnalls, we take the definition for the word 'holy' as "regarded with or characterized by reverence because associated with God; sacred; having a spiritual and moral worth; designated for religious worship; consecrated; evoking or meriting reverence or awe."

From the Seventh-day Adventist Bible Dictionary, we have more light on the term 'holy' explained in this way, holiness is ". . . the rendering of several closely synonymous Greek and Hebrew words which refer in general to that which is sacred or set apart from the common. Besides connoting a separation from all that defiles, the terms also include, when referring to people of God, the concept of moral perfection, and there is often a strong emphasis upon dedication to religious or sacred use". Other definition include: revered; solemnly undertaken; sacrosanct: deserving special respect or reverence; and so on. In short, whatever is associated with God is sacred; it is set apart from the common and merits reverence or awe.

God alone is worthy to make anything or anyone holy; no man, so powerful or learned he may be, has this power. If He does impute holiness, no one can change or modify it! Having this sense always present in mind, let nobody degrade what God has put apart, He expects it might be used with awe, honor and fear; such as His Name, His Word, His commandments and laws, His people . . .

If we can imagine the difficulty before us, we would cultivate a steadfast daily living; in this, the book of Psalms opens with a powerful counsel, "*Blessed is the man that walketh not in the counsel of the ungodly, nor standeth in the way of sinners, nor sitteth in the seat of the scornful. But his delight is in the law of the LORD; and in his law doth he meditate day and night. And he shall be like a tree planted by the rivers of water, that bringeth forth his fruit in his season; his leaf also shall not wither; and whatsoever he doeth shall prosper*" (chapter 1, verses 1 to 3, King James Version).

How we understand the holiness of God determines if we serve the True God of the Bible, or a false god of our own imagination. We are not at leisure to define God for Whom we want Him to be. He defines Himself, and gives sense of His nature and His holiness through His Word. He is the Standard by which we judge what is holy and what is sin. Holiness is unique, for holiness in man must be the same as holiness in God (Matthew 5 : 48), or else there is no significance in the command of Peter to 'obedient children' of God: ". . . *as obedient children, not conforming yourselves to the former lusts, as in your ignorance; but as He who called you is holy, you also be holy in all your conduct, because it is written, 'Be holy, for I am holy*" (1 Peter 1 : 14 - 16). We cannot take the position that the moral attributes of God may be wholly different from those of man. We do not worship a God of an unknown moral character, but the God to whom Jesus prays, saying, '*Holy Father*' and who has revealed

Himself as '*Light in Whom is no darkness at all*'. The light is a metaphor for purity, and darkness rhetorically stands for sin. Light as holiness is opposite to darkness and sinfulness; likewise as the day is opposite to night! A night lighted by stars and moon cannot be called day, even though this latter may be covered with heavy clouds and rain, it is always day! So we could be light or darkness, never altogether!

Here is an unquestionable truth: holiness in Scripture takes its essential meaning from what God is. God alone is holy in Himself. All other holiness is derived from a relationship with Him. In light of this, perhaps it would be clearer to some if we used the term 'godliness' or 'God-likeness'; that is what holiness is. The extent to which one is holy is determined by their likeness to the One True God, and sin is the extent in which we have departed from that character. It should suffice to say that God expects us to be in alignment, as His Spirit leads, with the divine character in as much as it is possible. God does not command us to be gods. He commands a likeness to His holy nature in as far as human limitations will allow.

Most deficient views of sin and grace are to be found in the imbalanced view of who God is. We know from Scripture that God is love. We know that He is all-powerful. We know that He is omnipresent. And we also know that God is omniscient. Nevertheless, not all of God's attributes are equal. Holiness is the primary attribute of God. All other attributes must be in subjection to His holiness. Holiness occupies the foremost rank among the attributes of God. Because the fundamental character of this attribute, the holiness of God, should be given first place rather than the love, the power, or the will of God. Holiness is the regulative principle of all of them, for His throne is established on the basis of His holiness. Indeed, if we put love as the primary attribute, then we can rationalize the idea that God accepts sin because of His love. We cannot say that God is first omnipotent so can do anything He wants, including sin. We can emphasize a God who is in everything, a God of pantheism and the environment, making the abuse of the environment the major sin.

All other attributes must fall in subjection to the primary attribute of God, which is His holiness. God is all-powerful, so He can do everything but which is perfect. God cannot sin. He cannot use that power to accomplish that which goes contrary to His holy nature. God may be omnipresent, but He is not 'in' that which is evil. God does not by nature reside in every blade of grass, or in evil human hearts such as the murders, the prostitutes, the demons, . . . With the purpose of holiness being primary, the ability to reside in evil people is an impossibility; the residing in isolation or in inanimate objects carries no moral purpose.

In my youth as student in Catholic schools, I was taught to adore and kiss the Cross, because it represents Christ, to veneer the church building as God's dwelling place, to have a cross around my neck to prevent Satan's defilement; but God's Word freed me from all this defilement. He gave me the understanding of His will and opened my eyes to find the Way through His Map that is His eternal Word.

Love is the most abused aspect of the nature of God that is constantly appealed to make God 'tolerant' of sin. Love, when it becomes the end in itself in isolation from holiness, becomes a means of many philosophers and preachers to treat the unregenerate and unrepentant sinner as being incorporated into the holy Body of Christ.

While it is said the love held Jesus to the Cross, it was holiness that necessitated it. Love alone could not reconcile us to God. God cannot freely forgive without the barrier of sin being removed that put a vast divide between Him and humans. Holiness is so central to understand sin. To arrive at Biblical truth concerning God's interaction with Man, it is essential to have a right concept of His holiness and the centrality of it in His plan of salvation for human beings.

He cannot more cease to hate impurity and He cannot cease to love holiness: if He should in the least instant approve of anything that is filthy, in that moment He would disapprove of His own Nature and Being; there would be an interruption in His love of Himself, which is as eternal as it is infinite. How can He love any sin which is contrary to His nature, but for one moment, without hating His own nature, which is essentially contrary to sin? Two contraries cannot be loved at the same time.

O yes, God so loved His children that He sent His only begotten Son to the Cross to restore purity in Man, as he became polluted by the intrusion of sin; because His holiness could not tolerate the presence of polluting sin and then, His love spared the rebels from eternal destruction.

If holiness can only well be understood in relationship to the nature of God, and the necessity of the atonement connected to holiness, then we must consider that all of God's dealings with Man are based upon this foundation. When we imagine the horrible sufferings of Christ on the Cross on our behalf as the terrible cost of sin, we can understand the gravity and the depth of our distance from God. How much far away from God must we be by sin, that God's holiness demands such a cost? Christ would not have suffered so unless it was not only necessary but also surely imperative to save us. We can also see in the atonement that the design of this reconciliation is more than just a mere judicial forgiveness, but a means to cancel the differences that keep Man from being at one with his Creator.

Holiness is the conformity to the character of God. To have fellowship with Him in His characteristic feelings and principles, to love what He loves, to hate what He hates, to desire what He promises, to rejoice in His will in all things always and anywhere!

Holiness prompted grace to Man. Unfortunately, grace by nature has always had the potential to lead people to a concept of license. This is why Paul advises in Romans chapter 6. ". . . *Shall we continue in sin that grace may abound? Certainly not! How shall we who died to sin live any longer in it?*" (verses 1 and 2). People are taking the words of Paul concerning grace abounding more as sin itself abound, as meaning that more sin would automatically increase grace, in such a way that sin may become tolerated and even cherished. This is far from the doctrinal conclusions many teachers draw from their theology of grace today. A salvation so gracious from the beginning to the end might be misconstrued as encouraging the continuance of sin in the Christian's life, a notion not only Christ denounces in the most vigorous terms, but also the apostle Paul and other apostles and prophets. By no means, those that have died to sin cannot go on living in it.

Exactly the opposite is true: while works of the Law (Galatians 2 : 16) have no part in justification, which is solely of grace (Ephesians 2 : 8 - 9), good works are to be the very centerpiece of the life of gratitude, which is to characterize those who have been saved by God's grace (Ephesians 2 : 10). Your works will go with you, say the Scripture! Indeed, Adam and Eve, after their fall, did not perform any good works to get God covering them of the innocent lamb's skin! It is not by Man's good works that Christ came to die to the cross for him. This is the divine grace, which speaks loudly that God first did His part, and then we too have to do ours.

In my Christian experience, I have found that few Christians may put any effort whatsoever in searching the Scriptures for a Biblical answer on this subject. For, when asked whether we must sin or not, their answer is, "of course we do, we all sin!" Is this argument based upon personal experience of some people, a viable substitute for what God says on the subject anything else?

God knows why He gives us laws, commandments, statutes, rules, ordinances. Our responsibility is but to obey without doubting, questioning or interpreting what is clearly explained by Him; for, thus says the Lord, "*For My thoughts are not your thoughts, nor are your ways My ways, . . . For as the heavens are higher than the earth, so are My ways higher than your ways, and My thoughts than your thoughts.*" (Isaiah 55 : 8, 9)

The Savior explains for us how to obey His commandments, saying ". . . *Whoever therefore breaks one of the least of these commandments, and teaches men so, shall be called least in the kingdom of heaven; but whoever does and teaches them, he shall be called great in the kingdom of heaven. I tell you that if you are no more obedient than the teachers of the law and the Pharisees, you will never enter the kingdom of heaven*". (Matthew 5 : 19, 20). Making it clearer He explains that he who will say to his fellow man '*fool*' will be judged and condemned to a death sentence according to the sixth commandment '*you will not kill*'. (verses 21 and 22)

To sin against the Lord's Law starts in our mind, God alone knows when and how and already imputes the sin; then our words or deeds express openly that inward sin. "*For from within, out of the heart of men, proceed evil thoughts, adulteries, fornications, murders, thefts . . . foolishness. All these evil things come from within and defile a man.*" (Mark 7 : 21 - 23).

If the thoughts are not properly employed, "religion cannot flourish in the soul. The mind must be preoccupied with sacred and eternal things, or it will cherish trifling and superficial thoughts. Both the intellectual and the moral powers must be disciplined and they will strengthen and improve by [right] exercise. In order to understand this matter aright, we must remember that our hearts are naturally depraved, and we are unable of ourselves to pursue a right course. It is only the grace of God, combined with the most earnest effort on our part, that we can gain the victory." (Ellen G. White, *Counsels to Parents and Students*, p. 544, *emphasis added*)

Let no one deceive himself with the belief that he can become holy while willfully violating one of God's requirements so small it may be.

When one commits a known sin, this silences the Spirit's voice to witness and then separates the sinner from his Creator, as Adam and Eve tried to flee and hide from God in vain.

Why should we obey God? The simplest reason is: It is our duty to express our love to Him who loves us first without measure. Through His death on the cross, Christ has purchased us (Acts 20 : 28), and made us children of God, so we are to do what He commands or asks us. Of course, we do not obey in order to be saved. Salvation comes first, and obedience should follow as the result of our acceptance of the salvation offered to all, to ". . . *bear fruits worthy of repentance*" (Matthew 3 : 8) in doing things that show we really have changed our hearts and lives.

Obedience goes deeper than duty or obligation. Obedience should come from the heart, done because we want to. Thus, there are three main reasons for our obedience. First, in faith, we believe that God's commands are for our own good. As our Creator, He has the wisdom to know how we should live, what works best and what causes the most happiness in our pilgrimage. Obedience expresses faith in His wisdom and love. Obedience is what He made us for, as it is written, "*For we are His workmanship, created in Christ Jesus for good works, which God prepared beforehand that we should walk in them*" (Ephesians 2 : 10), and life works better if we are in tune with the way we were made. Surely, we are created for good works, not to be sinners.

Second, obedience involves hope in a future blessed life. If there is no future life, then Christianity would be foolishness, for Christ ensured us, saying, ". . . *I have come that they may have life, and that they may have it abundantly.*", ". . . *My sheep hear My voice, and I know them, and they follow Me. And I give them eternal life, and they shall never perish, neither shall anyone snatch them out of My hand. My Father, who has given them to Me, is greater than all . . .* (John 10 : 10, 27 - 29). Jesus promised that His disciples would find eternal life worth far more than anything they might have to give up in their life: ". . . *there is no one who has left house or brothers or sisters or father or mother or wife or children or lands, for My sake and the gospel's, who shall not receive a hundredfold now in this time—houses and brothers and sisters and mother and children and lands, with persecutions—and in the age to come, eternal life.* (Mark 10 : 29 - 30). Everyone who is saved will have the joy of knowing God in eternal life, but there are also rewards in addition to eternal joy.

Finally, God is love and loved us before the world was. He loves us and wants to help us, not give us unnecessary burdens. In the gospel of John, chapter 14, verses 21 and 22, Christ said, *"He who has My commandments and keeps them, it is he who loves Me, and he who loves Me will be loved by My Father, and I will love him and manifest Myself to him . . . ."*

God wants each of us to be conformed to the likeness of His Son (Romans 8 : 29). We are in the process of 'being transformed into His likeness with ever-increasing glory' (2 Corinthians 3 : 18). As children of God, we are to become like the Son of God. He is not only our Savior, He is also our example, showing us what humans should be like. When we believe in Christ, we have a new identity and a new purpose of being and living. Our new identity is 'children of God', not 'being sinners'; our purpose is 'to be like God in true righteousness and holiness' (Ephesians 4 : 22 - 24) and to act like new creatures which we are.

XXV—BE YE HOLY AS HE IS

If anyone loves Me, he will keep My words; and My Father will love him, and We will come to him and make Our home with him (John 14 : 23)

WHAT AN ENORMOUS goal! We are to be like God! By His holiness, God is changing us to be like Himself, more like Jesus, His begotten Son, who showed us what God is like when living in the flesh. Obviously, we cannot make ourselves Godlike. But God can and He is willing to! He does not do this against our will, but only as we agree to what He is doing. And by the Holy Spirit working in our hearts and minds, He is helping us to agree what He asks. ". . . *Work out your own salvation with fear and trembling, for it is God who works in you both to will and to do for His good pleasure*", writes Paul in chapter 2, verses 12 and 13 of his letter to Philippians Christians.

Kindling fire, cooking or warming food, cleaning vessels, or talking our own words on Sabbath is breaking the fourth commandment of the Decalogue, even though we pretend having stopped our works at sunset Friday. For the Lord explains the sixth commandment, saying that ". . . *whoever is angry with his brother without a cause, shall be in danger of the judgment . . .*" (Matthew 5 : 22). Why? Because violating the sixth commandment is not only killing, but also getting angry or threatening your fellow man with words or gestures. In the same manner, you can pollute the Sabbath day even in speaking out vain words. Even planning for some everyday activities during those holy hours is breaking the Law. For "*You must be perfect, just as your Father in heaven is perfect*" (verse 48)

Yes, one is perfect if he is not cold or lukewarm, but he is hot; for the lukewarm and the cold have the same end at the divine judgment, '*I will spit you out of My mouth*', says the Lord. Instead, the perfection is attained in sanctification that is the grace of God revealed in character, and the graces of Christ brought into active exercise in good works: Christ implanting His divine nature in human heart and mind.

The light the Spirit of God had shed upon His Church is so great that we do not have the right to make mistakes. Not only His Will is clearly expressed in His Word; but also, through all Christian history, He sends to His children the messages of warning for the coming judgment. However, it is not enough to have the light. The most important thing is how people use the light; is it for God's glory and their salvation or for their shame and death?

Satan is so busy working with all who give him encouragement. Those who have the light but find the reason not to walk therein will become at last confused until darkness pervades their mind, and shapes the whole course of their action and life. Nevertheless, there are great privileges and blessings for all who humble themselves and fully consecrate their hearts to God. More light will be given to them. Then the spirit of wisdom and goodness of God as revealed in His Word will become brighter and brighter as they follow on in this path of true obedience.

When men are willing to be transformed, they will be exercising unto godliness, and the work of sanctification is the work of a lifetime; it must go on continually. Thus ". . . this work cannot go on in the heart while the light on any part of the Truth is rejected or neglected; the follower of Christ will seek for truth as for hidden treasures, and will press from light to a greater light, ever increasing in knowledge; he will continually grow in grace in the knowledge of the truth'. (Ellen G. White—*Selected Messages—1*, p.317)

The Decalogue is eternal as Its Author is: all its commandments, precepts and rules related to it to explain and complete, are in the same manner eternal. Breaking one spot of them annuls the whole Law.

For the Church as well for each faithful believer, the path of obedience is the path of safety and happiness spiritually and materially.

FORTUNAT TSHIMANGA-MUKADI

A diligent obedience is asked from us and we cannot choose the course of ease and self-indulgence. ". . . *'Surely I have taught you statutes and judgments, just as the LORD my God commanded me,'* says Moses, *'that you should act according to them in the land you are entering, in the land which you go to possess. Obey these laws carefully, in order to show the other nations that you have wisdom and understanding . . .'"* (Deuteronomy 4 : 5, 6)

Many verses throughout the Word of God echo this eternal theme, "*KEEP MY COMMANDMENTS, OBEY MY LAWS*"! God never instructed the Israelites 'to try to keep the Law', 'to do their best' or 'to do what they are able to'; but the message was and is still, "TO KEEP, TO OBEY". Despite their human weakness and even mingling with pagans, they never complained 'Why, Lord, do you ask us such a hard thing to keep the whole Law'? Instead, though they were disobedient and hardened their heart from time to time, they understood that the Law could and should be kept (Joshua 22 : 2, 2 Kings 18 : 6, Numbers 14 : 18). The Messiah stressed it clearly, saying, "*Love the Lord your God with all your heart, all your soul, all your mind, and with all your strength . . .* (Mark 12 : 30). For love makes obedience easier and sacrifice a pleasure.

True faith, which relies wholly upon Christ, is manifested by obedience to all His requirements; and from the beginning of creation until the end of World History, the great controversy is about obedience to God's Law, and especially to the Fourth commandment; for it points to God as the sole Creator of everything. And the Deceiver attacked directly in the beginning to this special creative character of God, deceiving our first parents with the promise, "*You will be as gods*".

When a man, by ignorance, self-confidence or pride, tries to choose and to do the contrary of what God requires, it is always counted to him as disobedience, sin and idolatry.

The Bible gives many examples of the consequences of breaking the Will of our God, even in the smallest jot possible!

Moses brought the Israelites into the wilderness and they needed drinking water. Moses prayed God. Then Moses was asked to smite the rock once that the people and their flocks may have water. He doubted, and then by false reasoning and self-sufficiency, he smote the rock twice maybe thinking that smiting the rock one time would not be enough to have enough water for the entire congregation! The judgment fell immediately upon him from the Lawgiver; because he did not fully obey the requirement of God. He preferred to change 'one jot', in smiting the rock twice instead of once.

Let us not be complaisant in doing God's will if we are asked to obey Him. Moses tried to correct God's words! Maybe he reasoned that no matter how many times he would smite the rock, the most important to his views was to smite it in any way. In so doing, he lost his part to the inheritance to enter into the Promised Land. (see Number 20 : 8 - 12)

Saul was told to destroy the Amalekites and all their herd and houses; but he thought that it was *'good'* to spare *'the best sheep and cattle to offer as sacrifices to the Lord your God'* (1 Samuel 15 : 9, 15) Perhaps Saul considered that it was not fair to destroy people and animals, when the victory was already at hand! Sometimes he thought of offering the good sheep as thanksgiving to the Lord. However, the judgment of the Lord fell without appeal, by the mouth of the prophet, *". . . What pleases the Lord more: burnt offerings and sacrifices or obedience to His voice? It is better to obey than to sacrifice. It is better to listen to God than to offer the fat of sheep. Disobedience is as bad as the sin of sorcery. Pride is as bad as the sin of worshiping idols. You have rejected the Lord's command. Now He rejects you as king"* (1 Samuel 15 : 22, 23).

The Bible is full of such stories teaching us that nobody has the liberty to bargain blamelessly the Word that proceeds out of the Mouth of the Lord. The great example is found in Eden and we are still reaping the fruit of that misconduct of our first parents.

Rejecting a small word of the Master's will, we but reject Him and we deserve the consequences of our deeds. Disobedience is rebellion, whatever your motive, whatever your reason; and disobedience is also idolatry, how great, highly educated and wise you may pretend to be.

For those who love the Lord, no one of His requirements and rules is burdensome (1 John 5 : 3); only the transgressor, the unrenowned heart ones, the backsliders are the ones who consider the law or commandment as grievous yoke, because the sinful mind cannot submit to God's will, nor can it do so (Romans 8 : 7).

To be really a 'peculiar faithful people', 'a remnant' to the Lord, as many like to claim it unceasingly, the leitmotiv must be, "I do 'this' or 'that' for the Lord has spoken". That is it! So did Abram and it was counted to him as righteousness.

Christ explained the living faith in the likeness of Abraham in giving to His disciples the parable of a father who had two sons whom he asked to go and work in the field: the first accepted by words but did not go, but the second who refused in words, and after reflection, obeyed and went to do what he was asked. This later son is considered as obedient to his father! In the same manner, our affirmation of faith avails nothing if it is not seen in our deeds and behavior! It is why the apostle James states clearly, saying, ". . . *Show me your faith without your works, and I will show you my faith by my works*" (James 2 : 18)! And beloved John to emphasize, "*For this is the love of God, that we keep His commandments. And His commandments are not burdensome*" (1 John 5 : 3).

Today, many teachers, doctors of the Law and philosophers annul good works for they are unable to produce them. They make their religion a mere formalism. They make void the very sayings of the Master (John. 14 : 23, 24).

More than any other factor, fruits produced by God's people could tell the story and send a message to the world, for, by our fruits, they will know who we are and what makes us to move: is it what God has spoken or what the demons dictate us; as it is written, "'*Therefore by their fruit you will know them. Not everyone who says to Me 'Lord, Lord, shall enter the kingdom of heaven, but he who does the will of My Father in heaven*" (Matthew 7 : 20, 21). We are special people to God, if we do His will, and the world will know we are His children if we have love for one another (John. 13 : 35). According to the Word, love and obedience are inseparable (1 John 5 : 3). Loving and doing go together and both are essential for the true followers of Christ (1 John 3 : 10). They willingly submit to God's will and love and obey Him and practice what they believe (James 1 : 22 - 25).

Our concept of God determines our response to who 'GOD' is. What one considers holy determines how he will live. How people understand the holiness of God determines also if they serve the True God of the Bible, or a false god of their own imagination. Nobody is free to define God as One they want Him to be: for God defines Himself and defines His nature and His holiness.

Restraining ourselves from polluting the Sabbath by not kindling fire on this Holy Day is not comparable to what was asked to Abram; but he obeyed without vain reasoning; and the Spirit of the Lord explains

Genesis 22 : 1 - 12 in this way: "Abraham's great act of faith stands like a pillar of light, illuminating the pathway of God's servants in all succeeding ages. Abraham did not seek to excuse himself from doing the will of God. During that three days' journey he had sufficient time to reason, and doubt God, if he had disposed to doubt. He might have reasoned that the slaying of his son would cause him to be looked upon as a murderer, a second Cain . . . He might have pleaded that age should excuse him from obedience. But the patriarch did not take refuge in any of these excuses. Abraham was human; his passions and attachments were like ours; but he did not stop to question how the promise could be fulfilled if Isaac should be slain. He did not stay to reason with his aching heart. He knew that God is just and righteous in all His requirements, and he obeyed the command to the very letter." (Ellen G. White— Patriarchs and Prophets, p. 153)

Notice the words ". . . he obeyed the command to the very letter"! Do we do so today?

As result for His matchless faithfulness, God sworn and said to Abram, "'. . . *because thou hast done this thing, and hast not withheld thy son, thine only son: that in blessing I will bless thee, and in multiplying I will multiply thy seed as the stars of the heaven, and as the sand which is upon the sea shore . . .*" (Genesis 22 : 16, 17, King James Version).

The patriarch did not seek 'his good', or the 'good of his only heir'; he obeyed the voice of the Lord by faith, sure that whoever he was and whatever he had, was from the same Lord, worthy of being fully obeyed, trustworthy and loved, able to resurrect his son from death, though he may be in the tomb since thousand of years! This Isaac's sacrifice is the lesson for us all, on how earnest we should obey our Creator, keep and do His Will as it is clearly expressed in His Word.

Jesus defeated the Devil with, "*It is written*", not by 'I say' (Matthew 4 : 1 - 11), even though He is the only begotten Son of God. Three times Jesus was tempted by the Devil and three times Jesus replied exactly by the same three powerful words that defeated the Devil: 'IT IS WRITTEN'.

If oral tradition or the authority of the Church were valid, then Jesus would have at least one time referred to oral human tradition, or used Himself as the authority, as many Christian church leaders do. Never did Jesus refer to oral tradition to prove or defend Truth, but every time, He refers to the Scriptures. The only times Jesus referred to Oral traditions, was condemning them: "*And in vain they worship Me, teaching as doctrines the commandments of men. For laying aside the commandment of God, you hold the tradition of men . . . All too well you reject the commandment of God, that you may keep your tradition . . . making the word of God of no effect through your tradition . . .*" (Mark 7 : 7 - 13)

During His earthly ministry. Jesus made over one hundred references to Scriptures and relied upon them alone, though He is the Son of God, Him who inspired them, always referred to them, ". . . *Have you not read . . .*" (Matthew 12 : 3) "*. . . have you not read in the law that . . .*" (verse 5) "*Have you never read in the Scriptures*" (Chapter 21 verse 42). Let us follow the Lord's pattern by relying always and solely on the Holy Scriptures!

The apostles, though inspired with genuine oral revelation, were always directing people to the Scriptures for the final determination of Truth. Oral tradition is worthless without the witness of Scripture! (Acts 17 : 2, 11 - 12; 18 : 28; 1 Timothy 4 : 13; 2 Timothy 3 : 15 - 17)

XXVI—WHAT IS SANCTIFICATION?

So Jesus said to them again, 'Peace to you! As the Father has sent Me. I also send you'. And when He had said this, He breathed on them, and said to them, 'Receive the Holy Spirit. If you forgive the sins of any, they are forgiven them; if you retain the sins of any, they are retained'. (John 20 : 21 - 23)

BORN IN SIN according to our human nature, our daily fight is to become holy as our heavenly Father. Therefore, we should be the one or the other, not sinner and children of God altogether; for "The eternal God has drawn the line of distinction between the saint and the sinner, between converted and unconverted. The two classes do not blend into each other imperceptibly, like the colors of a rainbow, but are as different as midday and midnight." (Ellen G. White, *Messages to Young People*, p. 390)

In my long time experience as a Roman Catholic Church believer, I never heard a priest stating during a mass, "We are all sinners". Instead, I was taught and encouraged to be 'saint' as I had to live performing good works, that, after death, I can be considered as 'saint', after a long process of inquiries, searches and polls! This act of recognition, called 'canonization', is reserved to the 'Holy See' and occurs at the conclusion of a long process requiring extensive proof that the person proposed for canonization lived and died in such an exemplary and holy way that he or she is worthy to be recognized as 'saint'. Even though in these days, the process had become shorter than before, the Church's official recognition of sanctity implies that the persons are now in heavenly glory, that they may be publicly invoked and mentioned officially in the liturgy of the Church, most especially in the 'Litany of the Saints'. Thus there are entitled to intervene to God for our forgiveness and our spiritual growing. This 'canonization' involves a decree that allows veneration of the 'saint' in the liturgy of the Church Rite throughout the world. For permission to venerate on a local level, only 'beatification' is needed, not canonization. "Beatification, in the present discipline, differs from canonization in this: that the former implies (1) a locally restricted, not a universal permission to venerate, which is (2) a mere permission, and no precept; while canonization implies a universal precept" (Beccari, Camillo. "*Beatification and Canonization*" Catholic Encyclopaedia. Vol. 2. New York: Robert Appleton Company, 1907. Retrieved 27 May 2009).

Such a process is particular to the Catholic (Roman and Orthodox) Church; therefore, the difficult questions now are:—in the Christendom, is the Catholic Church the only one that produces 'saints';—who should determine or confer the sanctity to a person if any;—Does the sanctity come to someone only after his death;—How does the sanctification occur . . . ?

Throughout the Word of God, the title of 'saint' is referred most of the time to the living person that is faithful to his Maker as the book of Revelation makes it so clear in its chapter 14 verse 12. It is what David sang in Psalms (30 : 4, 85 : 8 . . .); Luke emphasized in Acts 9 : 13, 32, 41 and Paul stressed in Romans 15 : 25, 26, 31, 2 Corinthians 9 : 1, 12; 13 : 13 . . .). Some different churches and beliefs have each one their lists of 'saints' set up in diverse manners with their own rules and processes to qualify someone as 'saint'.

In the beginning, around the fourth century, the first persons whom the newborn Christian Church honoured as 'saints' were the martyrs whose death for their faith was considered the supreme and undeniable witness to their faith in Christ, and also people, called confessors, who had confessed their faith not by dying but by word and life; the fame of many of them spread widely, leading to their veneration far outside the area in which they lived and died. While many churches consider generally as 'saints', the prophets, the apostles and writers of books of the Bible and other persons with some positive records of their lives, Catholic Church has a particular system of herself to produce 'saints' by the pope, through canonization.

This procedure of proclaiming 'sanctity' for a person as established around 10th century, and then ameliorated since 1983, is the act by which the Eastern or Roman Catholic Church or another religious group declares a deceased person 'saint' and is included in the canon or list of recognized saints. However, originally, individuals were recognized as 'saints' without any formal process. Later, the process changed through the centuries, and that which is used in the present time, took place in 1983, under pope John Paul II's apostolic constitution 'Divinus Perfectionis Magister' of January 25, 1983; and the norms issued by the Congregation for the Causes of Saints on February 7, 1983, for its implementation on diocesan level, continued the work of simplification already initiated by pope Paul VI. Those important regulations gave the process and rules that lead the Church to recognize one's sanctity, on one hand. On the other, as the Vatican's highest court, the Apostolic Penitentiary, the 'tribunal of conscience', deals with confessions of sins considered so grave that only pope has the authority to absolve. "A number of sins are considered as heinous by the Catholic Church that only the Pope can grant absolution. They include:—defiling the Eucharist, either by spitting it out or using it in a Satanic ritual;—Attempting to assassinate pope;—As a priest, breaking the seal of confession by revealing details about a repentant sinner;—as a priest, offering absolution to one's own sexual partner;—participating in an abortion, even by paying for it, and later seeking to become a priest." (Megan O'Toole, in *Toronto National Post*, January 16th 2009, sections A1 and A2)

Now, in the light of God's Word, how such a process is accurate and trustworthy? Before moving forward, as spoken in the twentieth and twenty-first chapters in this testimony, the Roman Catholic Church had obliterated the Holy Ten Commandments written by the Creator upon the tablets of stones, with the purpose to hide to their followers how she has fought against the unchanging Will of God! Therefore, to succeed in keeping their believers in ignorance, the Bible was forbidden to be read by the common people and considered as a deceitful book.

However, the message in God's Word is constantly the same, ". . . *there is One God and One Mediator between God and men, the Man Jesus Christ*" (1 Tim. 2 : 5); ". . . *you are the temple of God and that the Spirit of God dwells in you?*" (1 Corinthians 3 : 16); so ". . . *what agreement has the temple of God with idols? For you are the temple of the living God. As God has said: 'I will dwell in them and walk among them. I will be their God, and they shall be My people.*'" (2 Corinthians 6 : 16); because "*the idols of the nations are silver and gold, the work of men's hands. They have mouths, but they do not speak; eyes they have, but they do not see . . .*" (Psalms 135 : 15 - 18).

It is amazing enough that Catholic Church leaders could be erring so, as it is generally proven that this Church is the one among all Churches in the world which has a great number of leaders and believers with a higher level of instruction! Consider this only by the number of universities and schools of religious education which have formed the respectable emeritus around the world! Like in Christ's time with the learned Scribes and Pharisees, these Christians doctors and masters could not study the unchanging God's Word and hold its sayings with high respect as it deserves as being from the Mouth of the Most High Creator, who said repeatedly in His Word that not one jot or one point should be changed from His Word'!

The idea that a person can be "beatified" and be "canonized" and given status of 'saint' by a wanting and finite human being, is foreign to the Bible; but derived by a wrong interpretation of Matthew 16 : 17 - 17to give to the pope the power and authority to open the heavenly gates, Almighty God sacred Domain and let his 'saints' go therein. This Scripture states, ". . . *'Blessed are you, Simon Bar-Jonah, for flesh and blood has not revealed this to you, but My Father who is heaven. And I also say to you that you are Peter, and on this rock I will build My church, and the gates of Hades shall not prevail against it. And I will give you the keys of the kingdom of heaven, and whatever you bind on earth will be bound in heaven, and whatever you loose on earth will be loosed in heaven'"*. This rock (sometimes, the stone) is Christ Himself, for the eternal Church of Christ which is His Body, could not be built on finite man who had to pass away a time later (Matthew 7 : 24 - 25; Luke 6 : 48; Romans 9 : 33; 1 Corinthians 10 : 4 . . .).

A biblical 'saint' is a saint because of acceptance of the works of Jesus, and it is not based merely on individual efforts, nor upon prayers and human decisions, no matter how powerful and holy such man may pretend to be! For, we know by the Word of God, that the only living being who contended with God is Lucifer, so does he make his disciples to follow the same way.

A 'saint' is always someone through whom we catch a glimpse of what Christ is like and of what we are called to be (Ephesians 1 : 4; Colossians 1 : 22, 3 : 12 - 13; 1 Thessalonians 5 : 27; 1 Peter 1 : 15, 16 . . .). Only God 'makes' saints by His Spirit abiding within the person, as it is clearly stated in the holy Scriptures, *"and behold, I am coming quickly, and My reward is with Me, to give to everyone according to his work. I am the Alpha and the Omega, the Beginning and the End, the First and the Last."* (Revelation 22 : 12, 13).

The author and finisher of our faith is the only same Source of grace by which the saints live. The Word of God is so clear in the matter that no one can be misled by the powers of darkness working in this world. *"For this reason we also thank God without ceasing, because when you received the word of God which you heard from us, you welcomed it not as the word of men, but as it is in truth, the word of God, which also effectively works in you who believe."* (1 Thessalonicians 2 : 13). *". . . let it be known to you all, and to all the people of Israel, that by the name of Jesus Christ of Nazareth, whom you crucified, whom God raised from the dead, by Him this man stands here before you whole. This is 'the stone which was rejected by you builders, which has become the chief cornerstone'. Nor is there salvation in any other, for there is no other name under heaven given among men by which we must be saved."* (Acts 4 : 10 - 12). Do you get this message? If so, compare it to Matthew 16 : 17 - 19 quoted earlier in here.

As clearly described in Bible prophecy (Daniel 7 : 23 - 27;and Revelation), the pope, called by his followers 'Holy Father' (see John 17 : 11) is a visible contender of the Creator of the World and his symbols and armories describe so well how he makes himself equal to God. "Out of the ruins of political Rome, arose the great moral Empire in the 'giant form' of the Roman Church". (A. C. Flick, *The rise of the Mediaeval church*, New York, G.P. Putnam's Sons, 1909, p. 150). "Under the Roman Empire the popes had no temporal powers. But when the Roman Empire had disintegrated and its place had been taken by the papacy, a number of rude, barbarous kingdoms, the Roman Catholic church not only became independent of the states in religious affairs but dominated secular affairs as well". (Carl Conrad Eckhardt, *The papacy and World-Affairs*, Chicago, University of Chicago Press,1937, p. 1)

Wherever he goes, the insignia of the Pope is displayed, emblazoned on the 'pope mobile', hung from stages and high on posts at outdoor masses.

The various parts of the papal symbol describe the power of the papacy, one who, as Pope Leo XIII explained, occupies "the place on earth of God Almighty" (refer John 14 : 15 - 19; 15 : 26, 27; 16 : 12 - 15; Matthew 28 : 19). This makes our God a limited person, unable to get involved in our daily struggle and He needs someone powerful to take physically His place on earth! This is blasphemy and it denies profoundly the clear teachings of His Word. For, as Paul stressed it clearly in 1 Timothy 2 : 4 - 6 and Hebrew 9 : 15, our only Mediator is the Eternal Son of God, Jesus Christ through the Holy Spirit (see John 14 : 26).

FORTUNAT TSHIMANGA-MUKADI

Most notable in the papal emblem is the tiara, or Triple Crown. Until recently, during the coronation of a new pope, the tiara was placed on his head with the words: "Receive the tiara adorned with three crowns, and know that you are Father of princes and kings, guide of the world, vicar of our Savior Jesus Christ". This is sharply contrary to what the Lord had promised, *". . . I will pray the Father, and He will give you another Helper, that He may abide with you forever—the Spirit of truth, whom the world cannot receive, because it neither sees Him nor knows Him; but you know Him, for He dwells with you and will be in you. I will not leave you orphans; I will come to you. A little while longer and the world will see Me no more, but you will see Me. Because I live, you will live also"*; *". . . when He, the Spirit of truth, has come, He will guide you into all truth; for He will not speak on His own authority, but whatever He hears He will speak; and He will tell you things to come . . .")* (John 14 : 16 - 19; 16 : 13)

Therefore, it is good to understand the meaning of the three crowns that express loudly his self-entitled power over all creatures!

The first circlet, or crown, symbolizes the pope's 'universal episcopate'; as he claims to be ruler over all the Church of Christ: all priestly power, including the power to forgive sins, must come through him and his agents. This is why the pope John Paul II, felt justified to remind in his homilies, that everyone must be in submission to him in order to be saved; referring to *"No salvation outside the church of Rome"*, from the original saying by Saint Cyprian of Carthage (3rd century AD) found in his Letter LXXII, Ad Jubajanum de haereticis baptizandis, and in Latin reads: 'Salus extra ecclesiam non est'.

The second crown symbolizes the pope's claimed 'primacy of jurisdiction', meaning that he alone is complete ruler of the Church: he is the final judge, teacher and ruler. Over the Church of Christ, the pope claims to be more than a king. This is the reason why all other earthly kings, queens, princes, princesses, and even protestant and reformed church leaders alike have to bow before him and kiss his 'holy' ring!

The last circlet in the crown represents the pope's temporal power. This means that he is ruler of the entire world: all kings, presidents and governments are subservient to him. The papacy claims that all civil rulers have only that authority which the pope, as spiritual and temporal head, allows them to have.

Lest you think this to be an empty claim, consider how rulers and governments tremble at the opposition of the pope. In recent years, many rulers have been toppled when they lost papal favour. Once he turns against a government, the pope can raise up a mighty opposition of loyal Catholics to topple a government from within.

The papal emblem also contains a pair of crossed keys. These represent the supposed power of the pope to forgive sins and, as emphasized above, open heavenly doors to let his worshipers go in. Alexander Hislop (1807-1865), in his classical work, '*The Two Babylons*' in 1853, gives the fascinating background of how these keys helped the pope gain control over the pagans by the adaptation of the ancient keys of Janus and Cybele.

Another important part of the papal shield is the big letter "M" at the lower right quadrant of the shield. This stands for Pope John Paul II's undying devotion to the Virgin Mary.

While many Protestants believe that Rome is changing, the Vatican is actually bringing Catholic doctrine back to the old ways, with worship of Mary and many so-called 'saints' playing a key role.

The end of the matter is this: the popes still dream of world dominion. Claiming all authority and power, they strive to manipulate populations, governments and nations.

As clearly predicted and well described in God's Word (Daniel 7 : 23 - 25; 8 : 9 - 11; Revelation 17), the pope is now standing in the temple to receive the worship of the nations which should be only due to the Most High Priest, Creator and Saviour, Jesus Christ!

Bishops also wear a ring and so costly vestments. In the past, a distinction was made between the pontifical ring (which would have a gemstone, traditionally an amethyst), and the ordinary ring (which would have the bishop's coat of arms or some other design engraved on it). The ring, like a wedding band, symbolizes that the bishop is "wedded" to his diocese. The ring would also be used, at least in previous centuries, to make the important imprint of the bishop's seal in hot wax to authenticate documents. The 'Holy Father (God have mercy!)' does this today. Moreover, in Catholic tradition, to reverence or 'kiss' the ring of the bishop by their followers and civil and military authorities as a sign of respect for his authority, is still proper; interestingly, a partial indulgence was attached to the reverencing of the bishop's ring.

In comparing the Word of God and the most finished productions of men, there are spots and blemishes in the most admired productions of human genius. But the more the Scriptures are searched, the more minutely they are studied, the more their perfection appears; new beauties are brought into light every day; and the discoveries of science, the researches of the learned, and the labours of infidels, all alike conspire to illustrate the wonderful harmony of all the parts, and the Divine beauty that clothes the whole.

Let us conclude this part with this wonderful reflection which should be thoroughly read and understood: "If Rome is now to be admitted to form a portion of the Church of Christ, where is the system of Paganism that has ever existed, or that now exists, that could not put in an equal claim? On what grounds could the worshippers of the original Madonna and child in the days of old be excluded 'from the commonwealth of Israel,' or shown to be 'strangers to the covenants of promise'? On what grounds could the worshippers of Vishnu at this day be put beyond the bounds of such wide catholicity? The ancient Babylonians held, the modern Hindoos still hold, clear and distinct traditions of the Trinity, the Incarnation, the Atonement. Yet, who will venture to say that such nominal recognition of the cardinal articles of Divine revelation could relieve the character of either the one system or the other from the brand of the most deadly and God-dishonouring heathenism? And so also in regard to Rome. True, it nominally admits Christian terms and Christian names; but all that is apparently Christian in its system is more than neutralized by the malignant Paganism that it embodies. Grant that the bread the Papacy presents to its votaries can be proved to have been originally made of the finest of the wheat; but what then, if every particle of that bread is combined with prussic acid or strychnine? Can the excellence of the bread overcome the virus of the poison? Can there by anything but death, spiritual and eternal death, to those who continue to feed upon the poisoned food that it offers? Yes, here is the question, and let it be fairly faced. Can there be salvation in a communion in which it is declared to be a fundamental principle, that the Madonna is 'our greatest hope; yea, the SOLE GROUND OF OUR HOPE'? (The language of the late Pope Gregory, substantially endorsed by the present Pontiff.). The time is come when charity to the perishing souls of men, hoodwinked by a Pagan priesthood, abusing the name of Christ, requires that the truth in this matter should be clearly, loudly, unflinchingly proclaimed. The beast and the image of the beast alike stand revealed in the face of all Christendom; and now the tremendous threatening of the Divine Word in regard to their worship fully applies, "*And the third angel followed them, saying, 'If any man worship the beast and his image, and receive his mark in* his forehead, or in his hand, the same shall drink of the wine of the wrath of God, poured without mixture into the cup of His indignation; and he shall be tormented with fire and brimstone in the presence of the holy angels, and in the presence of the Lamb.'" (Revelation 14 : 9,10). These words are words of awful import; and woe to the man who is found finally under the guilt which they imply. These words, as has already been admitted by Elliott, contain a 'chronological prophecy,' a prophecy not referring to the Dark Ages, but to a period not far distant from the consummation, when the Gospel should be widely diffused, and when bright light should be cast on the character and doom of the apostate Church of Rome (verses 6-8). They come, in the Divine chronology of events, immediately after an angel has proclaimed, "*BABYLON IS FALLEN, IS FALLEN*". We have, as it were, with our own ears heard this predicted 'Fall of Babylon' announced from the high places of Rome itself, when the seven hills of the 'Eternal City' reverberated with the guns that proclaimed, not merely to the citizens of the Roman republic, but to the wide world, that "PAPACY HAD FALLEN, de facto and de jure, from the temporal throne of the Roman State." . . . (*The Two Babylons*, 1853, by Alexander Hislop).

Did we get the message!

Ought it not to lead us to say with the Psalmist, "*Therefore, I esteem all Thy commandments concerning all things to be right*"? The commandments of God, to our corrupt and perverse minds, may sometimes seem to be hard. They may require us to do what is painful, they may require us to forego what is pleasing to flesh and blood. But, whether we know the reason of these commandments or not, if we only know that they come from 'the only wise God, our Saviour', we may be sure that in the keeping of them there is great reward; we may go blindfold wherever the Word of God may lead us, and rest in the firm conviction that, in so doing, we are pursuing the very path of safety and peace. Human wisdom at the best is but a blind guide; human policy is a meter that dazzles and leads astray; and they who follow it walk in darkness, and know not whither they are going; but he that walks uprightly by the rule of God's infallible Word, will ever find that he walks surely, and that whatever duty he has to perform, whatever danger he has to face, great peace have all they that love God's Law, and nothing shall offend them.

Come quickly, Lord Jesus, for the prince of darkness comes so furious and smart and the battle so hard that many elected may fall!

". . . in the last days perilous times shall come. For men shall be lovers of their own selves, covetous, boasters, proud, blasphemers, disobedient to parents, unthankful, unholy, Without natural affection, trucebreakers, false accusers, incontinent, fierce, despisers of those that are good . . . lovers of pleasures more than lovers of God; Having a form of godliness, but denying the power thereof: from such turn away!" (2 Timothy 3 : 2)

THE FOURTH COMMANDMENT, 'to remember the Sabbath', concludes the section of the Ten Commandments that specifically helps define a proper relationship with God: how we are to love, worship and relate to Him. It explains why and when we need to take special time to draw closer to our Creator. Satan does not want us to accept these views because he hates God's Law, he does all he can to influence us ignore, avoid and even suppress it and makes us reason our way around it. Few people grasp the extent of society's indoctrination by Satan. As the real 'god of this age' (2 Corinthians 4 : 4), he has deceived most of humankind (Revelation 12 : 9). The whole world falls prey to his influence (1 John 5 : 19). His objective has always been to destroy the relationship between the true God and His creatures. He wants nothing more than to thwart people from developing a loving, personal relationship with their Creator, which is the purpose of the Fourth Commandment. He wants to prevent us from reaching our incredible destiny in God's family! The result of his work is that we forfeit the special understanding that God wants to develop in us by worshiping Him on that day.

It is by ceasing our normal labor and activities that we are reminded of an essential lesson every week. After six days of fashioning this beautiful earth and everything in it, our Creator ceased molding the physical part of His creation and rested on the seventh day (Genesis 2 : 1 - 3).

The Sabbath is a special day to concentrate on developing our spiritual relationship with God. It is a special day on which we should dramatically change the focus of our activity. God intended that it be a delightful period during which we busily draw closer to Him O yes, to 'delight ourselves in the LORD' is the reason we should cease, for the 24 hours of the Sabbath, the labour and normal activities that consume our time the other six days of the week. Relationships take time. Every successful association demands time. No close relationship can succeed without it: no courtship, no marriage, no friendship can be enjoyable without time. Likewise, in our relationship with God there is no exception, especially because the forces of darkness work hard to hinder people from obeying their Maker's commandments.

In another sense, the specific object of the Christian Sabbath is the commemoration of the resurrection of Jesus Christ from the dead. All the exercises of the day, therefore, should have a special reference to Him and to His redeeming work. It is the day in which He is to be worshipped, thanked, and praised; in which men are to be called upon to accept His offer of grace, and to rejoice in the hope of His salvation. It is therefore a day of joy; not that joy of carnal mind of relaxing, eating and dancing, but of concentrating our mind and spirit upon which is eternal. That joy and delight to be called by the name of our Creator; the joy which Christ had accepted to offer Himself on a cross that we may live. That joy which moved the heavenly beings to sing 'hosanna' when Christ came as a Baby in this world. Let us rejoice for what is greater and is still to be revealed at His second coming: *"Behold, I give you authority to trample on serpents and scorpions, and over the power of the enemy, and nothing shall by any means hurt you. Nevertheless do not rejoice in this, that the spirits are subject to you, but rather rejoice because your names are written in heaven."* (Luke 10 : 19, 20)

Some preachers teach with animosity, "It is utterly incongruous to make the Sabbath a day of gloom or fasting . . .", forgetting that Christ Himself spent forty days and forty nights fasting in the desert, praying and mourning upon the state of the lost Mankind, as He came on Satan's ground! The Word of God does not say anything about how He spent the Sabbath days during that period in desert, or Christ had stopped fasting on Sabbath days! For our guidance, let us follow the precepts and example of our Lord. First, He lays down the principle, "*The Sabbath was made for man, and not man for the Sabbath*". It is to be remarked that Christ says, "*the Sabbath was made for man*"; that is different from being made for the Jews, neither for the people of any particular age or nation, but for Man; for Man as God's creature, and therefore for all Mankind throughout the universe and times. Not for anybody to do of it whatever pleases him to do, for it is blessed by God Himself for the purpose to remind that He is the only Creator of all which is seen and unseen. No one can change that which bears the mark of holiness from the Most High. However, moral duties often conflict, and then, we should honestly know that the lowest must yield to the highest. God alone knows our higher interests and concerns, and He will provide all our needs on time, according to His own Will and purpose.

Again, we are told by the same Authority, that "*the priests in the temple profane the Sabbath and are blameless.*" (Matthew 12 : 5). The services of the temple were complicated and laborious, and yet were lawful on the Sabbath, because they were unabridged part of that time of worship as instituted by God Himself. What is not the same with the work performed in church kitchens every Sabbath! So, setting tables, chairs and utensils for communion service is lawful, baptism and all its services are lawful, caring for the needy and sick ones on Sabbath is lawful as their purpose is to minister and care for the spiritual and special needs to the local church members.

Many people jump to wrong conclusions about Jesus and the Sabbath in His confrontations with the scribes and Pharisees. Yet these confrontations were never about keeping or not the Sabbath, but how it should be kept. There is a crucial difference between the two! According to the Pharisees, rendering medical attention to someone, unless it were a matter of life and death, was prohibited on the Sabbath; and since none of Christ's healings (Mark 3 : 1 - 6; Luke 13 : 10 - 17; 14 : 1 - 6) involved a life—death situation, they thought Jesus was breaking the Sabbath. But the Savior Jesus understood the purpose of the Sabbath; that it was a perfectly appropriate time to bring His message of healing, hope and redemption to humanity and to live that message through His actions. So asked He the Pharisees the question, "*Is it lawful on the Sabbath to do good or to do evil, to save life or to kill?*" (Mark 3 : 4), in opposition of the work of kindling fire, cook or warm food, traveling from town to town for leisure!

He exposed their hypocrisy that they saw nothing wrong with working to rescue an animal that fell into a pit on the Sabbath day, or watering an animal on that day, yet they were condemning Him for helping a human being, whose worth was far greater than of any animal (Luke 13 : 15 - 17; Matthew 12 : 10 - 14). He was rightfully concerned for their inability to see that they placed their own traditions and interpretations above the true purpose of Sabbath observance (Mark 3 : 5). Yet they were so spiritually blind that they hated Him for exposing their distortions of God's commands (verse 6).

On one occasion, Jesus' disciples, as they walked through a field on the Sabbath day, picked handfuls of grain so they would have something to eat. The disciples weren't harvesting the field; they were merely grabbing a quick snack to take care of their hunger. But the Pharisees insisted this was not lawful. Jesus used an example from Scripture to show that the spirit and intent of the law were not broken and that God's law allowed for mercy (Mark 2 : 23 - 26). On another occasion, He said to His accusers, *"If a man receives circumcision on the Sabbath, so that the law of Moses should not be broken, are you angry with Me because I made a man completely well on the Sabbath? Do not judge according to appearance, but judge with righteous judgment."* (John 7 : 23, 24). So should we all do today!

Let me emphasize it! From all this, we learn that whatever is necessary for the due celebration of religious worship, or for attendance thereon, is lawful on the Sabbath. Preaching and evangelism on Sabbath is the main work, which should be done for the salvation of many, even travelling from a city to another for this purpose!

The frequency with which our Lord was accused of Sabbath-breaking by the Pharisees, proves that His mode of observing the day was very different from theirs, and the way in which He vindicated Himself proves that He regarded the Sabbath as a divine institution of perpetual obligation. If not so, it had been easy for Him to say that the law of the Sabbath was no longer in force; that He, as Lord of the Sabbath, will erase it from the Decalogue after His resurrection. Indeed, as the whole Mosaic Law was in force until the resurrection of Christ, or until the day of Pentecost, the observance of the Sabbath would be, as a matter of fact, no longer obligatory; but Christ regarded it differently. It is obvious to remark that Christ did not hesitate to abrogate those of the laws of Moses which were in conflict with the spirit of the Gospel or were fulfilled in His death. This He did with the laws relating to polygamy and divorce and others. The fact that He dealt with the Sabbath just as He did with the fifth, sixth, and seventh precepts of the Decalogue, which the Pharisees had misinterpreted, shows that He regarded the fourth commandment as belonging to the same category of eternal laws. His example affords us a safe guide as to the way in which the day is to be observed.

Many Christians do not give earnest heed to the sayings of their Maker! Then, go and watch the same people in their business office or in their workplace and see how they are very serious in the work, obeying earnestly the code of conduct and rules on the time, the cleanliness and noise, the respect of the boss . . . , all is done to please their earthly masters for a living bread which endures but a time. Listen to an evangelist complaining about 'Martha's distractions' during the holy Sabbath hours, saying, ". . . So many times I have sat on the platform during a church service or camp meeting, eagerly waiting to preach the Word, watching a seemingly endless parade of announcements, preliminaries, fanfare and 'special features' devour the precious time that should be dedicated to the proclamation of the Word. By the time, I finally open my Bible to expound God's Word, many in the congregation are restless and irritable, already eyeing their watches, ready to leave. Other people, suffering from low blood sugar, are unable to comprehend what I am saying anyway. The Lord is given our mental leftovers, a lame offering of our attention . . ." (Unknown)

To worship and pray Lord God must be more than coming before Him and kneeling by a mere formalism, even uttering rapidly some words of prayer by mouth, with heart, mind and thoughts remained in the world and its fame. Instead, the true worshipers must focus all their whole being to heaven; they must see the heaven opened and them be drawn nearer to the Mercy Seat; so feeling the presence of the Godhead and making sure that the dialogue between Him and them is really established. Having always in mind that *"God is Spirit, and those who worship Him must worship in spirit and truth."* (John 4 : 24), for, if *". . . you were raised with Christ, seek those things which are above, where Christ is sitting at the right hand of God. Set your mind on things above, not on things on the earth. For you died, and your life is hidden with Christ in God"* (Colossians 3 : 1 - 3). "As you enter the place of worship, ask the Lord to remove all evil from your heart. Bring to His house only that which He can bless. Kneel before God in His temple, and consecrate to Him His own, which He has purchased with the blood of Christ" (Ellen G. White—Testimonies to Church—6, p. 362). Let us make these principles ours!

The Bible tells us, "*Great peace, have those who love Your law, and nothing causes them to stumble, LORD. I hope for Your salvation, and I do Your commandments. My soul keeps Your testimonies, and I love them exceedingly*" (Psalms 119 : 165 - 167). Even more, God's Word tells us that His teachings are 'PERFECT' and His judgments 'are TRUE and are completely RIGHT' (Psalms 19 : 7, 9). Accordingly, the enthusiastic author above again affirmed, "*So shall I keep Your law continually, forever and ever*" (Psalms 119 : 44).

Let us walk in the way of life given to us in those principles.

Christ perfectly kept the Ten Commandments and completely filled their meaning. He showed their spiritual intent, explaining that unjustified anger equates murder, and lust is mental stealing and covetousness is emotional adultery. Jesus expanded the intent of the Ten Commandments. He also made it unquestionably clear that God treasures people who obey His laws. But anyone who transgresses His commandments quickly diminishes God's favor toward him. Jesus expects much more from us than lip service. He demands that we do as the Father has commanded. Jesus said, "*Not everyone who says to Me, 'Lord, Lord,' shall enter the kingdom of heaven. But he who does the will of my Father in heaven.*" (Matthew 7 : 21). By this, He plainly taught obedience to God's Law, showing that simply believing in Him is not enough.

Entering into everlasting life means to be redeemed, to be a newborn again Christian, to be a part of the invisible congregation of saints when still in this world of sin. Thus we have to bear the image of our heavenly Father and must walk as Christ walked. How did He walk in this world? According to Isaiah 53, Christ, during His ministry here below, showed the exceeding riches of divine grace; the world beheld His glory, "*the glory of the only begotten Son of the Father, full of grace and truth*"; He had become for the lost race, wisdom from God, and righteousness, sanctification and goodness, with forbearance, humility, longsuffering, love and kindness, self-denial . . . that we might follow His footsteps and give to the dying world His right example.

Justifying our lack of honor and fear for our Creator before Whom we come to worship in quoting selfishly the sacred Scriptures is a sin. Instead, let us keep in our mind that the Tempter uses the very Scriptures to deceive those that claim to be saved and makes them forget to be vigilant. Knowing that on earth He was in Satan's dominion, Jesus went every night in the calm places to call upon His Father for power and protection, not with unnecessary noises, jumps and crying, but in reverence and humility and perseverance. If as a people, the Christians make no effort to remain alert and so resist, by God's grace, Satan's alluring and powerful suggestions; if the indifference prevails in the heart and life of people, in the church and in the sacred things; Satan becomes triumphant. If on the contrary, the church member attention is, day by day, called to heavenly things and holy deeds, the Enemy is in sinking sand and he trembles.

Let us emphasize it; the first Satan's deception to Man pointed directly to the creative power of God, meaning against the fourth commandment: "*You shall be as gods*", said He to our first parents. Thus, the issue of Sabbath observance must be considered more crucial in our days of the end than in ancient times, as we watch the fulfillment of all prophecies concerning the time we are living in. Satan wanted Adam and Eve feel that, in breaking God's command, they had opportunity to become equal to Him. Yes, this is the same attitude adopted by a disobedient child who would want to prove to his or her parents that he or she had become their equal, after his or her eighteenth year of age, and he or she can no longer be bound to their will and discipline. Yes, I heard a Christian girl boasting to her parents which were concerned about her misconduct, saying, "I am eighteen, I can do whatever I want . . .". Lord, have mercy!

Those that know the value of God's Law including Sabbath observance must also know that they are on the battlefield (read Revelation 12 and 14) against the Prince of darkness; they are the target of his fiercest attacks. Because of this, they must be more vigilant and more prayerful in this time of the end than in any other period of Christian history.

Some other brethren assert that, "We cannot make the Sabbath burdensome for the Church members"! Wow! Could a wise, almighty and unchanging God set up the Sabbath which He calls "*My holy Day*" and established, through His Word, the rules how to keep it to make it burdensome for His children? No, this is deceitful lie. As a loving and holy God, He cannot ask what is burdensome to us. Only a disobedient child finds as burdensome obeying his parents; only a lazy person finds burdensome to accomplish his duty; only a pleasure lover can find it burdensome to refrain from evil pleasures . . .

Loving God means obeying His commands. And God's commands are not too hard for us, because everyone who is a child of God conquers the world. And this is the victory that conquers the world, our faith (refer to 1 John 5 : 3, 4).

The Sabbath rest is not only because of the fatigue from hard work, or how long time it takes to perform our weekly task, or because of our own choice . . . For the Creator made everything by word, however He rested; He does not get tired, however He rested; He says and the thing is done, and He rested and calls this day His Sabbath day and commands His creatures to keep it holy, not only during the service in the church, but also in all their dwellings, from sunset Friday to sunset Saturday. Isaiah shows better this in chapter 40 verses 28 - 29 when he depicts for us the power of our Maker, "*. . . the everlasting God, the Lord, the Creator of the ends of the earth, neither faints nor is weary. His understanding is unsearchable. He gives power to the weak, and to those who have no might He increases strength!*". And David completes the picture in his own terms, saying, "*By the word of Lord the heavens were made, and all the host of them by the breath of His mouth . . . For He spoke, and it was done; He commanded, and it stood fast.*" (Psalms 33 : 6 - 9). However He rested on the seventh day of the creation week.

With such a powerful Creator, there is no need for rest. It is why Christ gave the light on the necessity of the Sabbath commandment, saying that '*the Sabbath was made for man*'. The life, the health, and the one's well-being are higher ends in a given case, than the punctilious observance of any external service. For "*I desire mercy and not sacrifices, and the knowledge of God more than burnt offering.*" (Hosea 6 : 6). Our Lord quotes twice this passage in application to the law of the Sabbath, and thus establishes the general principle for our guidance, that it is right to do on the Sabbath whatever mercy or a due regard to the comfort or welfare of others or ourselves requires to be done. Christ, therefore, says expressly, "*. . . Therefore it is lawful to do good on the Sabbath*". (Matthew 12 : 12. See also Mark 3 : 4.) However, whatever we need on Sabbath (meal, clothing, showers . . .) should be planned and done ahead in preparation of this Holy Day. For, the truth is not what we know solely, but, most importantly, it is what we do, how we use the knowledge we possess.

As God's people, bought from the world by a High Price, we must *"love the Lord our God with all our heart, and with all our soul, and with all our mind"* (see Mark 12 : 30). This love for our Lord God is found on the first tablet of stone of the Decalogue, to which belongs the fourth Commandment. The obedience of His commandments proceeds from this love.

Do you want to determine how the Sabbath is to be observed, or to decide what is and what is not lawful on that holy day? First humble to the will of God, put aside all selfishness and false philosophy, then ask for guidance and then find out the design of the commandment. What is consistent with that design is lawful; what is inconsistent with it, is unlawful. The design of the command is to be learned from the words in which it is conveyed and from other parts of the Word of God. From these sources, it is plain that the design of the institution was in the main twofold:—to secure rest from all worldly cares and avocations; to arrest for a time the current of the worldly life of men, not only lest their minds and bodies should be overworked, but also that opportunity should be afforded for other and higher interests to occupy their thoughts!—God should be properly worshipped, His Word duly studied and taught, and the soul brought under the influence of the things unseen and eternal.

It should be repeated and emphasized. Any man who makes the design of the Sabbath as thus revealed in Scripture his rule of conduct on that day, can hardly fail in its due observance. The day is to be kept holy unto the Lord. As said earlier, in Scriptural usage 'to hallow' or 'make holy' is to set apart to the service of God. In this sense, the Sabbath is holy and to be devoted to the duties of religion, and what is inconsistent with such devotion, is contrary to the design of the institution.

Many professed Christians are boasting for being children of apostles, of prophets, of pastors, of elders and of any church leaders, or for being born in the church, as proof of their spirituality! To such ones Christ replies, *"Do the things that show you really have changed your hearts and lives. Don't begin to say to yourselves, 'Abraham is our father'. I tell you that God could make children for Abraham from these rocks. The ax is now ready to cut down the trees, and every tree that does not produce good fruit will be cut down and thrown into the fire."* (Luke. 3 : 8, 9; New Century Version Bible, 1996)

Sabbath is a day devoted to rest from our everyday work and admire God's work of creation and above all our salvation with its image in the deliverance of the Jewish people from Egyptian bondage, that they sang:

"Who is like You, O Lord, among the gods?
Who is like You, glorious in holiness,
Fearful in praises, doing wonders?
You stretched out Your right hand;
The earth swallowed them.
You in Your mercy have led forth
The people whom You have redeemed;
You have guided them in Your strength
To Your holy habitation".
(Exodus 15 : 11 - 13)

Soon and very soon, this song will be ours in front of the Pearly Gate! Will you be there?

And He would not allow anyone to carry wares through the temple. Then He taught, saying to them, 'Is it not written, "My house shall be called a house of prayer for all nations?" But you have made it a den of thieves'". (Mark 11 : 17)

IT IS NOT enough to claim to be 'remnant', 'peculiar' people by the fact that we are Christians. The Word of God urges people to walk, speak and act as Christ whose name they bear walked in this world, ought to be judged by the 'Law of freedom'.

"As the memorial of creation, Sabbath observance is an antidote for idolatry. By reminding us that God created heaven and earth, it distinguishes Him from all false gods. Keeping the Sabbath, then, becomes the sign of allegiance to true God, a sign that we acknowledge His sovereignty as Creator and King [and Saviour]." (Seventh day Adventists believe, *A Biblical Exposition of 27 Fundamental Doctrines*, 1988, by the Ministerial Association General Conference of Seventh-day Adventists, p.251, *emphasis added*)

The use of the verb 'remember' in the very beginning of the fourth commandment is very important by the fact that people are always inclined, let us say tendentious, to forget their duties and responsibilities toward their heavenly Master and toward each other. By this emphasis, God would like His creatures have present in their mind not to take this holy Day as all other days of the week, nor to keep the Sabbath in a light manner. The verb 'remember' indicates most importantly that the Sabbath observance had not begun with the adoption of the Israelites by God as His people at the mount Horeb, as many Christian leaders tend to teach, and thus argue that they cannot be concerned by a Jewish observance; this shows that the sacredness of the seventh day starts at creation as the Creator Himself rested in it.

In the mouth of the prophet Isaiah, our Lord insists, ". . . *If thou turn away thy foot from the Sabbath, from doing thy pleasure on my holy day; and call the Sabbath a delight, the holy of the LORD, honourable; and shalt honour him, not doing thine own ways, nor finding thine own pleasure, nor speaking thine own words: Then shalt thou delight thyself in the LORD; and I will cause . . .*" (Isaiah 58 : 13, 14, King James Version). The Sabbath is a natural ordinance given to man before he sinned and had no need of the Saviour. As such, it is equally enjoined on all races, tribes and tongues and should be observed by all people of all ages and dispensations, including even the sinless ones in Paradise. It was and is still God's means for maintaining in the human family His knowledge and fear as the Maker, the Ruler and the coming Judge of the universe. Therefore, men are naturally bound to keep the Sabbath simply as men, and not only as Christians.

Why should it be so? Why the seven-day week and the continual cycle of day and night? Is there a message for modern men and women in the way our planet is designed to operate?

Science had proved that as it needs naturally a daily rest and sleep, our body, after a cycle of six days of work, needs a full day to rest. The researchers call it 'the body biological clock'. Indeed, we rush from one appointment to another, and from one task to the next. Many of us are perpetually in search of materialism and money as we charge up the ladder of success. Many executives are routinely expected to put in at least 14 hours daily at the office or on the road. One man recently said that he was in the office by 6 a.m. and worked weekends, and he's certainly not alone. Long hours at work are harming our mental health, psychologically and emotionally, by raising stress levels and reducing emotional well being. We do not easily come to terms with the discipline of deferred gratification. We impatiently want everything done now, while we all need to sit down, breathe easily, relax and take time to think rationally and constructively.

Clearly, human beings were designed to rest at appropriate times. Many great cities around the world never sleep, as many services, industries, manufactures and shops are open around the clock, the TV stations and the Internet are available anytime and we expand our control over time to do things whenever it is convenient for us, regardless of what the clock tells us.

What's the solution?

Jesus Christ tells us that if we will adapt to His way of life, He will give us rest from our burdens (Matthew 11 : 28). On one occasion, He encouraged His disciples to ". . . *come aside by yourselves to a desert place and rest a while*" (Mark 6 : 31). Once, in a while, we all need to come to a complete halt, to totally stop what we are doing, take time to rest and reflect, and take stock of our lives. To cope successfully, we need valuable time for sustained thought, periods in which we really have time to think things over and prioritize our commitments. Also we need time to truly appreciate the wonders of creation. Solomon said that God ". . . *has made everything beautiful in its time*" (Ecclesiastes 3 : 11). While Paul does tell us that we are to be "*redeeming the time, because the days are evil*" (Ephesians 5 : 16).

How are we to accomplish this task? A key lies in a God-given pattern that has been with us since creation: each twenty-four hour period was divided into night and day for special purposes; and naturally speaking, the nighttime is for rest and sleep.

Nevertheless, we also need rest from our general labors. So the Creator commands us to rest every seventh day (Exodus 20 : 8 - 11; Deuteronomy 5 : 12 - 15). This twenty-four hour period is holy to God, and He tells us to cease from carrying on with our normal working lives and devote this time to rest and reflection on His ways. It is also a time for assembling with others for collective worship (Leviticus 23 : 1 - 3; Mark 6 : 2; Acts13 : 44; 16 : 13; Hebrews 10 : 24 - 25 . . .).

Spiritual fellowship with others of like mind is one of the most beneficial tonics to the human psyche. We all need it! Of course, this can only succeed in and through our fellowship with God the Father and His Son Jesus Christ (1 John 1 : 3; 1 Corinthians 1 : 9; John 17 : 21).

Any successful relationship requires time: quality time with God in prayer and Bible study; quality time with husband and wife; quality time with family, friends and fellow churchgoers; the weekly day of rest provides such a time and enables us to use the other six days much more profitably. It also gives us sufficient time to meditate and think about those things that can bring special meaning and divine purpose to our busy lives. It provides time and space for families and couples to draw closer together. It provides precious time to read and study the Bible, the Book that tells us how to live in a way that is infinitely rewarding, purposeful and fulfilling.

The principle of activity preceding rest is an important one for our health. Physical and mental activities both require energy and create waste products. As our energy level goes down and wastes accumulate, we experience fatigue and a desire for rest. During rest, energy is restored, and the waste buildup is diminished. An important difference between physical and mental activities is that physical activity usually leaves the muscles relaxed, whereas prolonged mental activity alone leaves the muscles tense. Fatigue is protective in that it serves to make us aware of our need of rest; as fatigue increases, efficiency and performance decrease. It is not a good idea to ignore this signal or to try to counteract it with drugs.

Rest and relaxation cannot take the place of sleep. Human beings were designed to be awake during the day and asleep at night. Enzymes and hormone systems within the body, which remain fairly fixed, even if one were to remain isolated in total darkness or total light, normally control wakefulness and sleepiness. These 'internal clocks' can be nudged forward or backward a few degrees. They may also be ignored, but not without negative consequences. Yes, to rest means to cease all activity; it also means to cease from our worries and the cares of the day. We are given only one day at a time, and no one knows what the next day will bring. It could be better than we think, especially if we heed the invitation of the loving God: "*Come to me, all you who labor and have heavy laden, and I will give you rest. Take My yoke and learn from Me, for I am gentle and lowly in heart, and you will find rest for your souls. For My yoke is easy and My burden is light.*" (Matthew 11 : 28 - 30)

After Man fell in sins and came to need redemption, the Sabbath became more efficiently a means of grace and a gospel institute; but this did not repeal or exclude its original use. The obedient Christian has two reasons for observing the Sabbath and every human being has one. Both as human beings needing rest after six days of labor, the second for the Christian is to keep the holy Ten commandments of the Lawgiver (Matthew. 5 : 17 - 19).

Not only we keep a holy rest all the day from our own works, words and thoughts, about our own worldly employments and recreations, but also we take up the whole time in the public and private exercises of God's worship and in the duties of necessity and mercy. It is a time set aside to concentrate on the things that are pleasing to God and nourish our relationship with Him and with our fellow men. It is a day set aside for rest and worship. God commanded a Sabbath day because human beings need to spend unhurried time in worship and rest each week. A God who is concerned enough about us to provide a day each week to rest is indeed so wonderful. To observe a regular time of rest and worship in our fast-paced world demonstrates how important God is to us, and it gives us the extra benefit of refreshing our spirits.

Jesus Christ showed by His example the proper way to observe the Sabbath. It was never intended to be a rigid, joyless day constrained by endless restrictions detailing what could and could not be done . . . He used it as a time to delight in sharing with others the joy of God's Word and way of life, showing it to be a time for strengthening our relationship with His Father and with our brethren. He used it as a time for healing of physical, mental, emotional and spiritual sickness. He used this time for encouraging and helping those who were less fortunate. The Master made it clear there was nothing wrong with doing good on the Sabbath, pointing out that God's Sabbath command had never forbidden it. He emphasized what the day is for, rather than listing all the things we cannot do. His actions on the Sabbath pointed to the coming age He referred to as 'THE KINGDOM OF GOD' in which all humanity will share in God's promised healing, joy and freedom (Matthew 4 : 23; 9 : 35; Luke 4 : 16 - 19; 9 : 11; 10 : 9). Christ's example showed that the Sabbath is to be a day of physical rest and spiritual rejuvenation. It is meant to be a welcome, refreshing rest from our weekly labors, a time during which we must no longer be absorbed in our ordinary daily cares and concerns.

Let us insist that a day consists of twenty-four hours, and when God commands us to sanctify one day to Him, as we devote the other six to all our own work, the honest conscience will find no difficulty in concluding that holy time should not be abridged by unnecessary sleep or by needless recreations any more than any other day. Let true faith possess the soul with a scriptural sense of the arduous task to be finished in the believer's own life, in fitting it for the everlasting Sabbath, and of the multitudinous claims of misery and ignorance surrounding him among his perishing fellow-men, the holy occupations of the Sabbath day will appear so urgent and so numerous that there will be no room in it for either worldliness or indolence.

Let us hear the law and the testimony, which we have shown to be unrepealed: "*Observe the Sabbath day, to keep it holy, as the Lord your God commanded you. Six days you shall labor and do all your work, but the seventh day is the Sabbath of the Lord your God. In it you shall do no work: you, nor your son, nor your daughter, nor your male servant, nor female servant, nor your ox, nor your donkey, nor any of your cattle, nor your strangers who is within your gates . . .*" (Deuteronomy 5 : 12 - 14, Isaiah 58 : 13, 14).

If the Bible is considered by Christians as a guidebook for human behavior, the Ten Commandments serve as the main headings in its table of contents. By themselves, the commandments do not tell the whole story, but they clearly summarize it. According to Matthew 5 : 17, Jesus, by the word 'FULFILL' meant that His teachings would fill out or expand the application of the commandments of God. He so emphasized to His hearers that His mission and purpose was to show or fill to the full the intended meaning of the Ten Commandments, not to annul or take away anything from them. Then, in this same passage, He affirms some specific commandments and then greatly expands their application, such as the commandment forbidding murder. "*You have heard that it was said to those of old, 'You shall not murder and whoever murders will be in danger of judgment.' But I say to you that whoever is angry with his brother without a cause shall be in danger of judgment. And whoever says to his brother 'Raca!' shall be in danger of the council. But whoever says, 'You fool!' shall be in danger of hell fire.*" (verses 21 - 22). The Lord Jesus showed that the principle embodied in this commandment goes far beyond the taking of human life. It includes the destructive effects of anger and bitterness. Christ explained that condemning and hating someone only in our hearts could prevent us from inheriting eternal life. In other words, Jesus explained that His teachings amplify and explain the required behavior summarized in the Ten Commandments. So did also the teachings of prophets and apostles. In the same manner, in Isaiah 58 : 13, 14, the prophet teaches not to keep the Sabbath according our human and selfish philosophy, looking for the worldly joy and pleasure, even speaking of our own words. Instead, in keeping the Sabbath accordingly we honour the Lord that He will make us ride upon the high places of the earth and He will feed us with the heritage of our spiritual father Jacob. Thank you, Lord!

When Christ referred to 'doing good on Sabbath', He did not mean the work of cooking or kindling fire during the Sabbath hours which is planned week after week and done during these holy hours every week, without any case of emergency, or accident, or surprise, or threat of life. For, to prevent all misunderstandings and false interpretations, God had set up a day of preparation, the sixth of the week. Our responsibility as people of God is to simply keep in mind that which is holy belongs to God. Our Maker recommends us that in every hour and minute of the Sabbath, 'TO DO NO WORK'. We do not have the right to rob God of His time, so minor it would be; by doing so, we also break the eighth commandment, altogether with the first, the second, the third, and so on.

What is seen in many churches where members come to worship the Lord? While the worship service is going on in the sanctuary, they eye the time on their watches to leave the assembly, to go in church kitchens and give themselves to turn on stoves or microwaves; they stay to watch and care after the food from being burnt. One of their friends join them, they start to chat about their own business; if one or two more come in for the same purpose and join them, a little marketplace is opened and the talk and the laughs become noisier and noisier. Thus Satan opens, in the church kitchen and aisles, another cult to himself beside to the one dedicated to the Most High in the sanctuary! Then, the members of Satan's church, and they are many, are constantly working to justify themselves and try to cast off the divine Law by confusing 'doing good on the Sabbath' and 'fearing the Lord in keeping His laws, statutes and ordinances'.

All good or delight is found in God alone. Any 'good' which contradicts or suppresses the commandments and pushes men to disobey and to sin, is but evil. ". . . the place that should be holy, where a holy stillness should reign, and where there should be a perfect order, nearness and humility, is made to be a perfect Babylon and a place where confusion, disorder and untidiness reign. This is enough to shut out God from our assemblies and cause His wrath to be kindled . . ." (Ellen G. White—Selected Messages—3, p.257)

After having so profaned the Sabbath hours, people still flatter themselves having kept the Sabbath accordingly! Instead, we should mourn over our blindness and vain boasting.

Fortunately, among the Sabbath-keeping Christians, there are some devoted and Spirit-led leaders who do not encourage such practices, permitted and even justified only by the greedy and arrogant ones. Why?

Because there are those that are more confident in their instruction than in what the unchanging Word of God teaches!

O GOD, HAVE MERCY!

What else?

People become so busy to clean stoves, plates, tables and floor; they remove garbage, bringing in and out their heavy utensils and vessels; for they are unable to wait patiently the end of the Sabbath hours or they do not want to waste the least of their own time, after sunset. One wrong step making the next easier!

The Sabbath service programs are not respected, as it should be: the early morning services are ignored even by those that are supposed to stand for them; so-called 'peculiar' people prefer to attend the worship service in a time after their convenience, for they come late and leave earlier.

Some are unceasingly walking to and fro the church aisles. Seated in disorder, they are speaking of their weekly affairs, while the lessons or sermons are given . . . What about the noisy greetings that take much time during the service!

Let us look at this paper found in a Toronto church foyer in 2001, to the intention of the Sabbath-keeping worshipers therein.

BEHAVIOR IN THE HOUSE OF GOD

That thou mayest know how thou oughest to
behave thyself in the House of God
1 Timothy 3 : 15
Ye shall keep my Sabbaths, and reverence my Sanctuary—I am the Lord
Leviticus 19 : 30
Keep thy foot when thou goest to the House of God
Ecclesiastes 5 : 1
There should be rules in regard to the time,
the place and the manner of worship
5 T. 491

RULES

1. Be always on time.
2. Maintain a spirit of praise and worship.
3. God is here. Be silent. Common talking and laughing
will not be permitted in the House of God.
4. Bow in silent prayer as the ministers enter the rostrum.
5. Avoid careless and irreverent postures when
sitting, standing or kneeling.
6. Keep your seat during the service. Avoid interrupting.
Give rapt attention to the proceedings.
7. Parents, keep your children by your sides.
8. If late (a) Never enter while prayer is being offered.
(b) Do not walk up the aisles except
during the singing
(c) Sit on the nearest seat to the door.
9. Walking across front aisles during service will not be permitted.
10. After the benediction and silent prayer, wait to be ushered
out and leave building reverently. Do not crowd the aisles.
11. Loitering on church precinct before or after service is to be avoided.
12. Cooperate with deacons and ushers in the
maintenance of order and reverence.

REMEMBER
This is the House of God

Go into that church and others across that North America great City and you will be amazed of the behavior of the members and of their leaders in the presence of the One to Whom they come to worship! For the human beings, it is one thing to set up rules and it is another to keep and obey them, except toward civil authorities and in their workplace to avoid human punishment or to please their boss and get paid!

XXIX—FIGHT A GOOD FIGHT OF FAITH

"Ye are of God, little children, and have overcome them: because greater is he that is in you, than he that is in the world" (1John 4 : 4, KJV)

THE FORCES THAT have obliterated the hours of a day are the same that have obliterated the days of the week. The Sabbath was kept by Adam and Eve; it was kept by Abraham, our father in faith; it was kept in the Exodus from Egypt, when God tested His children if they would keep the Ten Commandments, including the Fourth as part of them, and this, before the Mount Sinai ceremony when the Ten commandments were given to the Israelites, as chosen people of God. It was kept by Jesus, Paul and all the twelve apostles. It was kept in the early Church by both Jews and Gentiles until year 70 AD when the Temple was destroyed. The very true and unbiased history sources show that it had still being kept until the year 120 AD when some Christians first changed to Sunday to avoid persecution. Then the emperor Constantine finally changed the sanctity of the day officially by the year 321 AD, in favor of sun worship. The Sabbath was almost murdered out of existence through the dark ages by the Roman Catholic Church ruling as State Church during the prophetic dramatic 1260 dark years, according to the prophecy of Daniel chapter7 verses 23 through 25.

If the Church, through the dark centuries, tried to put an end to the testimonies of the Word of God by burning the books and the people that were standing for God's Truth; the Christian church leaders today destroy it by teaching their human philosophy and worldly ideas instead of the unchanging sayings of the Bible! Such teachers do not understand the evidences of their faith (Read Revelation 22 : 12 - 14). Confronted to the sayings of the Word of God, they but deny the Bible truth saying that ". . . it is not our Church teachings" or ". . . that is contrary to our Church doctrine . . ." or ". . . we are not the Jews" or ". . . the Church as the Body of Christ is above the Scripture", and so on . . . forgetting a simple reality that the Bible itself is from Jewish people to which God revealed Himself; also Abraham, Moses, Isaiah, Jeremiah, Simon Peter, John, Paul . . . and above all, Jesus Himself are Jews! So came He to do His heavenly Father's Will, Which is really and clearly expressed in His Word.

The term "*turn away your foot from the Sabbath*" (Isaiah 58 : 13 - 14) means that you should not walk over the Sabbath, or not forget it is holy time set aside by the Creator. "*Not doing your pleasure*" (Idem) refers to misusing the Sabbath for hobbies, sports activities, or other personal pursuits. When we understand and keep the Sabbath as God intended, it will indeed be A DELIGHT. Keeping the Sabbath would most likely lead to keeping the other nine commandments of God. Using the Sabbath for the purposes He intended would focus people's minds on His way. This would leave this world's false religions in shambles, because God's laws would then replace their own laws, twisted reasonings and false interpretations. This is why Satan has gone to such great lengths to blind the world from the benefits of keeping the Fourth Commandment.

The Enemy has succeeded in keeping many Christians away from the true doctrine and have them confused. Ignorance or refusal to know rightly the Word of God is rampaging among Christians, starting from the church pulpits all around the world. They refuse to be students of the Word, although a true child of God should live by His Sayings! Nevertheless, we are recommended to "*Preach the word; be ready in season and out of season. Convince, rebuke, exhort, with all longsuffering and teaching. For the time will come when they will not endure sound doctrine, but according to their own desires, because shall they have aching ears, they will heap up for themselves teachers; and they will turn their ears away from the truth, and be turned aside to fables*" (2 Timothy 4 : 2 - 4)

The Law of Ten Commandments was given to the Jews as God's testimony to the dying world. How can only one of them be Jewish and the other nine be Christian? The Bible is clear in this matter: The salvation comes from the Jews, (Acts 3 : 25; Romans 9 : 4, 5; Galatians 3 : 8) "The Lord calls upon all who believe in His Word to awake out of sleep. Precious light has come, appropriate for this time. It is Bible truth, showing the perils that are right upon us. This should lead us to a diligent study of the Scriptures and a most critical examination of the positions that we hold. God would have all the bearings and positions of the truth thoroughly and perseveringly searched, with prayer and fasting. Believers are not to rest in suppositions and ill-defined ideas of what constitutes the Truth. Their faith must be firmly founded upon the Word of God . . ." (Ellen G. White, *Testimonies for the Church*, vol. 5, pp. 707, 708)

To be saved from being deceived and getting astray out of the Way of all Truth, our Savior urges us to search the Scriptures, which testify of Him. Because He is Spirit, only by lifting our all heart, spirit and mind to God, imploring the aid of His Holy Spirit, we may be carried above all the fictitious teachings of the would-be teachers that are not sustained by the Word of our mighty and everlasting God. The first step to make is to empty ourselves and become ignorant before the Almighty God; to pray as did Solomon, saying "I AM BUT A LITTLE CHILD, I KNOW NOT HOW TO GO OUT OR TO COME IN", that He may find a place in the heart and mind to fill with His knowledge and wisdom; as nothing more can be put in a full bottle: so may He complain that the Son of Man has no place where to lay His head in the heart . . . or will He find faith on earth when He comes! . . . *"Look to yourselves, that we do not lose those things we worked for, but that we may receive a full reward. Whoever transgresses and does not abide in the doctrine of Christ does not have God. He who abides in the doctrine of Christ has both the Father and the Son. If anyone comes to you and does bring this doctrine, do not receive into your house nor greet him."* (2 John 8 - 10). For God is not the Author of confusion and He is not mocked. Whatever men will sow, they will surely reap also.

We are called to stop idle words when speaking of sacred things. Out of many pulpits, are uttered the words such as, "We need to be progressive . . .", "We need to keep up with the times . . .", "We need to advance in faith . . .", "Times are changing and we must change with . . .", "We should not be so closed-minded . . .", "What makes us think that we have a monopoly on truth and let us try to draw as close to these other people as we can, that we can better reach them . . ."

To progress or to advance is one thing for him that does not move forward regresses; but to do so in the right direction is another thing. The best direction is to grow to reach the likeness of Christ. If our growth is to meet the worldly standard, we are but dead spiritually. For God inspired His Word to reveal light and truth which enable us to know the proper steps to take, when we lean upon His mercies and His love toward us. As it is written, *"Teach me Your way, O Lord, I will walk in Your truth: unite my heart to fear Your name."* (Psalms 86 : 11)

Those that have privileges and responsibilities in the Church must be aware of the influence they exercise on the people not firmly rooted in Bible teachings, mainly the writings from the pen of apostle Paul, to fall deeply and quickly in corruption and open sins under their wrong understanding (2 Peter 3 : 14 - 17). For, "If we cultivate spiritual thoughts here, our minds will be filled with spiritual thoughts throughout eternity. The process begun here will continue there. We cannot expect a spiritual mind-set in heaven if we have a carnal mind-set on earth. For the committed Christian, heavenly-mindedness begins right now" (Mark Finley, *Solid Ground*, daily devotionals 2004)

All deviation from the explicit Word of God causes people to war against the Truth. Every idle word is recorded in heaven, in such a way that for obedience we reap blessings and for disobedience, trouble. It is written, *"Lord, who may abide in Your tabernacle? Who may dwell in Your holy hill?"*, and the answer is clear: *"He who walks uprightly, and works righteousness, and speaks the truth in his heart. He who does not backbite with his tongue . . ."* (Psalms 15 : 1 - 3). Yes, our words are the expression of our heart, of our spirit and of our personality and the Savior makes it clear, *"Brood of vipers! How can you, being evil, speak good things? For out of the abundance of the heart the mouth speaks . . . But I say to you that for every idle word men may speak, they will give account of it in the day of judgment . . ."* (Matthew 12 : 34 - 37)

Those who claim that new days of the week cycle are not the same as in the beginning of the world should review their position. Has the annual calendar been changed? Yes, "the calendar has been changed in the reign of pope Gregory XIII in the year 1582 and our present calendar is named after him when he made that change. In fact, before 1582, the Julian calendar had been in effect since instituted by Julius Caesar about year 46 BC. But the Julian calendar calculated the length of the year as 365 ¼ days, which was incorrect as the length of a year was really 11 minutes less than 365 ¼ days. Those 11 minutes accumulated throughout the centuries, and by the year 1582 the numbering of the calendar was 10 days out of harmony with the solar system. Pope Gregory fixed the problem by simply dropping those 10 days out of numbering of the calendar. It was Thursday, October 4th, 1582 and the next day

Friday should have been October the 5th, but Gregory made it October 15th instead, dropping exactly 10 days to bring the calendar back into harmony with the heavenly bodies" (Ben Snowden, *The Curious History of the Gregorian Calendar*, Infoplease site web).

Here, it is clear that the days of the week were not confused. Friday still follows Thursday, and Saturday still follows Friday! And this, according to "*Thus saith the Lord*".

To maintain confusion and get the weak ones lost, the calendar makers today and many French and other language dictionaries define actually Sunday as the seventh day, Monday the first and Saturday the sixth day of the week. It is what I was taught in my Elementary school in the 1950s. However, there are two infallible and unchangeable witnesses against this foolishness: the Bible and the Jewish people. By the Bible, we know that Christ raised from the tomb on the first day of the week; for this, the Christendom, though many sanctify Sunday as the 7th day of the week, celebrate their Easter on Sunday instead of Monday! On the other hand, the Jewish people have been observing the Seventh day Sabbath from Abraham's time, and they still keep it today; that this prophecy may be fulfilled, "*But you shall receive power when the Holy Spirit has come upon you; and you shall be witnesses to Me in Jerusalem, and in all Judea and Samaria, and to the to end of the earth.*" (Acts 1 : 8). Those ones are millions of people who have been counting off time meticulously, week after week, calendar or no calendar, for thousands of years! True, the course of the days of the week had never changed.

The names given to the days of the week confuse somehow some Christians. According to the History, the names of the days of the week are linked to Roman mythology. The Romans saw a connection between their gods and the changing face of the nighttime sky, so it became natural to them to use their gods' names for the planets: the ones they were able to track in the sky were Mercury, Venus, Mars, Jupiter and Saturn. Those five planets plus the moon and the sun made seven major astronomical bodies seen in the sky. Therefore, when the seven-day week was imported from Mesopotamia early in the fourth century, it was a natural thing for them to use those astronomical names for the days of the week. Thus, the first day of the week was named after the sun, the brighter planet in the sky, and became Sunday (also to honor their Sun god), followed by the moon for Monday, Mars for Tuesday, Mercury for Wednesday, Jupiter for Thursday, Venus for Friday and Saturn for Saturday. These names of the weekdays were adopted with little change throughout most of the Roman Empire and even beyond. In only a few cases were some changes made for cultural and political reasons.

Contrary to the duration of the day, month or year, which depends upon some calculations and planet movements, there is no scientific or astronomical reason for measuring time in a cycle of seven days. Indeed, a year comes from the time it takes to the Earth to fully orbit the Sun; a month is the time it takes for the Moon to orbit the Earth, and a day of course, is the time for the Earth to complete one full rotation on itself.

Then, what astronomical reason does make a week to have seven days? Glory be to the Creator of the Universe! It comes only from the time God took to complete His creative work. Is it not marvelous? This is why the Seventh day of the week is the eternal sign between the Creator and His creatures (Exodus 31 : 13 - 17); trying to explain this otherwise could be but blindness or rebellion. Thus, the origin of the week is solely found in the creative story and it is an arbitrary arrangement of God alone since creation, so is the Sabbath which has been miraculously preserved to eternally point out to the creative power of the only true God! It is indeed a sign of His sovereignty over the world, and over the life and death!

Any blasphemies against the Word are against its Author. All sins shall be forgiven unto the sons of men, and blasphemies wherewith so ever they shall blaspheme, but he that shall blaspheme against the Holy Ghost has never forgiveness, but is in danger of eternal damnation (refer to Mark 3 : 28, 29). Why is it so, Lord? Because, while the Spirit of God was upon the Son and He spoke by the Holy Spirit, they said that He had an unclean spirit (verse 30). The Bible is composed of the Old Testament and the New Testament. Each of these two parts is sealed with the signature of the Author of life. In Deuteronomy, chapter 4 verses 1 to 3, we read "*Now, O Israel, listen to the statutes and the judgments which I teach you to observe, that you may live, and go in and possess the land which the LORD God of your fathers is giving you. You shall not add to the word which I command you, nor take from it, that you may keep the commandments of the LORD your God which I command you. Your eyes have seen what the Lord did at Baal Peor: for the LORD your God has destroyed from among you all the men who followed Baal of Peor . . .*". In the last book of the New Testament, the Revelation, chapter 22 verses 18 and 19. Christ declares solemnly "*I warn everyone who hears the words of the prophecy of this book: If anyone* adds anything to these words, God will add to that person the disasters written about in this book. And if anyone takes away from the words of this book of prophecy, God will take away that one's share of the tree of life and of the holy city, which are written about in this book . . ." (New Century Version)

Christ spoke clearly by the Spirit to those that were saying of Him being under Satan's influence that they were blaspheming against the Holy Ghost. In the same way, the Bible being inspired by the same Spirit of Truth, those that try to add, to subtract anything or to alter of its sayings, are under woe for blasphemy! The Bible interprets itself. It is real that evil and sins of different kinds are increasing worse and worse as the end of time is approaching: unless one would have to be blind and deaf or devoid of proper mind in order not to be aware of world conditions; doubtlessly, ". . . *evil men and imposters will grow worse and worse, deceiving, and being deceived.*" (2 Timothy 3 : 13). The world is fast becoming comparable to the prevalent conditions in the time of Noah just before the Flood. Although the knowledge increases in many sciences and technology, although science and technology advance greatly in every area of life, although there are more high learned people than ever before in the past centuries, unfortunately they are still ". . . *never able to come to the knowledge of the truth. Now as Jannes and Jambres resisted Moses, so do these also resist the truth: men of corrupt minds, disapproved concerning the faith.*" (Idem, verses 7 and 8)

We should be sure that our physical welfare is Lord's business (Luke 12 : 22, 23). We must know that we are not at our disposal to do whatever that pleases us to be alive, or to be healthy. Him, who counts each of our hair and knows their number, cares for each of His creatures. Our breath belongs to Him. So let us stop to burden ourselves of the useless care of our wellbeing. We have no right of ourselves to anything, not even our existence. All our health, time and wealth are the Lord's: we cannot make it a business to serve ourselves and become indifferent to our Creator. Only the heathen need all these things. The earth is not filled only with wealthy people or with those that awake early morning to work for the living bread; but also with those that need the daily bread and lack the place to lay their heads; nevertheless, their heavenly Father cares for them (Matthew 6 : 25 - 32), regardless of their ignorance or neglect of Him.

Let us stop robbing God and pawn His holy time of worship; let us give to Him our affections for the provisions He gives us in each instance of our life; let us keep our satanic appetite under the control of enlightened conscience; let us wrestle against so much lust of vain pleasure. For man will live not only of bread, but also of all the Word that is from God. *"Be anxious for nothing, but in everything by prayer and supplication, with thanksgiving, let your requests be made known to God"* (Philippians 4 : 6).

The Sabbath is a weekly rest for Man, his family, his servants, and his animals; it is a day to rest and do good, and to get blessings if observed to the will of the Lord. Someone had said of this holy day 'my weekly vacation'. O, be careful, not a mundane vacation to do whatever you want, according to the flesh. By its very nature, observing the Sabbath is a way to remember and worship God as Creator, who rested from His work in creation. This is not something relegated to the Old Testament saints. Worshipping God as Creator is part of the everlasting gospel to Mankind found in Revelation 14 : 6 - 7 at the end of the world, *"Then I saw another angel flying in the midst of heaven, having the everlasting gospel to preach to those who dwell on the earth—to every nation, and tribe, tongue, and people—saying with a loud voice, 'Fear God and give glory to him, for the hour of his judgment has come; and worship Him who made heaven and earth, the sea and springs of waters'"*. It is important to remember God as our Maker. Observing the weekly Sabbath allows us to do that. This truth also means that we work six days per week, not five; at Sunday sunset, which we call in our modern culture Saturday 7:00 PM, is time to prepare for a productive six-day week of work.

Though the plan of salvation rests only upon the work of Christ on our behalf on Calvary, still we have a role to play, as we debated about it in previous chapters. By our words, our actions, even our attitude, we can help to bring glory to our Creator. For ". . . in the precepts of His holy law, God has given a perfect rule of life; and He has declared that until the close of time this law, unchanged in a single jot or title, is to maintain its claim upon human beings." (Ellen G. White, *The Acts of the Apostles*, p. 505)

We feel it is not an attractive choice to go out and physically bring people to Jesus in cutting deep in our personal week time, or to take away from the things we want to do for ourselves and use that time to lead souls to Christ; but we find it pleasant to accomplish our own tasks and speak vain words during these sanctified holy Hours! In so doing, we have not kept the Sabbath and we are but liars.

God did save us to have intimacy with Him and to work with Him in the beauty of His holiness. When He teaches us, *"Be holy"*, it is not a mere wish, it is a command. And God doesn't command us to do anything that He won't empower us to accomplish. He will empower us to be holy as He made the Sabbath holy. Listen to this: "*And I gave them My statutes and showed them My judgments, which if a man does, he shall live by them. Moreover also I gave them My Sabbaths, to be a sign between Me and them, that they might know that I am the LORD who sanctifies them. Yet the house of Israel rebelled against Me in the wilderness; they did not walk in My statutes, they despised My judgments, which if a man does, he shall even live by them; and they greatly defiled My Sabbaths . . . ."* (Ezekiel 20 : 11 - 13). Now is the time for us as a people, to be more doers of His Will than steadfast listeners. "The salvation of the soul requires the blending of the divine and human strength. God does not propose to do the work that man can do to meet the standard of righteousness. Man has a part to act . . ." (Ellen G. White, *Christ's Object Lessons*, p. 331).

Many preachers today lead their listeners and their admirers to disobedience and sins in affirming at their pulpits that the Christian life is not about "to do or not to do, but only to believe" to be saved! Adam was asked not to eat of the fruit of tree, but he ate and we still reap the results of that sin. Cain killed by jealousy his brother and he was cursed. Abram was asked to offer his only begotten son Isaac, he obeyed and his Maker counted it as righteousness on his behalf. To give water to the Jewish congregation in the desert, and we know consequences Moses reaped by smiting the rock twice instead of once. The very holy Law of our Legislator is made of "DO THIS THAT YOU MAY LIVE" or "IF YOU DESPISE THIS YOU WILL DIE". Obedience to God is guiding and submitting our conduct to God's standards, rather than our own. We have to obey in the hope that this obedience helps us avoid the failures and sins. We believe in God and we obey Him by His saving grace imputed freely to us! Obedience is recognizing the love of our Creator toward us; in this, He cannot ask us to do what is impossible to us. Obedience is the revelation of our faith as did our ancestor Abram in faith in yielding his own pleasure and reasons to the claims of the Lord upon Isaac, the son that he loved the most. Obedience means for the Christians that God is true and His Word is eternal and He rewards everyone according to his works. Obedience is the living trust of Him who cannot lie nor be mistaken!

As stated early in this Testimony, history confirms there were Christians around the year 120 AD that changed to rest on Sunday to avoid the intense persecution against Judaism, by using Christ's resurrection day as their alternative. In the same manner, there are and will be always those who will do their own things contrary to the Lawgiver's instructions; but obviously, it is not Man's prerogative to change God's clearly expressed Will, for any reason. Jesus said to the Pharisees ". . . *All too well you reject the commandment of God, that you may keep your tradition*" (Mark 7 : 9)

Surely, events worthy to be honored occurred on certain days of the last week of Christ on earth, but we have no command to make any of them holy. Jesus died for us on the cross on Friday; we know this is the very important event of His mission on earth, which for centuries was prefigured by sacrificial system in Israelite temple and made our eternal death penalty removed and eternal life assured. Should we honor Friday as holy day on behalf of our Savior's crucifixion, when Christ dying for the world, cried, "*IT IS FINISHED*"? Nobody on earth or in heaven has the power to make holy a day of the week, except the Creator! Instead, the Lord Himself instituted communion to celebrate His death (Matthew 26 : 26 - 28), which could be celebrated any day of the week. In addition, resurrection on Sunday morning is important too, for, if He did not rise from death according to the Word, He would be a liar, not the true Messiah waited for. Therefore, how do we honor this event according His Will? Baptism is the memorial of the death to sin and resurrection to newness of life (Romans 6 : 4); communion commemorates Jesus' Friday crucifixion and death, while baptism represents altogether Christ's Friday burial and Sunday resurrection. Full stop.

Nobody can enter into the kingdom of heaven, which is our destination, while mixing up things and then keeping to hail always "*Lord, Lord*", even performing some wonders or building big beautiful churches; only he who '*does the will*' of the Father in heaven, could stand blamelessly at the judgment (Matthew 7 : 21). And the will of the Father is clearly expressed in His Law of Ten commandments, which is repeated in divers manners throughout all the Bible: 'You Israel in all ages and in all dwellings', meaning all people which will bear His Name, listen to the statutes and to the judgments, which your Heavenly Father teaches you, to do them, that you may live, and go in and possess the eternal and beautiful land that the Lord God of your fathers will give you. To His Holy Sayings which He commands you, You shall not add neither shall you diminish one point from it, that you may keep the commandments of the Lord your God which He commands you . . . For Christ, the Word made Flesh, who has come as Light in this world affirms, "*He who rejects Me, and does not receive My words, has that which judges him—the word that I have spoken will judge him in the last day . . . And I know that His command is everlasting life. Therefore, whatever I speak, just as the Father has told Me, so I speak*" (John 12 : 48, 50).

Some false teachers explain that, since the Law is spiritual and we being carnal (Romans 7 : 14), no human being will ever be able in this life to meet its requirements. The question is, has the Law been given by God as some idealistic impossible goal, toward which converted souls should struggle to fulfill but never be able to attain? No! In writing to Roman Christians (see Romans 7 : 7, 8, 12, 18, 19, 24, 25), Paul shows that he desires with all his heart and mind to obey the Law, but in the flesh he still fails. However, by the grace of God through faith in Christ, and sincere repentance, he is seen by God as righteous. Therefore, knowing the holy Commandments, but refusing to obey them is a willful sin and such an attitude cannot reflect in any case a genuine repentance. This is what the same Paul clarifies in Hebrews 10 : 26 - 31, stating clearly that sinning willfully provokes punishment that is without appeal.

To the Bible teachers and modern prophets, it is said, "*You, therefore, who teach another, do you not teach yourself? You who preach that a man should not steal, do you steal? You who say, 'Do not commit adultery,' do you commit adultery? You who abhor idols, do you rob temples? You who make your boast in the Law, do you dishonor Yahweh through breaking the Law? For 'the name of Yahweh is blasphemed among the Gentiles* [pagans] *because of you,' as it is written.*" (Romans 2 : 21 - 24, *emphasis added*). Denying the claims of our God upon us to make His commandments and His requirements void and to call sinfulness goodness, is to turn away our ears from the truth and change it unto fables made of men's devices! Instead, fight the good fight to finish the course and keep the living faith. "*If anyone comes to you and does not bring this doctrine, do not receive him into your house nor greet him; for he who greets him shares in his evil deeds.*" (2 John 10, 11).

Christ came on this earth and died on the cross to fulfill the law, for His food was to do the will of His Holy Father who sent Him, and to finish His work. In this, Paul has this hope "*. . . there is laid up FOR ME the crown of righteousness, which the Lord, the righteous Judge, will give to ME on that Day, and not to me only, but also to ALL WHO HAVE*

LOVED His appearing." (2 Timothy 4 : 8, *Emphasis added*). Therefore ". . . *everyone who has this hope in Him, purifies himself, just as He is pure.*" (1 John 3 : 3).

Paul in Galatians 1 : 6 - 9, stresses "*I marvel that you are turning away so soon from Him who called you in the grace of Christ, to a different, which is not another; but there are some who trouble you and want to pervert the gospel of Christ. But even if we, or an angel from heaven, preach any other gospel to you than what we have preached to you, let him be accursed . . .*". For, if we choose to proclaim the Good News, the message we proclaim must be true. Otherwise, we are building a foundation on falsehood. Christ Jesus is the Way, the Truth and the Life.

XXX—LET US WALK AS HE DID

Jesus said to him, I am the way, the truth, and the life: no man comes to the Father, but by me. If you had known me, you should have known my Father also: and from now on you know him, and have seen him. (John 14 : 6, 7)

LET NO ONE be deceived by the words of the to-day prophets and teachers, saying, "the salvation is by grace alone, man does not have anything to do to be saved; all was accomplished on the cross . . .". This kind of teaching, the more and more popular in Christianity, is the roots of many errors and heathen behaviors among those that claim to be genuine Christ's followers.

To sustain their erroneous teachings, they quote deceitfully Pauline writings, such as:

- *"For by grace you have been saved through faith, and that not of yourselves; it is the gift of God, not of works, lest anyone should boast."* (Ephesians 2 : 8 - 9).

  However, it is clearly stated that the faith alone is insufficient, as Christ the Saviour clearly states in Matthew 5 : 15 - 17and 7 : 21 - 27 and in Revelation 3 : 1, 2, 20 : 12, 13; 22 : 12 ; 19 : 16, 17; see also James. 2 : 14, 17 - 22)

- *". . . not by works of righteousness which we have done, but according to His mercy He saved us, through the washing of regeneration and renewing of the Holy Spirit"* (Titus 3 : 5). O yes, because the plan of salvation was set up even before humans were created and any sin was committed (John 1 : 29, 36 Revelation 13 : 8).

- *"Therefore we conclude that a man is justified by faith apart from the deeds of the law"* (Romans 3 : 28). Ask yourselves 'Which law is it about?' It is the law dealing with blotting out of sin, but not the not the law of Ten Commandments; see verse 31 of the same chapter!
- *"And the scripture, foreseeing that God would justify the Gentiles by faith . . ."* (Galatians 3 : 8)
- *"For you are all the sons of God through faith in Christ Jesus"*, according to Galatians 3 : 26; however the demons believe and tremble but they are not God's children and Abraham's seeds.
- *". . . knowing that a man is not justified by the works of the law but by the faith of Jesus Christ, even we have believed in Jesus Christ, that we might be justified by faith in Christ and not by the works of the law: for by the works of the law no flesh shall be justified . . . I do not set aside the grace of God; for if righteousness comes through the law, then Christ died in vain"*, (Galatians 2 : 16, 21). *"And if by grace, then is it no longer of works; otherwise grace is no longer grace. But if it is of works, is it no longer grace; otherwise work is no longer work."* (Romans 11 : 6). Compare with the sayings of the Messiah Himself in Luke 6 : 46 - 49, John 14 : 14 and Revelation 2 : 2 - 5 and find out what this means; also what Paul himself has to say about good works in Ephesians 2 : 10 and 1 Timothy 5 : 10, 25; and he praised good works in Acts 9 : 36 and 1 Timothy 2 : 9, 10. Did he contradict himself? No, instead, he affirms the same thing in different ways, that the faith without works is dead.
- *"Therefore, being justified by faith, we have peace with God through our Lord Jesus Christ."* (Romans 5 : 1) *". . . who has saved us and called us with a holy calling, not according to our works, but according to His own purpose and grace which was given to us in Christ Jesus before the world began"* (2 Timothy 1 : 9).
  For, to our Maker, everything is present and He foresees our life before we would be born.

Sometimes they cite pompously but wrongly the infallible words spoken by the Master of the Universe, such as:

- *"He who believes in Him is not condemned: but he who does not believe is condemned already, because he has not believed in the name of the only begotten Son of God"* (John 3 : 18); *"And this is the will of Him that sent Me, that every one who sees the Son and believes in Him, may have everlasting life . . ."* (John 6 : 40)

The Word of God, because it is spiritual, should be read, better studied steadfastly. Let us stop running through verses to find what fits to our thinking, by lack of the least sincerity. Instead, by love of our God as the Author of the Scriptures and the honor due to His eternal Word, we should take It in our hands with fear and reverence and ask the Holy Spirit as its Inspirer to teach us. We should notice that, in some scriptures quoted above, the matter spoken by Paul is, most of the time different from what people want to draw from them. If not, let us listen to the same Paul in many other Scriptures.

- He told believing Christians that those who committed various sins could not be saved in the kingdom of God (1 Corinthians 6 : 9 - 10; Galatians 5 : 19 - 21; Ephesians 5 : 3 - 5).
- He tells us through the Philippians to work out our own salvation with fear and trembling (Philippians 2 : 12, 13).
- When discussing the grace of God that brings salvation, he emphasized that the Spirit teaches that denying ungodliness and worldly lusts, we should live soberly, righteously, and godly, in this present world (Titus 2 : 7 - 12, 14)
- To the Hebrews he said that Jesus was the author of eternal salvation unto all them that obey Him. (Hebrews 5 : 9)
- He told the Romans, to confess and believe with their heart Christ unto righteousness and to cast off the works of darkness. (Romans 10 : 9, 10; 13 : 11 - 14)
- He told king Agrippa that when gentiles are converted, they should do works that meet their repentance, (Acts 26 : 20)
- He encourages us to do good works in many places, (Titus 8, 14; Hebrews 10 : 23, 24)
- He explains the purpose of the Gospel to make us righteous through our good works, (2 Timothy 3 : 15, 16)

As said above, it is clear that grace alone is insufficient and that it must be coupled at least with faith and with one act, confession.

Friend, did you learn something from these Scriptures enough to change your mind? If not, let us listen to other disciples of

Christ.—James stressed strongly that faith alone is dead, (James 2 : 14, 17 - 26)—What Peter is telling us is not different from what we have read above, (1 Peter 2 : 11, 12)—John the beloved of the Lord says that Cain slewed his brother because of his evil works, (1 John 3 : 12).

Friend, do you still hold to your false doctrine of faith alone as a sum? Listen to Peter warning us of Paul's writings that we should study them carefully, not running over verses, but praying the Almighty to enlighten us that we may understand what His Spirit wants us to know and do, for "... *we, according to His promise, look for new heavens and a new earth in which righteousness dwells. Therefore, beloved, looking forward to these things, be diligent to be found by Him in peace, without spot and blameless ... as also our beloved brother Paul ... speaking in them of these things, in which are some things hard to understand, which unstable people twist to their own destruction ... You therefore, beloved, since you know this beforehand, beware lest you also fall from your own steadfastness ...*" (2 Peter 3 : 13 - 18).

If Paul taught that our works have nothing to do with our salvation, how are we to understand passages like those found in Revelation 14 : 13 and 20 : 12, 13, which say that God will judge men *"according to their works"*? Surely, if one cannot be held responsible for his behavior, why should he be judged and how can it be?

The plan of salvation set up by God from eternity does not change. Before Eden, the constant message is still the same, 'Love your Maker ... Keep and obey His commandments and do them ... you will live'. Some angels failed by their deeds and became devils; Adam and Eve failed to do God's Will and reaped the consequences for them and for their seed. The Israelites failed the obey their Deliverer and only two persons among all who came out from Egypt reached the Promised Land.

Because of His love for His creatures, God sent untiringly messengers from time to time to bring back His rebellious people to Him, with the same message. 'You shall keep all my statutes . . .' (Exodus 15 : 26; Leviticus 20 : 22; 1 Kings 9 : 4; 1 : 33; Ezekiel 18 : 21), 'Keep all my commandments always . . .' (Deuteronomy 4 2 - 6, 5 : 1 - 10, 11 : 8; Joshua 22 : 5; 1 Kings 6 : 12, 2 Chronicles 34 : 31; Nehemiah 9 : 1; Psalms 119 : 115; Daniel 9 : 4), etc . . . The message of John the Baptist was so simple and clear that those that misunderstood it were lost, "*Therefore bear fruits worthy of repentance, and do not begin to say to yourselves, 'We have Abraham as our father ... every tree which does not bear good fruit is cut down and thrown into the fire.*", he said (Luke 3 : 8, 9).

FORTUNAT TSHIMANGA-MUKADI

The same fire that awaits those who will get lost.

Let us now sit at the feet of Him who paid the high price for our redemption, for He spent more than three years teaching people day and night, the principles by which they should live their lives, never once mentioning grace alone as mean of salvation. To the very simple and clear question of the rich young man, who was born and grown in Jewish nation, the Messiah went directly to the point, "*If you want enter into life, Keep the commandments.*" (Matthew 19 : 16 - 19)

Christ requires His disciples to follow His teachings and obey His commandments, ". . . *why call ye me, Lord, and do not the things which I say?*" (Luke 6 : 43 - 46, *King James Version*). He said that one would be rejected at the judgment day if he did not do His Father's will, suggesting that confession of His Name, while necessary, is insufficient for salvation (Matthew 7 : 21 - 24). He declared boldly that our love for Him must utter keeping His commandments, (John 14 : 15, 21 - 24; 15 : 10). His Testimony to John for the seven churches in chapter 2 of Revelation is so clear that nobody cannot misunderstand His message. He is the same yesterday, today and forever.

The grace is free, since Eden: Adam and Eve were created at God's image, without any work on their part; but they made void that grace by breaking its conditions. Abraham is considered as our father in faith, because he obeyed and did what his Creator asked him to do. Israelites became chosen people, special treasure for Yahweh without any work from them, but still they had to obey and do the Will of their Heavenly Father to remain in His love. When evangelism is held, the Gospel is brought freely to everyone, but only those that believe and are baptized and remain in the race, may be saved.

Therefore, in our daily struggle, trial or danger set on our way by the Enemy, we have in our side, the Father and the Son and the Holy Spirit who abide in us, if He finds place in our heart. So, throughout the Word of the Creator are these words, 'If you obey . . . So you will . . . , If you do . . . So I will . . . , If you listen . . . then you are'; ". . . *if you diligently obey the voice of the Lord your God,*" says Moses, ". . . *to observe* 'carefully' *all His commands which I command you today, that the Lord your God will set you high above all nations of the earth. And all these blessings shall come upon you and overtake you, because you obey the voice of the Lord your God.*" (Deuteronomy 28 : 1, 2, *emphasis added*)

The role that must be played by Man in the plan of salvation, in other words, the work of his transformation from natural sinfulness to holiness, ". . . is a continuous one. Day by day, God labors for man's sanctification, and man is to co-operate, *also daily*, with Him, putting forth persevering efforts in the cultivation of right habits, *meaning works*. He has to add grace to grace; and as he thus works on the plan of addition, God works for him on the plan of multiplication" (Ellen G. White—Acts of the Apostles, p. 532, *emphasis added*)

Obedience characterizes the Saints who wait for the soon coming of their Lord; they drink at the Source of all knowledge and wisdom and do not lean on the earthly philosophy and fables. Obedience to God is very important in the Christian growth. Jesus is very concerned about us and He wants us to do more than participate in good works. He wants us to believe in Him. He wants us to come up higher and be '*like*' Him.

When we are being obedient to God, we are doing just this, knowing Him, loving Him and having a personal, intimate relationship with Him. To do this, we must be attentive to God's Sayings. This is not an option, because we cannot have an intimate relationship with Jesus and trample on the words He taught. Obedience to God is living God's Word because we want to enjoy being filled with the love of Jesus and for Him and our fellow brethren.

God endowed Man with the freedom to choose the life or the death, to choose the right or the wrong, to obey or not. We are not the automaton. However, the natural man always chooses the wrong, for the spiritual things ". . . *are foolishness to him; nor can he know them, because they are spiritually discerned.*" (1 Corinthians 2 : 14). This makes the way to perdition so large that many walk on it. Therefore, "the part of the Christian is to persevere in overcoming every fault. Constantly he is to pray the Savior to heal the disorders of his sin-sick soul. He has not the wisdom or the strength to overcome; these belong to the Lord, and He bestows them to those who in humiliation and contrition seek Him for help.

So the true and earnest longing of the Christian is to accept Christ "as a personal Savior, and following His example of self-denial, this is the secret of holiness" (Ellen G. White, *Our High Calling*, p. 214), and before, "the believer is held out the wonderful possibility of being like

Christ, obedient to all the principles of the Law" (Ellen G. White—*Acts of the Apostles*, p.532.)

"*The grass withers, the flower fades, but the word of our God stands forever*" (Isaiah 40 : 8). "*He who has My commandments, and keeps them, it is he who loves Me, and he who loves Me will be loved by my Father, and I will love him and manifest Myself to him*" (John 14 : 21 . . .) "*I am the true vine and my Father is the vinedresser. Every branch in Me that does not bear fruit He takes away; and every branch that bears fruit, He prunes, that it may bring forth more fruit*" (idem, chapter 15 verses1, 2 . . .)

Believe in His words and do them, you will surely live!

XXXI—THEN SERVE HIM WITHOUT GUILE

"And when the chief Shepherd shall be manifested, ye shall receive the crown of glory that fadeth not away." (1 Peter 5 : 4, *King James version*)

SIN REQUIRES REPENTANCE. Repentance is a change of mind, a determined commitment to cease sin and obey God (Acts 8 : 22; Matthew 21 : 28, 29; Acts 17 : 30; 11 : 23). Before one can change his conduct, he must change his mind. He will never change until he makes up his mind to pursue the means God provides until he succeeds. The decision to do so is repentance, and no one will change to please God without it. All the good attitudes in the world will not get the job done until one follows through with action. Such a change will not be easy, but our Heavenly Provider promises it is possible if we work diligently according to His Word. Apostle James advises us to be doers of the word, not just hearers (James 1 : 22 - 25). Habits are formed by repeated action. Yes, repetition produces a habit that then one feels natural and enjoyable. So, we change to serve God only when we compel ourselves to do what we know is right and repeat it until it becomes 'second nature'. (refer to Romans 6 : 1 - 23; Matthew 7 : 21; Luke 6 : 46)

Another danger is that you cannot change a bad habit while continuing to run with the 'crowd' that caused the habit. Changing the habit will require changing your friends because the friends are part of the habit! For example, suppose you determine to watch less TV, so you turn it off; but sitting in front of it with nothing else to do, soon you will turn it on again. However, if you become actively involved in family activities, Bible study, etc., soon you will replace it with other habits. For every bad habit you put off, find some useful activity to put on in its place.

One day you would wish that you had to live your life for God. If you are not living it for Him now, I urge you to find out what His will requires of you. If you already know, I urge you to obey while you are still here. The question must always be, Are we keeping the Sabbath the way Christ instructed? The Sabbath made for man, is a vital part of what God has given us to develop His Love, His Mind, His Character, that we may be properly be born into His Family and be called His children. It is lawful to do things that are of benefit to the welfare of those around us on the Sabbath Day, if there is no other way to save one's threatened life. We must live by every word of God, applying the rest of mind and body from Friday sunset to Saturday sunset; as the Preparation Day starting Thursday at sunset prepare us and allows us to rest entirely during the Saturday twenty-four hours, that the Holy Rest may be a refreshing to us and to all those that are around us, even our herd; as Exodus 23 : 12 puts it clearly, "*Six days thou shalt do thy work, and on the seventh day thou shalt rest: that thine ox and thine ass may rest, and the son of thy handmaid, and the stranger, may be refreshed.*" The refreshing to take place on Saturday is part of the application of all the commands and words of God concerning the Sabbath.

Christ's custom was to go to the synagogue, to gather together on the Sabbath with the people (Luke 4 : 16, 31), for on Sabbath, there should be a "*holy convocation*" (Leviticus 23 : 2, 3). The word 'convocation' means 'commanded gathering', a gathering that is commanded by God. This sounds the sense of obligation. Thus the Sabbath is a time of commanded assembly. It is the time we should gather together.

In this, the epistle to the Hebrews chapter 10, verses 22 to 25 recommend: "*Let us draw near with a true heart in full assurance of faith, having our hearts sprinkled from an evil conscience and our bodies washed with pure water. Let us hold fast the profession of our faith without wavering, for He who promised is faithful. And let us consider one another in order to stir up love and good works, not forsaking the assembling of ourselves together, as is the manner of some, but exhorting one another, and so much the more as you see the Day approaching*". O yes, as we approach the End Time, assembling together should be more and more important and more beneficial to us. The specific time that God has given us for assembling together is the Sabbath, that we may fellowship with the Father, and with his Son Jesus Christ (1 John 1 : 3).

Surely, we fellowship with one another, but that fellowship is also with God the Father and Jesus Christ, if we do not come together to please ourselves and make useless noise and display! When we assemble together on the Sabbath Day, the very Spirit of God is there if we gather in His Name and, God the Father and Jesus Christ fellowship with us. The words that a pastor or a teacher speaks are not to be his own but should be the words of Jesus Christ. They are to be the words of God the Father. The preacher is to be led by the Spirit of God; his speech is to be inspired, using the Word of God, not handling it deceitfully by seeking to please the people or to provoke the unnecessary and useless applause of men. To 'prophesy,' in Greek, means to speak under inspiration and is therefore the word used when describing someone preaching in the Church. "*Blessed is the man who walks not in the counsel of the ungodly, nor stands in the way of sinners, nor sits in the seat of the scornful; but his delight is in the law of the Lord, and in His law he meditates day and night*" (Psalms 1 : 1 - 2) A blessed Man's delight is in God's law, and part of that law is the Sabbath. His delight needs to be in the Sabbath, part of the principle of not "*walking in the counsel of the ungodly*"; but instead, walking in the counsel of God is what that makes the Sabbath a delight.

Making the Sabbath a delight is to make sure that it is a rest, that it is God's day and there is a way to worship Him on this sacred day; that every word spoken brings honor to His holy Name; that it is refreshing for us and for our children, including people who come into contact with us as visitors and strangers. It is making the Sabbath Day a delight, not just for ourselves, but for those around us as well, and making sure that the Way of God is applied on the Sabbath Day. It is easy to get lost when you get wrapped in the false happiness or worldly delight: so, make sure that your happiness, your delight, leans upon your Maker's Will.

The very delight we find on the Sabbath day is our worship. Worship involves not only some sort of public service with hymns of praise, prayers and a well-planned liturgy. Such services epitomize for many what is involved in worshiping God, but it should also to render, to express reverence to our Creator. The word 'worship' comes from an old English word meaning "worth-ship" and refers to worthiness, respect and reverence directed toward God. Our worship of God would therefore literally mean showing our appreciation of God's worth. Certainly, we must pay careful attention to what God tells us in His Word, the Bible. He seeks those who will worship Him in spirit and in truth (John 4 : 23, 24). When Satan sought to tempt Christ to worship him, Jesus Christ sharply rebuked him, saying, "*You shall worship the LORD your God, and*

Him only shall you serve" (Matthew 4 : 10). The apostle Paul equated his worship of God with ". . . *believing all things which are written in the Law and in the Prophets*" (Acts 24 : 14), that is the Word of God. God wants His people to worship Him in truth. We do this by honoring Him, serving Him and giving heed to His instructions and His Holy Law.

God asks us to live '*by every word that proceeds from the mouth of God*' (Matthew 4 : 4). Our worship of God is shown in how we live our daily lives. Christianity is a way of life. It is a way of thinking, acting and living. It affects every aspect of our life. (Acts 18 : 25, 26; 19 : 9, 23; 22 : 4; 24 : 14, 22). True worship of God involves nothing short of the inward transformation of the human heart by faith in Jesus Christ and His sacrifice. External worship practices alone are inadequate. God is looking for those who will worship Him in spirit, from a converted and transformed heart.

True worship, then, is much more than praise of God in a public worship service. "The worship of God is nowhere defined in Scripture. It is not confined to praise; broadly it may be regarded as the direct acknowledgement to God, of His nature, attributes, ways and claims, whether by the outgoing of the heart in praise and thanksgiving, or by deed done in such acknowledgement" (W.E. Vine, *Vine's Expository Dictionary of New Testament Words*, Worship).

Jesus Christ sharply rebuked the religious leaders of His days because they misrepresented God's commands and substituted their own humanly devised teachings (Matthew 15 : 9; Mark 7 : 7). He said such worship was in vain. Christ reserved the harshest words of warning for those who would profess to worship God, who say "*Lord, Lord,*" (Matthew 7 : 21), but refuse to do God's will or obey His laws (verses 21 - 23). Such worship is empty and without merit, unacceptable to God and Jesus Christ. We live at a time when many people are disillusioned with traditional worship services, which are vacuous, without meaning and irrelevant to their lives. It is time to take a fresh look at what true worship is all about. When we come to understand its real significance, true worship becomes supremely relevant to our lives now and to our future destiny as a people.

Abraham's our pattern of faith demonstrated by his obedience to God that he is the model of living faith. His manner of life was that of obeying God from the heart. Also, God's servants in all ages, because of their faith, refused to sin at the risk of their lives. They had to do what God commands regardless of personal risk and hardship. Indeed, the devil cannot force us to sin. He simply influences us through our fleshly weaknesses. Several major areas of our fleshly nature could be easily manipulated by Satan, if we allow him to do so. We naturally look for ways to justify our lusts, our sinful desires, and the behavior that arises from them. We deceive ourselves into believing that, since our desires are natural, they are not so bad after all. But God's Word reminds us that "*there is a way that seems right to a man, but its end is the way of death*" (Proverbs 14 : 12; 16 : 25). Death is the end result of living that wrong way (Romans 6 : 23).

We must change the direction of our lives as a prerequisite for receiving God's gift of salvation. That is what both Christ and the apostles taught. Paul declared we ". . . *should repent, turn to God, and do works befitting repentance*" (Acts 26 : 20). Works demonstrate our repentance to God, but, in themselves alone, they will never earn for us the right to the eternal life.

James explicitly states that "*faith without works is dead*" (James 2 : 20, 26), and Paul makes it plain that God saves us '*by grace through faith for the very purpose of producing good works. For we are His workmanship, created in Christ Jesus for good works, which God prepared beforehand that we should walk in them*" (Ephesians 2 : 8 - 10). Why should this be so difficult for people to believe and accept?

It is simply walking in Christ's footsteps, following His example that makes us fit for eternal life (1 John 2 : 6). Jesus said, "*Let your light so shine before men, that they may see your good works and glorify your Father in heaven*" (Matthew 5 : 16). Though works do not earn us eternal life in themselves, they do glorify and honor God, and God requires that we honor Him by the way we live. People who refuse to include works in their lives are dishonoring God, whether they realize it or not. "*They profess to know God, but in works they deny Him, being abominable, disobedient, and disqualified for every good work*" (Titus 1 : 16).

Through submission to God, allowing His Spirit to lead us, and living a Christlike life, we build righteous, godly character that will enable us to rule with Jesus Christ in His Kingdom. Jesus explained this in His parable of the talents in Matthew 25 : 20 - 29 and also in Revelation 22 : 12 when He said, ". . . *I am coming quickly, and My reward is with Me, to give to every one according to his work*"; and further in verse 14 of

FORTUNAT TSHIMANGA-MUKADI

the same chapter He added, "*Blessed are those who do His commandments, that they may have the right to the tree of life and may enter through the gates into the city.*" Through God's grace, the gift of eternal life is given to those who demonstrate their faith in God by their obedience to his commandments.

God's Spirit working within us helps us change and begin producing right fruits in our lives. Paul in Galatians 5 : 22, 23 lists the fruits of God's Spirit, love, joy, peace, kindness, gentleness and self-control, among others, that become increasingly evident in us as we grow spiritually.

Producing the fruit of righteousness is important. When God calls us to be His children, He initiates a change in us from our formerly proud, selfish, disobedient ways. He transforms us by the renewing, or the changing of our mind if we let Him do so. It is not always easy or spontaneous as we live in this sinful world; however, we should understand that adversity and discontentment do not build the character; instead, they reveal it; instead good habit builds good character for eternal life.

Paul told the Romans, "*Do not be conformed to this world, but be transformed by the renewing of your mind, that you may prove what is that good and acceptable and perfect will of God*" (Romans 12 : 2). Then he explained that this transformation is not instantaneous. It requires ongoing changes in our thinking and outlook that permanently affect the way we live. We become "*a living sacrifice, holy, acceptable to God, which is our reasonable service*" (verse 1).

In Ezekiel 36 : 26 - 27, Our Maker tells us how He will accomplish this: "*I will give you a new heart and put a new spirit in you; I will remove from you your heart of stone and give you a heart of flesh. And I will put my Spirit in you and move you to follow my decrees and be careful to keep my laws*" (NIV).

We need God's help, through His Spirit, to obey Him from the heart and to bring our thoughts, attitudes and actions in line with His. We must allow His Spirit to become the guiding force in our lives so that we might have this '*new heart*'. Through God's Spirit, which He gives us, we can be influenced by God for good, while our free will is involved. This is living in stark contrast to the world around us and our own nature which influence us toward evil.

God's Spirit also helps us come to a deeper comprehension of His Truth. When Jesus promised the apostles He would send the Spirit to them, He said this Spirit would *"guide* them *into all truth"* (John 16 : 13, emphasis added). God's Spirit inspires a deeper understanding of His Word, purpose and will. Without God's Spirit a person cannot fully understand God's Word and Will, for ". . . *they are foolishness to him; nor can he know them, because they are spiritually discerned"* (1 Corinthians 2 : 14). The Holy Spirit makes overcoming evil possible. Nothing that God asks of us is too difficult to achieve by His power working in our lives. Romans 8 : 26 tells us that God's Spirit helps us in our weaknesses. Paul speaks for all of us when he said, *"I can do all things through Christ who strengthens me"* (Philippians 4 : 13). Jesus assures, *"With God all things are possible"* (Matthew 19 : 26; Mark 10 : 27).

The Christian life is to be one of overcoming evil of all kind. God doesn't want you to remain just as we were when He called you; instead, He tells you through apostle Paul not to ". . . *be conformed to this world, but be transformed by the renewing of your mind"* (Romans 12 : 2).

Christianity is a lifetime of overcoming and growing, of transforming our thoughts and mind to become like Jesus Christ (Philippians 2 : 5). As shown through this Testimony, the seventh-day Sabbath, which God blessed and made holy for Man to rest and to worship the true God upon it, was gradually set aside and the festival day of Pagan Sun worship was taken into the Christendom. Paganism with all of its pomp, and ceremonies, and holy days crept silently into the Christian Church until it developed into an apostate system of religious worship. Notice this statement, "Not a few pagan habits crept into the church concealed by new names. This is conceded by the most earnest of the Fathers. Leo the Great speaks of Christians in Rome who worshiped the sun, before repairing to the church of St. Peter. In the celebration of Sunday, as it was introduced by Constantine, and still continues on the whole continent of Europe, the cult of the old Sun god Apollo mingles with the remembrance of the resurrection of Christ." (Philip Schaff, Church History, page 375)

This is the story concerning the devil's most masterful deception of all History. Not only did he bring in the Church the Pagan forms of worship, but he managed to install the old heathen day of sun worship in place of the holy Sabbath of the Lord. And he continues to blind people that they may ignore what the Bible teaches on this subject, that they will still follow pagan tradition instead of the commandments of God. No wonder Jesus exclaimed *"But in vain ye do worship me, teaching for doctrine the commandments of men.*" (Matthew 15 : 9, King James Version).

The Spirit of God within us convicts our conscience and helps us see sin as it really is (John 16 : 8). He works with our conscience, helps us to recognize and avoid sin. And then, He produces godly fruit in us; just as an apple tree produces apples, God's Spirit produces a particular type of fruit in our lives (Galatians 5 : 22 - 23). The Spirit of God also comforts, encourages and otherwise helps us; which is the purpose Jesus Christ promised to send to His followers a '*Helper*' or '*Comforter*' (John 14 : 16). We need not to be unduly worried about what may happen to us. If we allow Him, God's Spirit gives us the assurance that whatever happens will work for good "*to those who love God, to those who are the called according to His purpose*" (Romans 8 : 28). After baptism and the laying on of hands, the same Spirit that leads us to repentance continues to work in us even more powerfully to help us see and overcome our sins and shortcomings, unless we shut Him out.

As emphasized in this book, some people mistakenly believe that, once a person is baptized, God takes over and does everything for such a person who has nothing else to do but his faith. This is a misleading and dangerous concept. God expects us to resist sin and strive to make His Spirit an active part of our daily life. Remember the assumptions of Satan against Job, "*. . . Does Job fear God for nothing? Have not you made an hedge about him, and about his house, and about all that he has on every side? you have blessed the work of his hands, and his substance is increased in the land. But put forth your hand now, and touch all that he has, and he will curse you to your face*" (Job 1 : 9 - 11).

In 2 Timothy chapter1, verse 6, Paul urged Timothy to "*stir up the gift of God, the Holy Spirit, which is in you through the laying on of my hands*" (emphasis added), showing that we have a personal responsibility in our salvation. Timothy needed to 'stir up' God's Spirit, not just sit back and let God take over. Paul restated, in Philippians 2 : 12 that we must work out our own salvation with fear and trembling.

We should remember that the Kingdom of God is the heart of the gospel message Jesus Christ taught. It is the end of our spiritual journey; that is to say, the real reason for us being Christians (Revelation 11 : 15; Daniel 2 : 44). Now that you know what to do, will you act on it, or will you let this precious calling from God go unheeded? Through the prophet Isaiah, God gives us an invitation and a promise: *"Seek the Lord while He may be found, call upon Him while He is near. Let the wicked forsake his way, and the unrighteous man his thoughts; let him return to the Lord, and He will have mercy on him; and to our God, for He will abundantly pardon"* (Isaiah 55 : 6, 7).

In 2 Thessalonians 2 : 13, 14, Paul writes, *"But we ought always to thank God for you, brothers loved by the Lord, because from the beginning God chose you to be saved through the sanctifying work of the Spirit and through belief in the truth. He called you to this through our gospel that you might share in the glory of our Lord Jesus Christ. So then, brothers, stand firm and hold to the teachings we passed on to you, whether by word of mouth or by letter"* (NIV Translation).

The apostle Peter also wrote, *"Therefore, my brothers, be all the more eager to make your calling and election sure. For if you do these things, you will never fall, and you will receive a rich welcome into the eternal kingdom of our Lord and Savior Jesus Christ"* (2 Peter 1 : 10, 11, NIV Translation).

This is the only road to eternal life.

In looking at the Preparation Day before the Sabbath, there is a principle we need to apply as to the way we keep the Law, to keep God's way, to understand His mind and His character in order to rest and have the time to spend with His Family and do the things that are important on the Sabbath Day. Exodus 16 : 4 reads *"Then said the Lord to Moses, 'Behold, I will rain bread from heaven for you. And the people shall go out and gather a certain quota every day, that I may test them, whether they will walk in my law or not."* This was a test, given before Israel came to Mount Sinai. God was going to give them manna from heaven, from the sky. And it is written *"And it shall be on the sixth day that they shall prepare what they bring in, and it shall be twice as much as they gather daily"* (verse 5). Here is the Preparation Day, the sixth day of the week. Then here comes the divine regulation to us today as in the time of old, *"So they laid it up till morning, as Moses commanded: and it did not stink, nor were there any worms in it . . . , but on the seventh day, the Sabbath, there will be none"* (Exodus 16 : 24 - 27). However, some hardened their heart and they ". . . *went out on the seventh day to gather, but they found none. And the Lord said to Moses, 'How long do you refuse to keep My commandments and My laws? See! for the Lord has given you the Sabbath; therefore He gives you on the sixth day bread of two days . . ."* (verses 28 and 29)

FORTUNAT TSHIMANGA-MUKADI

For 40 years, in 2,080 occasions, the children of Israel had a Preparation Day. It was shown to them by the miracle that on the sixth day they had twice the amount of manna, and that manna could be kept through the Sabbath. Any other day they would not be able to keep the manna more than one day from Sunday to Friday, because it would spoil quickly. How do these events apply to us? Why is it important? How do you rest? How do you apply the principle of a right rest? When do you start preparing for the Sabbath? When does the Preparation Day start for you, your family or your church? It has been said here that the Preparation Day starts on Thursday evening at sunset. If you come home late on Friday from work, you are not going to have time to prepare for the Sabbath. You will be going straight into the Sabbath. The biblical principle is that we are to start preparing 24 hours before the Sabbath, and that preparation starts Thursday (the fifth day of the week) evening. We are to be prepared and get things ready for the Sabbath, food, things needed for the children, clothing . . . However, as we live in this time of the end, things grow weary and we find ourselves so busy some Fridays that we do not have enough time to get really prepared before Friday sunset, it is wise to start preparing your coming Sabbath day, from the previous Saturday sunset and it will truly make the coming Sabbath day, a rest day. That is the essence of the Sabbath Day rest.

We need to analyze our own situations, with the help of the Spirit of God. We know the Sabbath is a rest day blessed by our Creator. We need to prepare for it, so that it is indeed, a rest day. The Judgment is going on right now (see 1 Peter 4 : 17); we are being judged by how we apply the principles established by the Great Lawgiver, how we apply the sayings of His Word, as we are to live by every word that proceeds from the mouth of the Almighty Creator and Savior (see Matthew 4 : 4). God's Laws must be kept by submitting our will to the Spirit of God, not merely using a Pharisaic tick list of points that are compiled. For 40 years, the principle of the Preparation Day was implemented in the case of Ancient Israel in the wilderness. We need to look at it and see if we can apply the principles in a New Covenant sense today. To apply it in the new agreement where the Law is in our heart, where we are, in fact, to do what we have to do and make sure we are spiritually obedient to the very Word of God.

Let us sing with the psalmist:

The law of the Lord is perfect, converting the soul;

The testimony of the Lord is sure, making wise the simple;
The statutes of the Lord are right, rejoicing the heart;
The commandment of the Lord is pure, enlightening the eyes;
The fear of the Lord is clean, enduring forever;
The judgments of the Lord are true and righteous altogether.
More to be desired are they than gold, yea, than much fine gold;
Sweeter also than honey and the honeycomb.
Moreover by them Your servant is warned,
And in keeping them there is great reward.
Who can understand his errors?
Cleanse me from secret faults.
Keep back Your servant also from presumptuous sins;
Let them not have dominion over me.
Then I shall be blameless,
And I shall be innocent of great transgression.
Let the words of my mouth and the meditation of my heart
Be acceptable in Your sight,
O Lord, my strength and my Redeemer.

(Psalm 19 : 7 - 14)

To God be the Glory! Amen, Amen, Amen.

FORTUNAT TSHIMANGA-MUKADI

IMAGES REFERENCES

I mages used in this Book are taken, except otherwise, from the website Google, as this: go to Google and make search images after the words found in every Chapter title. They come up many images according to the words used in the search. Then, one of them responding best to the message I want to send to the readers is chosen. Finally, after pasting the image in the document, its shape and size are adapted to the document only highlight the Chapter Title. The *image names* used here below are not those of the Chapter Title in the Book but those used in the search.

Chapter

1. Page 11: Image, *The Ark of the Covenant*
2. Page 21: Image, *Walk With Jesus*
3. Page 30: Image, *Alpha And Omega*
4. Page 38: Image, *Then, What?*
5. Page 46: Image removed and changed by, *Sunset*
6. Page 56: Image, *Nature's worship*
7. Page 65: Image, *Praying*
8. Page 72: Image, *Seven Candlesticks in Revelation*
9. Page 80: Image removed and changed by, *Thunderstorm*
10. Page 86: Image removed and changes by, *Christ Risen*
11. Page 101: Image, *The Cross*
12. Page 112: Image, *God Is Love*
13. Page 119: Image, *The Ten Commandments*
14. Page 126: Image, *Prepare The Way*
15. Page 132: Image, *Two Paths*

FORTUNAT TSHIMANGA-MUKADI

CPSIA information can be obtained at www.ICGtesting.com
Printed in the USA
LVOW07s0711201114

414365LV00001B/10/P